Voice

READINGS IN THEATRE PRACTICE

Series Editor: Simon Shepherd

Published:

Jane Boston: Voice

Ross Brown: Sound

Jon Davison: Clown

Penny Francis: Puppetry

Alison Maclaurin and Aoife Monks: Costume

Eleanor Margolies: Props

Scott Palmer: Light

Simon Shepherd: Direction

Forthcoming:

Joslin McKinney: Construction

Readings in Theatre Practice
Series Standing Order ISBN 978–0–230–53717–0 hardcover
Series Standing Order ISBN 978–0–230–53718–7 paperback
(*outside North America only*)

You can receive future titles in this series as they are published by placing a standing order. Please contact your bookseller or, in the case of difficulty, write to us at the address below with your name and address, the title of the series and the ISBN quoted above.

Customer Services Department, Macmillan Distribution Ltd, Houndmills, Basingstoke, Hampshire, RG21 6XS, UK

Voice

Readings in Theatre Practice

Jane Boston

First published 2018 by
PALGRAVE

Palgrave in the UK is an imprint of Macmillan Publishers Limited, registered in England, company number 785998, of 4 Crinan Street, London, N1 9XW.

Palgrave® and Macmillan® are registered trademarks in the United States, the United Kingdom, Europe and other countries.

ISBN 978–1–137–30195–6 hardback
ISBN 978–1–137–30194–9 paperback

This book is printed on paper suitable for recycling and made from fully managed and sustained forest sources. Logging, pulping and manufacturing processes are expected to conform to the environmental regulations of the country of origin.

A catalogue record for this book is available from the British Library.

A catalog record for this book is available from the Library of Congress.

Contents

Acknowledgements

Grateful thanks to my friends, family, students and colleagues at the Royal Central School of Speech and Drama and to readers of draft chapters who helped me to get through the loneliness of the long-distance page: Gilli-Bush-Bailey, Kate Elswit, Tash Fairbanks, Rosemary Malague, Jac Mathews and Tanya Zybutz.

Grateful thanks to Simon Shepherd for his patient and inspirational guidance; to Ella for being an ever-vibrant cheerleader; and to my dear Jac for keeping in dialogue with me, for sustaining me and flying the flag of home, and without whom – literally – this book would not have come to life.

And Liz and Ray, here's one for you, too – with love always.

Series Preface

This series aims to gather together both key historical texts and contemporary ways of thinking about the material crafts and practices of theatre.

These crafts work with the physical materials of theatre – sound, objects, light, paint, fabric, and – yes – physical bodies. Out of these materials the theatre event is created.

In gathering the key texts of a craft it becomes very obvious that the craft is not simply a handling of materials, however skilful. It is also a way of thinking about both the materials and their processes of handling. Work with sound and objects, for example, involves – always, at some level – concepts of what sound is and does, what an object is and does … what a body is.

For many areas of theatre practice there are the sorts of 'how to do it' books that have been published for at least a century. These range widely in quality and interest but next to none of them is able to, or wants to, position the *doing* in relation to the *thinking about doing* or the thinking about the material being used.

This series of books aims to promote both thinking about doing and thinking about materials. Its authors are specialists in their field of practice and they are charged to reflect on their specialism and its history in order, often for the first time, to model concepts and provide the tools not just for the doing but for thinking about theatre practice.

The series title 'Readings in Theatre Practice' uses the word 'reading' in the sense both of a simple understanding or interpretation and of an authoritative explication, an exegesis as it were. Thus, the books first gather together people's opinions about, their understanding of, what they think they are making. These opinions are then framed within a broader narrative which offers an explanatory overview of the practice under investigation.

So, although the books comprise many different voices, there is a dominant authorial voice organising the material and articulating overarching arguments. By way of promoting a further level of critique and reflection, however, authors are asked to include a few lengthy sections, in the form of interviews or essays or both, in order to make space for other voices to develop their own overviews. These may sit in tension, or indeed in harmony, with the dominant narratives.

Authors are encouraged to be sceptical about normative assumptions and canonical orthodoxy. They are asked not to ignore practices and thinking that might question dominant views; they are invited to speculate as to how canons and norms come into being and what effects they have.

We hope the shape provides a dynamic tension in which the different activities of 'reading' both assist and resist each other. The details of the lived practices refuse to fit tidily into the straitjacket of a general argument, but the dominant overview also refuses to allow itself to fragment into local prejudice and anecdote. And it's that restless play between assistance and resistance that mirrors the character of the practices themselves.

At the heart of each craft is a tense relationship. On the one hand there is the basic raw material that is worked – the wood, the light, the paint, the musculature. These have their own given identity – their weight, mechanical logics, smell, particle formation, feel. In short, the texture of the stuff. And on the other hand there is theatre, wanting its effects and illusions, its distortions and impossibilities. The raw material resists the theatre as much as yields to it, the theatre both develops the material and learns from it. The stuff and the magic. This relationship is perhaps what defines the very activity of theatre itself.

It is this relationship, the thing which defines the practice of theatre, which lies at the heart of each book in this series.

Simon Shepherd

Preface: What the Book Does

This book sets out a number of textual evidences that define the practice of voice within Anglo-American theatre performance and theatre training academies over the twentieth and early twenty-first centuries.

In keeping with the ethos of the series, of which this book is a part, the main thrust is about why and in what ways the practices in voice have developed rather than a detailed investigation of the methods they have given rise to. This provides a useful counterbalance to the prevailing documentation of voice practice with its explanation of how-to-do-it as opposed to why. This approach encourages reflection on the subject within theatre and theatre training more widely and provides an opportunity both to examine the prevailing orthodoxies and to think more specifically about new ways of conceptualizing the voice and its function in theatre.

The book examines the formation and development of theatre-based voice practices that can be linked, among other things, to the anatomical, physiological and 'holistic' principles found in a range of well-known, largely biomechanical, approaches. (By biomechanical, I mean those approaches that use vocal anatomy as a baseline, with a reliance on observable realities over abstract theories.) It explores the dynamic interplay between these approaches and the spoken voice aesthetics they generate, with particular focus on the ways in which orthodoxies of the voice become established. It also examines the ways in which the voice is shaped by both the poetic and the dramatic canon that are central to mainstream interpretive theatre practice.

The category voice collectively refers to the practitioners, their practices and the theory underpinning the work in theatre. This allows for a distinction to be made between voice in theatre and voice as it is featured in the speech and language sciences, the medical sciences, linguistics, philosophy, literature and drama studies. A discussion of this problem continues in Chapter 1.

The historical backdrop of Aristotle's 330 BC *Poetics*, Renaissance rhetoric and Shakespeare's seventeenth-century canon all provide frameworks within which to identify both the evolution of the practice and the theory of the contemporary theatre voice. They also form a collective benchmark for voice in the public domain and offer a useful vantage point from which to better appreciate the approaches taken by subsequent twentieth- and twenty-first-century theatre voice practitioners.

The hierarchy of value placed upon the written word over the spoken word, from the Middle Ages onwards, provides a key to understanding contemporary conservatoire voice in actor training. As a voice practitioner researcher in the conservatoire context of actor and voice training in the UK, I am interested in an examination of what happens when embodied voice practice finds its way into print and how this is engaged with in both the academy and the studio. In particular, I am interested in problematizing the hierarchies of theatre production in which voice gets subordinated to the interests of the author and the director. I examine the social preference for the reliability of the word in print, over the perceived inconsistencies of that which is simply voiced, particularly as it supersedes individual speaker agency in the interpretive traditions. The transformational possibilities imbricated in the word are traced back to its medieval origins, and this enables distinctions to be made between a poetics of voice and the physiological instructions about the voice.

Contemporary philosopher Adriana Cavarero, in her 2005 book *For More than One Voice: Toward a Philosophy of Vocal Expression*, offers some key thought about the 'permanence' of logos and the 'ephemeral' nature of voice. In her critique of cultural binaries from Aristotle onwards, she provides the critical underpinning that, in part, helps to explain the dominance of print over voice and the ways in which this has impacted on voice in theatre.

History, as ever, is important in this account. A brief contextualization in the classical and medieval periods helps to identify the ways in which the transformational power of the Latin liturgy is carried into contemporary vocal practice and its poetics. An important question here is about the ways in which Latin liturgical expectations are perpetuated within secular environments, such as voice training, where, it is argued, parallel expectations about the educational and transformational effects of the word in English are generated.

The story of English in the later Middle Ages, informed in part by a rise in nationalism in the 1570s and 1580s and the rhetoric of Protestantism, suggests that those with access to specific language forms are able to achieve more than they can within the prosaic function of ordinary communication (Dillon 1998: 163). This is, in part, attributed to the elevated position of Latin in civic and cultural life. Latin was traditionally considered to be the exemplary model of eloquence, whereas spoken English in many instances was 'regularly accused of being too "rude" and "barbarous" to render the great classical texts adequately' (Dillon 1998: 141). This view serves as a useful cultural barometer. The reference suggests that if the spoken form via the 'ordinary' voice was deemed too *rough*, then those who spoke formal text – first in Latin and then later in English – stood a better chance of having their voice accepted and listened to by those in authority. It indicates the importance of consideration given to the ways in which widening access to written forms has an impact not only on the process of writing but also on the spoken voice within theatre.

Similarly, many centuries later, it is important to consider how specialized categories of voice practitioners have structured their practice in order to bring parallel notions of 'sacred' values onto the 'ordinary' tongue. In the obituary of Elizabeth Pursey, a twentieth-century voice teacher at the Royal

Academy of Dramatic Art (RADA) in London, links are made between her religious faith and her work with actors. There is a suggestion that it informed her pedagogy:

> Her devout Catholicism was a great source of strength to her and fueled her keen dramatic insight. Her advice was not only technically precise but also seemed to come from a deep well of truth.
>
> (Trott 2012)

Speech and language science provides a parallel discourse about the human voice that runs alongside the one in theatre. Despite the growth of the scientific view from the Enlightenment onwards, the vocal sciences were late starters, due, in part, to the fact that the inner workings of the larynx were not easily observed until as late as 1854. It was then that Royal Academy of Music singing teacher Manuel Patricio Rodríguez García invented the laryngoscope (Boston 2007: xiii). After this date, biomechanical processes, where authenticated by science, have at times garnered greater credibility over other humanities-based vocal processes, precisely because of their capacity to measure and quantify vocal functioning.

In the second half of the twentieth century and into the twenty-first century, the predominance of scientific evidence-based voice theory over any other artistic or philosophical theory about voice in the academy has continued. Otolaryngologist Jo Estill (1921–2010) is notable in this category. The high regard that has been given to her work has been due, in part, to the closeness with which it is associated with 'science'. Similarly, Arthur Lessac's (1909–2011) kinesensic voice work for theatre in the USA is regarded in some circles as 'scientific' and has a parallel application in the sports sciences. The theatre voice work of Catherine Fitzmaurice engages with both holistic and scientific-based psychological, anatomical and physiological vocal understanding, and speech science knowledge underpins a number of other voice approaches on both sides of the Atlantic. The US-based Lessac–Madsen Resonant Voice Theory, for example, uses speech and language science to support work on vocal remediation, and author and voice practitioner Christina Shewell, in the UK, applies both arts-based approaches and speech and language therapeutic approaches to her work in and out of the voice clinic. While some of these approaches fall short of scientific evidence-based protocols, many present their credibility in terms that stem from the medical sciences rather than from the humanities. It is important to note that while many of these practitioners stress the importance of their application to the vocal arts, the arts and humanities do not themselves provide the main theoretical underpinning for their work.

The binary between science and the humanities affects the verification given to theatre-based voice training and links to a wider matter about hierarchies of knowledge and arguments about the nature of empiricism. It also contributes to the challenge of the location of an identifiable knowledge base for the expressive voice. British cultural historian Raymond Williams draws attention to the debate about empirical versus scientific knowledge that helps to explain why some voice practitioners have gravitated towards the 'scientific'. In an attempt to dispel any negative association with the amateur, the ignorant or the untrained that might be linked to the arts-based voice practitioner, some have sought the regulatory 'safety' of science. Williams illustrates the problems of the binary in his discussion about the conflictual meanings in the word empirical:

> In one important sense, of observation and experiment as the primary scientific procedure, empirical has remained normal in English to our own day.
> But the word became complicated by two factors. First, the specialized sense of the Empiriks, and the derived English sense of untrained and ignorant, indicated not only a reliance on observation and experiment but a positive opposition or indifference to theory. Secondly, a complicated philosophical argument, about the relative contributions of experience and reason to the formation of ideas, produced as a description of one side of the argument the terms empiricism and empiricist to indicate theories of knowledge as derived wholly from the senses – that is from experience (not experiment) in a now special sense.
>
> (Williams 1976: 100)

In order to better understand theatre voice as an object of study, the empirical versus scientific debate is clearly an important starting point. The location of a range of cultural, social and historical factors as they intersect with the materiality of the voice is similarly important. Voice as it is material on the one hand and voice as it is part of a range of socially activated abstractions on the other remain prevalent themes throughout the book. In the following extract by historian Gina Bloom, important consideration is given to the notion that the early modern representation of voice, for example, is stronger in terms of its material associations than it is with abstraction:

> While early modern writers recognize the voice as ephemeral and often invisible, they represent vocal matter as taking on a variety of forms (breath, seed, and so on) that are alienable from the speaking subject.
>
> (Bloom 2007: 2)

Bloom gives credibility to another important theme, that I return to often, about the material voice as an unsettled and potentially rebellious force:

> If the voice is produced by unstable bodies, transmitted through volatile air, and received by sometimes disobedient hearers, how can voice be trusted to convey an individual's thoughts to a listener? And in a cultural climate in which speech marks political and social power, who stands to lose and who to gain when speech assumes this unsteady material form?
>
> (Bloom 2007: 3)

This book, therefore, will appraise a weave of theories and protocols about voice that include both the material and the abstract. As such it provides an opportunity to reflect on not just how and where voice presents itself but also the influences behind emerging trends and changes in the codification of voice practice in theatre.

Early twentieth-century pedagogy and performance training protocols, several now out of print, form some of the key textual extracts. These are found in interview transcripts, vocal manuals and treatises. The tone, style and content of the extracts from Western twentieth-century training manuals for voice provide an opportunity to observe both the historical specificity and the focus of their application. This comparative approach enables the reader to better consider how a variety of ideas and practices in society and theatre, as well as science, have influenced not just the audience reception given to theatre voice but also its training protocols and values.

Part I
Introductions

Chapter

1   Voice Locations

CONTEXT, PROBLEMS AND DEFINITIONS

Voice is significant to theatre in the same way that voice is significant to life itself. Many expressive forms combine social and artistic functions – the cave painting, the socialist mural and the communal chant – but none so completely as voice. It is the means by which some of the most ordinary and the most sophisticated of human expressions are communicated. Voice is the channel and the amplification, the impulse and the expression, the thought and the sound. It is art and it is life. It is, however, also hard to define.

In this chapter, I examine some of the core principles that inform a better understanding of the production of voice in both art and life. I briefly consider a number of the key influences involved in the definition of theatre voice in order to develop them further in subsequent chapters.

I begin with the problem posed by history, where, as the role and function of theatre practice changes, so, too, do the aesthetics and conventions of voice. Voice is never one thing in any one epoch and where it is present in one form within the religious rituals and pageants of the ancient past, it is transformed into a number of specialized vocal registers in the contemporary era. In classical text-based theatre, for example, at a distance from that which is 'ordinary' and 'familiar', the voice reflects some of its ancient roots. In contemporary realism, however, the voice is asked to mirror the familiar. On the one hand sit highly trained or specialized voices that are distinguishable from conversational norms, and, on the other, are those that are imitative of them. Clearly, the better the historical and sociocultural detail, the better the understanding of the individual voice in its own time and place.

Exceptional feats of vocal duration and range are the norm within interpretive classical theatre work. A hyperfunctionality sets it apart from the conversational dimensions of civic vocal life. In forms such as social realism, by way of a contrast, the voice takes on a replication of the 'ordinary'. Both rely on skilful production, however, and even conversational norms need work. 'Conversational elocution' is a term applied to a certain type of verse speaking in the early twentieth century. It provides a further clue about the artful expectations for the voice in theatre in whatever form it takes (Webb 1979: 50).

The key to successful realization at both ends of the spoken voice spectrum is the actor. It is the actor who holds the knowledge and skill necessary
to organize and articulate the voice in performance and to sustain it for the
duration of any given run. It is the actor who negotiates the acoustic space
of the Greek amphitheatre, judges the company style of the Shakespearean
company and anticipates the demands of the actor manager. The art of the
voice in theatre, then, rests primarily on the actor.

A small number of contemporary producing theatres, in addition,
enlist a voice specialist to assist actors both within the rehearsal process
and in performance. This is consistent with the professionalization of
theatre in the twentieth century in which an increase in the discrete roles
involved in the professional theatre brings together specialists from a
number of disciplines. Prior to the twentieth century, training for the
voice was haphazard and lacked system. From the turn of the twentieth
century onwards, it is a story of increasing systematization in which
precedents are set for the role of the voice specialist within both theatre
training and professional productions.

As the role of the voice specialist evolves over the twentieth century it
is possible to locate the impact of a number of influences associated not
only with the values, finances and purpose of specific companies or productions, but also with a shift in cultural priorities. A voice specialist is
more likely to be employed in the theatre company with a strong public
profile associated with canonical theatre, as in the case of the UK's Royal
Shakespeare Company. They are less likely to be employed in low-profile,
small-scale companies for whom the voice specialist poses an expensive
'extra'.

A different priority is evidenced, however, when voice practice forms the
core of a company's ethos, as in eastern Poland's Centre for Theatre Practices
'Gardzienice'. Voice in this context is as indelibly marked by ensemble process as by the individual, and the voice specialist as a guide comes into their
own. They offer the actor an opportunity to unhook voice from the formal
concerns of the canon in interpretive theatre, and to form, instead, a fulcrum
of energetic and holistic expression in the laboratory. Zygmunt Molik, the
voice teacher at the heart of Grotowski's company when it formed in the
late 1950s, talks of his 'shaman'-like role in effecting change within the actor
(Campo and Molik 2010: xi).

I note this phenomenon across theatre history. On the one hand, voice
is shaped by a specific ethos under the guidance of a specialist teacher or
trainer. In the laboratory theatre settings of the Gardzienice company, the
Grotowski Institute, the Roy Hart Theatre, Nadine George's Voice Studies
International and others who work outside dominant orthodoxies, the voice
is often a key element in the work. In mainstream theatre, on the other hand,
voice is often regarded as a sign of an individual's expressive capacity and

is not subject in the same ways to the training protocols of the specialist. In this latter context, it is the actor's interpretive ability with the dramatic text that is called upon instead. In mainstream theatres, such as the RSC and the National Theatre, and in London's West End, one of the distinctive features of the voice specialist is the fact that they guide but do not lead.

Broadly speaking, there are two main approaches that underpin the concept of voice in theatre. The first regards voice as the product of an individual's expressive capacity and relates primarily to function. The second regards it as part of a wider ethos that relates to the aesthetics of its production and includes speech. At the level of function, theatre voice engages an individual actor in the management of the vocal instrument, in acoustic sensitivity to the theatre space and in vocal nuance in relation to audience response. The functional 'triangulation' that arises serves as an operational baseline for effective vocalization. It provides a distinction between optimal voice, or voice that is voice, and the vocal ornamentation that arises out of a particular ethos, textual impulse or speech act from within the frame set by the aesthetics of the production.

The individual actor, then, operates within the two broad approaches taken to theatre voice as mentioned above, and also within a set of specific micro vocal 'frames' that refer both to the instrument and the individual. At a micro level this includes an actor's personal relationship to the functional or healthy voice, an understanding of their expressive ability to give voice, and a capacity to work within an ethos of voice production, often generated in relation to specialist trainers. The three manifestations of voice are linked but also distinctive in their own right. Where one is highlighted or impacts more than the other, it is also important to clarify the wider historical and social context within which any specific choice is made.

There is clearly no one type of expressive theatre voice outcome and it is, therefore, more beneficial to locate a number of pluralistic evidences in a range of specific contracts negotiated between individual voices and artistic principles across theatre history. Important in this process is a close examination of the ways in which the principles are understood, how they are enacted by the specialists and performers who shape and express the voice and how they are received by different audiences.

DEFINITIONS OF VOICE

Before I further investigate the evidences of voice across theatre history, it is important to engage with the problem presented by the term voice itself. What, at the outset, is voice? For many, voice remains one of the most elusive and invisible factors among all the visible and measurable knowledge about the body. Rocco dal Vera and Robert Barton, in the first chapter of their voice manual *Voice: Onstage and Off*, for example, state that the voice is the entity least known of all the physical arts:

> Your voice is hiding in a cave. The cave is your body. You will never know your voice as well as your body because there is no photograph, scale, measuring tape, full-length mirror or zipper to help you. No one will ever kiss, slap, caress or shove your voice. It hides well.
>
> (Barton and dal Vera 2011: 3)

Whilst there is no one definition, it is useful to appreciate that voice is best understood in relation to several historical, social, scientific and cultural paradigms. Once these are stated, it is easier to see how they illuminate the specific codes, values and terminologies that collectively construct theatre voice. This approach corresponds with the wider terms used in the book, in which the provision of a range of readings offers a set of multidisciplinary pathways through a complex terrain of divergences and, of course, convergences. The project parallels cultural historian Raymond Williams' task in his book *Keywords: A Vocabulary of Culture and Society* (1976), in which he asserts the following about his attempt to locate and define the terms by which cultural and social institutions function:

> It is not a dictionary or glossary of a particular academic subject. It is not a series of footnotes to dictionary histories or definitions of a number of words. It is, rather, the record of an inquiry into a vocabulary; a shared body of words and meanings in our most general discussions, in English, of the practices and institutions which we group as culture and society.
>
> (Williams 1976: 13)

In my project here, I, similarly, examine the vocabulary that circulates in a range of contexts in order to better locate and describe the particular practices and meanings that pertain to theatre voice. The examination of voice follows a procedure outlined by Williams for his own task:

> Notes on a list of words; analyses of certain formations: these were the elements of an active vocabulary – a way of recording, investigating and presenting problems of meaning in the area in which the meanings of culture and society have formed.
>
> (Williams 1976: 13)

My own enquiry begins with a definition provided in *The Shorter Oxford English Dictionary*. It starts simply enough:

> Voice: (1) Sound, or the whole body of sounds, made or produced by the vocal organs of man or animals in their natural action; esp. sound formed in or emitted

from the human larynx in speaking, singing, or other utterance; vocal sound as
the vehicle of human utterance or expression.

(Onions et al. 1965: 2368)

The dictionary definition, however, is just a beginning. In order to better understand the histories, aesthetics and actions of voice in theatre, a
range of other definitions needs to be activated. By so doing, theatre voice
is understood both alongside and within existing thought and practice,
including the philosophical, the anatomical, the scientific, the literary and
so on. The following categories, therefore, are introduced as a response
to this challenge. They are not exhaustive or conclusive but offer, instead,
the beginnings of a formulation that demonstrates the relationship of the
subject voice to a wide range of meanings, contexts and knowledge. Whilst
the terminologies of voice stem from many different disciplines, and do not
necessarily speak to each other, this book more explicitly maps out their
commonalities. As Williams has already suggested, this will bring the terms
more readily to a broader table for further discussion and amplification:

The work that this book records has been done in an area where several disciplines converge but in general do not meet. It has been based on several areas of
specialist knowledge but its purpose is to bring these, in the examples selected,
into general availability.

(Williams 1976: 15)

ANATOMICAL VOICE

The humanities, as opposed to the medical sciences, provide the main
framework for understanding voice in theatre. Since voice is a key factor
in the condition of being human, its home in the humanities makes sense.
The voice also fits neatly into a range of scientific categories across a spectrum, including the surgical, the acoustic and the therapeutic, amongst
others. And this also needs to be acknowledged.

Anatomical and physiological definitions of voice are useful at the outset
because they are broadly democratic and allow the voice to be named and
located within a shared understanding of the functionality of the body. It is
important to note, however, that concepts of the body and the voice within
the body differ across cultures, and issues of cultural assumption also
need to be factored into any detailed intercultural discussion about voice
(McAllister-Viel 2009: 433). Although Eastern philosophies and practices
inform the work of many contemporary voice practitioners, it is a Western
approach to vocal anatomy and physiology that contributes to the majority
of the vocal practices that are devised within the theatre contexts discussed
over the course of the book. The widely known actor's research tool that

defines given character circumstances, referred to here as the *who* and the *what* of a given persona, serves as a useful schema towards the identification of the relevant principles of vocal anatomy and physiology.

First I consider the '*who*' as a way of designating individual actors' consciousness about the physical body. Whilst this opens up interesting questions about a Cartesian mind–body binary, to be discussed at more length in further chapters, for the time being it is important to note that the *whole* body of the individual is the concern of the voice practitioner and not just its specific vocal apparatus. Why is this so? It is due, largely, to a twentieth-century revision of the mind–body relationship that, in turn, serves as a guiding rationale within voice practice. In this view, the voice *is* the body as the body *is* the voice, as further discussion illuminates. Kristin Linklater says something akin to this in her seminal work *Freeing the Natural Voice*: 'To free the voice is to free the person, and each person is indivisibly mind and body' (Linklater 2006: 8). It is now a widely held precept within most voice practice in the Western training academies.

The anatomist, on the other hand, does something quite different. The anatomist separates and isolates the parts of the body in order to understand their discrete function. Its study is defined in *The Shorter Oxford Dictionary* as: 'The artificial separation of the parts of the organized body, in order to discover their position, structure and economy' (Onions et al. 1965: 63). The use of the term 'artificial' is of interest and serves as a reminder that it is the reconnection of the parts to the whole (after their 'artificial' separation on the dissection table) that remains one of the primary remedial objectives of the voice practitioner. It reminds me, too, that an understanding of the skeletal structure in its entirety, and not partially, is directly related to the voice, and thus the individual. It is not just about an abstract understanding of its more than six hundred isolated bones; it is about a 'felt' sense of its bearing in time and space:

> A person's voice usually is an integral part of his or her self-perception. Therefore it is wise to consider the whole person rather than isolate the production of sound from personality.
>
> (Bunch 1993: 7)

In what ways does vocal anatomy relate to the voice in theatre? In a European context, the knowledge of vocal anatomy emerges, in part, out of visual art associated traditions. Whilst several branches of knowledge contribute to the understanding of vocal form and function, the branch that links visual arts to the sciences contributes a particular importance because of the way it helps to illuminate existential meanings. In many ways, the synthesis of humanistic and scientific principles *is* voice knowledge:

> Italian Renaissance artists became anatomists by necessity, as they attempted to refine a more lifelike, sculptural portrayal of the human figure. Indeed, until about

1500–1510, their investigations surpassed much of the knowledge of anatomy that was taught at the universities … In the words of the Florentine sculptor Baccio Bandinelli (1493–1560), who was trying to impress a duke to hire him, and who also appears to have run an academy for the teaching of young artists, 'I will show you that I know how to dissect the brain, and also living men, as I have dissected dead ones to learn my art'.

(Bambach 2017)

The skeleton itself, and the muscles and cartilages it supports, serves as the *'what'* in the narrative and provides the material structure around which voice practice in an artistic environment is structured. As part of an individual's genetic endowment – a *given* for the individual – the lived experience of the skeletal structure has a role to play in the overall production of the voice. Additionally, environment, nutrition, lifestyle and so on impact on an individual's physiological well-being. It is the overall combination of factors, including the theatre environment and its behavioural values, that contributes to the vocal function of the individual actor and its impact on the listener:

[E]ffective integration of psychological, physiological and acoustic factors when combined with the intellect, will give the singer or speaker balanced communication. The listener, responsive to the same factors, then integrates these with what is being communicated.

(Bunch 1993: 9)

The anatomy and physiology of voice matter because they ensure that discussion also includes questions that relate to its materiality such as timbre, pitch, rhythm and so on, as well as its abstract associations. In later chapters, for example, I will examine the esoteric and the metaphorical, amongst some of the other more ineffable notions of the voice. The first principles, though, sit with the physical systems of the body. Here, where the voice is both materially knowable and susceptible to practical and cognitive instruction, sit some of the most important factors that pertain to the development of vocal artistry and vocal health.

PHYSICS OF VOICE

The complexities of physics are no stranger to the actor. Part of the actor's task is to convert slow-moving breath (gas) into rapid sound wave motion. The gas is then transformed by vocal tract resonance in order to produce a series of explicable and finely tuned phrases and sounds for the communication of meaning to the audience.

The knowledge that there is more to voice than meets the eye is, arguably, one of the main factors that separates the actor from their civic counterparts.

Many actors are trained to perceive and develop the voice based upon a conscious deployment of the laws of physics. Whereas all voice users are subject to 'natural' laws, it is usually only the professional voice user who stands to exploit them effectively for their own artistic purposes. The conscious application of the laws of physics makes a difference not only to the actor but also to the theatre audience itself. The fine-tuning involved in the projection of an actor's sound to the listener in any particular theatre space is both part of an intuitive sense of physics and a conscious awareness of acoustics. If the voice fails to carry, it is both a problem with the way in which the vibration of breath turns into 'glottal wave motion' (Linklater 2006: 380) and how it travels through space and arrives at the listening ear. It is a delicate matter of conversion:

> Converting acoustic vibrations in the air to a nerve signal that is sent off for processing in the brain is the job of the cochlea, a spiral chamber of bone in the inner ear that looks like a tiny snail shell ... Our perception of the sound depends on how those signals are processed.
>
> (Ball 2010: 37)

The phenomenon of voice, then, is partially explained in the account provided by physics. The actor's relationship to physics and its effects, however, are different matters and, although physics provides an account of the voice in a range of performative actions, it does not provide the instruction to effect the desired changes. It is the voice trainer who does this via the mechanism of voice training protocols. Kristin Linklater, notable in this, includes an appendix on vocal anatomy in her theatre-based work *Freeing the Natural Voice* (2006). It consists of a brief description of the science of sound production and provides a useful digest of the physics involved. As such, it signifies the importance given to the scientific underpinning of an overtly arts-centred voice practice. The appendix is formed of excerpts from *Anatomy and Physiology of the Voice and Choral Pedagogy* by Dr Robert Sataloff (Linklater 2006).

PSYCHOLOGICAL VOICE

> ... there is in man a dubble Speech; the one in the mynd, which they call the inward Speech which wee conceive afore we utter it; and the other the sounding image thereof, which is uttered by our mouth and is termed the Speech of the Voyce.
>
> (Sidney and Bellings 1724: 267)

The importance of psychology to the voice user is, in the main, a twentieth-century concern. This is not to say that the connection was unnoticed prior to the twentieth century, as we can see from the quotation above. But, prior to the advent of psychoanalysis at the turn of the twentieth century, the majority of voice practitioners placed their attention on the production and mechanics of sound production and the exercise of relevant musculature. This is different to the approach that values (or recognizes) an *interiority* of engagement. The following key passage in the preface to *Freeing the Natural Voice* gives a clear idea of the importance given to this in the latter part of the twentieth century on both sides of the Atlantic. It also provides a clear signal of Linklater's interest in the incorporation of psychological awareness in her voice practice:

> When I moved to America in 1963 to set up my own voice studio, I found that the voice work I brought with me had evolved over the years to the point at which it would marry well with American methods of acting. There was still an imbalance between the creative use of inner self and communicative skill in both America and Britain: British theatre was still suffering from a lack of emotional and psychological demands, while American training placed little value on physical and vocal skills, but all this was changing.
>
> (Linklater 2006: 2)

The transatlantic exchange between voice practitioners in the twentieth and twenty-first centuries is significant in the development of voice training in the West. It is described in greater detail in the later chapters about individual practitioners and their influences. For now, it is important to note the significance of the bridge made between psychological understanding and technical vocal virtuosity. Such a bridge, most notably, was inspired by the work of Iris Warren, one of the main influences in the early career of Kristin Linklater in the UK:

> In the late 1930s, Iris Warren … did not deal directly with the suffering voice but with the physical and mental tensions caused by blocked emotions. She administered voice exercises, but she altered their nature by shifting the controls from external, physical muscles to internal, psychological impulses. The criterion for assessing progress lay in the answer to the question 'How does it feel?' rather than 'How does it sound?' The ultimate emphasis was 'I want to hear you, not your voice.' This was happening at a time when the 'voice beautiful' was still very much in vogue, when pear-shaped vowels and technical skill were preferred to 'vulgar' emotion.
>
> (Linklater 2006: 5–6)

A similar bridge between mind and voice is found in the European-based work of German psychotherapist and singing teacher Alfred Wolfsohn (1862–1962). His London-based training school in extended vocal technique, drawing in part from his own memories of the sounds of suffering in the trenches of World War I, proved to be a potent influence on the career of the actor Roy Hart. The subsequent synthesis of Wolfsohn's techniques and therapeutic principles, along with his own RADA-trained vocal virtuosity, formed the basis of an influential mid-century voice and acting process known as the Roy Hart technique, more of which is discussed in Chapter 7.

Finally, I want to point to the importance of connections between psychoanalytic understanding and voice and the ways in which they relate to understandings and expressions of gender. Whilst I will not examine the intersections in any great detail, it is important to signal the importance of their impact. The modes of thinking and theoretical modelling they collectively give rise to contain the possibility for opening up new perspectives on the voice that are not necessarily made within theatre practice. To be made conscious of them is to extend the concept of the voice itself.

NEUROSCIENTIFIC VOICE

In her workshops and in her writing, Kristin Linklater frequently refers to the work of neuroscientist Antonio Damasio. His science-based verifications support some of the instinctual codifications in her voice practice and underline the importance of training techniques that engage with the subtle and complex neurology of the voice in relation to the recent discoveries about the plasticity of the brain and visual imaging, amongst other factors. It is now almost commonplace, for example, to draw attention to the scientific verification of long-standing voice and theatre exercises based upon the conscious image-making process of the individual actor. Recent research on the brain has reinforced what actors have always known: the creation of a strong imaginary image in the mind has an influence on the transmission of clear intentions with impact on the voice:

> Research has shown body-sensing areas of the brain reflect not only body states, but can also manufacture and deal with 'false ones' … These 'as if' body states can be thought of as imaginary ones that are essentially based on memory, i.e., recollections and reconstitutions of conscious and somatic experiences. Humans have some control over these as-if states.
>
> (Blair 2008: 79)

It is of note that future developments in voice understanding are now perhaps more closely aligned to neuroscience than they have ever been, precisely because of the verifications it has provided about the effectiveness of voice exercises in modelling the mind–body relationship. This proposition is something voice has claimed for decades but it is only in recent years that scientific disciplines have been found to offer the authority of proof. Voice in the humanities studio, it seems, is never far from its counterpart in the scientific lab.

SOCIOCULTURAL VOICE

> The voice positions me in space, and establishes the space of social relations; but the voice also by its nature makes the positioning of the self less than wholly certain.
>
> (Connor 2000: 43)

In this account, Steven Connor positions voice as representative of personal certainties and uncertainties, as well as of individual material interpretations involving complex social interaction. I am reminded, again, that voice is never one entity and it is never fixed. His ideas about the 'spatial and sensory fields' of the voice as they relate to 'the apprehension and embodiment of different forms and conceptions of power' (Connor 2000: 43) provide a view that brings together a recognition of the impact society has on the individual voice and on the material voice where, '[i]n each case, the voice is a means both of integration and of disturbance' (Connor 2000: 43). I argue that voice is both constituted of something and yet is always in the moment of formation. The pervasive creative tension this represents allows for a more nuanced view of the social and interpersonal connections that arise in the voice itself.

French sociologist Pierre Bourdieu, in the relationship he makes with notions of place and event, similarly allows for a dialectic between voice, the individual and society. His theory of *habitus*, applied in relation to the voice, shows how it is formed as much by its materiality as by the sociocultural event in which it functions as part of the body's 'learnt bearing' (Wallis and Shepherd 2004: 191). Bourdieu's theories, as well as those of others like him, serve to remind us of the important fact that whilst the voice in theatre is part of a narrative that celebrates the unique expression of the individual, its actual embodiment is also framed by the regulations and expectations of the society within which it performs.

In one of her earliest publications, *The Right to Speak*, voice practitioner Patsy Rodenburg states: 'Voice work is for everybody' (Rodenburg 1992: iv). Her position as a vocal coach and director at the National Theatre in London and at the Guildhall School of Music and Drama is supported by a view that the expression of voice is about participation in a wider political act, particularly in relation to class, race and gender as they have inhibited or silenced the right to speak:

> What I have noticed as a teacher does support the notion, however unscientifically posited by me, that environment and social background leave us culturally possessed or dispossessed. The voice we have is a by-product of that background and an expression of it in every way. We are judged when we speak and we are also categorised ... Through voice and speech we portray ourselves.
>
> (Rodenburg 1992: 7)

One of the more under-discussed aspects of voice is the role played by the listener or interlocutor. This issue has its origins in a number of sociopolitical discussions about voice. These link not only to a range of philosophical debates between theorists and practitioners, in which attention is drawn to the importance of the actual sound of the voice, as compared to the 'soundless' voice in written language, but also to the fundamental question of the voice that is listened to or excluded. Consequently, it is vital to consider the impact of receptivity on the individual's voice both in life and in the theatre.

PEDAGOGICAL VOICE

A prominent feature of theatre voice is the influence effected by the specialist teacher. The studio presence of the voice teacher is regarded as highly significant to the development of the individual's voice, even if the practitioner concerned has also produced written documentation about their work. What this amounts to is that the phenomenon of a teacher's presence serves as an additional key to their historical reputation. This factor is, in many ways, equal to or even more influential than their writing.

The ephemeral nature of the studio experience is common to all the performing arts, but none more so than in the voice studio where the sought-after experience of the expression of voice at the level of pure sensory awareness outweighs any other outcome. In other words, there is rarely anything to verify the outcome of voice other than the 'felt' vocal sensations themselves. As a consequence, theatre voice training often requires that the teacher engage in a dialogue with the individual in order to assist with meaningful development and to offer a discernible outcome. The dialogical role of the teacher in helping to make manifest the changes to an individual's voice is regarded by many as fundamental to vocal transformation.

An examination of some of the defining principles of leading pedagogues in the UK and the USA allows parallels to be drawn between studio training aesthetics and some of the juridical, political or educational principles that also have an influence on the outcomes of the expression of voice in the student. In particular, as already shown, late nineteenth- and early twentieth-century voice pedagogy is readily associated with science. This is in line with mid-nineteenth-century positivism and notions of scientific reasoning, and offers the means to legitimate a given vocal aesthetic. It is present in both late nineteenth- and early twentieth-century voice practice in the UK and parallels the newly emerging science of the musicologist, the laryngologist and the speech scientist.

The issue of the legitimization of a vocal *aesthetic*, however, is only one part of the challenge. There is an additional issue posed by the need to legitimate the *role* of the voice teacher at the outset. The tension this generates is evident in the very first paragraph of a manual by voice specialist H.H. Hulbert at the turn of the twentieth century. Leading UK voice practitioner Elsie Fogerty features in the prefatory remarks of the first edition in 1907: 'The author's thanks are due to Miss Elsie Fogerty for … valuable suggestions' (Hulbert 1912: ix). Her remarks provide a valuable validation of Hulbert's artistic credentials. What is most notable, however, about the next passage from Hulbert, is the insecurity it indicates about the epistemology of voice. Hulbert, a teacher with scientific leanings, reflects on the importance of the verification of voice knowledge with a scientific method:

> An endeavour is herein made to place voice-training upon a safe scientific foundation; hitherto its principles have been very imperfectly understood ... The training of the voice is the tuning of the vocal organ, and the removal of defects, whereby the instrument is enabled to do its work efficiently and easily. It would be better to call it voice-building or voice-renovating ... This involves a theoretical knowledge, not necessarily of an exhaustive nature, but sufficient to ensure intelligent practice.
>
> (Hulbert 1912: v)

Hulbert's argument indicates a need for strong links between science, health and voice. In this way he anticipates the emergence of the professionalization of discrete strands of voice work later in the twentieth century, in which voice practitioners in the arts sit on one side, and voice and speech trainers in therapeutic and medical settings sit on the other. At the outset, however, they sit together: 'What is good for the health of a part of the body is good for the body as a whole; each part is dependent for its well-being upon every other part' (Hulbert 1912: vi).

So far so good. It is in the following passage, however, that signs of the juridical rear their head, featuring the assignment of value to vocal outcomes. In this, the matter of health (as with so many Victorians and early Edwardians) becomes associated with social improvement. His conflation of vocal health and morality ushers in the idea of a vocal aesthetic that equates vocal health to moral well-being:

> Hence, the voice becomes a valuable and delicate index of what is perfect and imperfect in physical education; for even ordinary physical movements badly executed very soon exert an evil influence upon the voice, making it hard and unmusical.
>
> (Hulbert 1912: vi)

Hulbert's equation of health with 'good' vocal sound sits on one side and ill health, dysfunction and 'bad' sound sit on the other. It remains a persistent binary distinction throughout the twentieth century and on into the twenty-first. In his role as lecturer on voice production and breath, as well as an examiner in physical education, he starts a dialogue about voice that links not only health and science, but also culture and class.

Like Hulbert, other writers of voice manuals in the late nineteenth and early twentieth century also reveal an insecurity of subject 'newness' with regard to the legitimacy of voice in a humanities context. Detectable is the question of value and whether voice work constitutes part of a formal scheme of academic knowledge. Hulbert clearly felt it necessary to declare his work a 'treatise' in order to underscore its credibility, afford it the appropriate gravitas and ensure the broad reach of his work beyond the arts and education:

> The treatise is intended for voice users generally, singers, clergymen, barristers, actors, public speakers, and lecturers, but more especially for teachers, who are probably the greatest voice-users, and therefore most in need of voice-training.
>
> (Hulbert 1912: 1)

The importance of his declaration is in the way it highlights a mutuality of interest between voice work for actors and voice work for other professionals in the community, especially teachers. It is interesting, too, that he points to the actor as a model of best vocal practice: 'Sir Henry Irving made such intelligent use of his rhetorical pauses that it has been said of him that "he was eloquent in his pauses"' (Hulbert 1912: 77). The value given to the pause puts it on a par with utterance itself. I suggest that the ability to hold a pause is indicative of a speaker's ability not only to manage the contours of rhetorical delivery but also to hold their authoritative position in public. In fact, they are often one and the same thing and represent a feature throughout the history of voice that shifts interchangeably between the platforms of theatre and public office. Churchill, in the twentieth century, for example, is noted for the use of the pause in his public oratory and the poet Tony Walsh used it to underscore the significance of his words at the public memorial for the Manchester bombings in 2017.

Hulbert's pluralistic view, in which the actor, the cleric and the teacher's voice provide vocal models for the rest of society, is one that can be traced in the philosophy of the Central School (later the Royal Central School of Speech and Drama) in London in 1906. At its foundation, links and comparison are made between actor training, theatre education and speech therapy. Hulbert, present at Central's inception, put emphasis on the importance of training the teacher's voice. Key above all is his belief in the value of ensuring verifiable standards in voice training:

> The treatise includes all the voice training that is mentioned in the regulations of the Board of Education for the Teacher's Certificate Examination. It is absolutely necessary that all who have to use their voices much in their work should have definite instruction in voice-training, and the necessity of it for teachers is being gradually realised by the educational authorities ... Teachers are often appointed to teach voice-production who themselves do not know what voice-production is, and in consequence voice-training is frequently branded as useless; whereas if properly taught it is potent and sure.
>
> (Hulbert 1912: viii)

SPEECH AND VOICE

In a book about voice, the discrete elements of speech are also a major focus. It is important, therefore, to establish the ways in which the two elements correspond. Hulbert's position as an early twentieth-century standard bearer for voice and speech training prefigures a long-running twentieth-century transatlantic debate about the adoption of formal voice and speech models. His stance, in turn, is prefigured in UK elocutionary publications from the mid-1700s onwards in which, again, science is used to verify speech and physical standards for public life. The fact that Hulbert felt it necessary to redeem elocution from the hands of amateurs demonstrates the newness of formal speech voice training, even as late as the early twentieth century, and shows how robust assertions of its importance were seen as necessary in order to ensure its uptake as a serious branch of study:

> The combined efforts of scientists have done much in the past to elucidate the hidden mysteries connected with voice, and as new paths of investigation are opened out there is a rapid exit of fads, secrets, and tricks of the charlatan. Anatomists, physiologists, hygienists, throat specialists, voice producers, phoneticians, physicists, and even pathologists and chemists have special lines of original research still waiting investigation in connection with the voice.
>
> (Hulbert 1912: ix)

Hulbert's robust beliefs are paralleled in the USA in the late nineteenth and early to mid-twentieth century. Under the influence of English phonetician William Tilly at New York's Columbia University, phonetics is deployed in order to ensure the scientific verification of voice, similar to that sought by Hulbert in the UK. Tilly's student in the 1920s, Margaret Prendergast McClean, 'expressed that the science of phonetics "is the only way pronunciation can be properly studied and accurately represented"'(Withers-Wilson 1993: 8):

> Her book *Good American Speech*, first published in 1928, became a popular text used in American high schools, universities and drama schools. In it she stresses that a sound knowledge of the science of phonetics can assist students in acquiring good American speech free from regionalisms.
>
> (Wilson 1993: 8)

The Theatre Speech or Transatlantic dialect borrowed from both Standard British and Standard American pronunciations (Wilson 1993: 9) and influenced by the science of phonetics from the 1920s to the 1940s, however, retained, for many, echoes of colonial and elitist oppression. Many also regarded it as overly prescriptive in contrast to the constitutionally enshrined principles and rights of the freedom of speech: 'The Transatlantic dialect, with its inherent suggestion of affectation and superiority, was inappropriate for the majority of characters in ... modern realistic plays' (Wilson 1993: 12).

I consider, though, that whilst the US debate about speech standards is informed by a more active awareness of democratic entitlement than in the UK, it is clear that the influence of the early elocutionists and the phoneticians still counts. It isn't until much later, in the middle of the twentieth century, that a theatre voice, bespoke to the 'spirit' of the US constitution, emerges. Even then, whilst more broadly democratic, it remains one that reflects the tastes of a small, white ruling elite and the influence of speech standards are never far away.

The transatlantic interest in a literary and theatrical canon, with its associated acting aesthetics, further contributes to the complexity of the debate about speech standards. It has contributed to at least two major directions in American theatre practice, and has had a profound impact on the training of voice and speech on both sides of the Atlantic.

In the USA, the first impact is seen in the development of the Method, a mid-twentieth-century American acting method derived from Stanislavski's principles. It challenged perceived notions of the add-on affectations of received speech and eschewed all associations with the obviously trained voice. The second impact is seen in the successful dissemination of the codification of American speech by Edith Skinner. Her book *Speak with Distinction*, first published in 1942 and reprinted multiple times, was widely influential with respect to standard setting. In Skinner, it is possible to read a range of sub-textual anxieties about North American identity that echo Hulbert's turn-of-the-century anxieties about scientific approval given to voice and speech work. I suggest that the reinforcement of a set of standards offers a partial alleviation of some of those same anxieties.

Even though the Skinner standard retained much of its premier position as a model of speech work well into the late twentieth century, and still retains a position in the twenty-first century, its persistence in the training frame raises important questions about standard-setting in voice and speech. They include questions not only about why prescriptive voice and speech standards last as long as they do on both sides of the Atlantic, although more so in the UK, but also about why they are needed in the first place.

Skinner's combination of detailed and codified speech analysis and exercise regimes seemingly resolved the problem of defining speech in relation to voice as they became one and the same thing in the end. For many others, however, the mere fact of such a speech standard has had a counterproductive effect on their voice practice and they have, consequently, sought other ways of working with voice and the speech it ushered in.

The separation of voice from speech is a complex task. Both pertain to the individual and society, are open to multiple understandings and have associations with many academic disciplines and codifications. As a consequence, they both require scrupulous definition at the outset. In setting out some of the key associative disciplines and theories, the qualitative effects of both voice and speech in the theatre are better revealed. By showing that formations of voice and speech are made in direct relationship to a range of social and political constructs outside the theatre, it is possible, as stated at the outset, to better ascertain the terms on which voice operates in theatre practice. In this way, its history, its lineage of practice and its expressions – as it emerges from and is shaped by external social and cultural factors but also returns uniquely to the theatre – are better understood.

Part II
Histories

Chapter
2
Voice as an Instrument of Theatre

This chapter examines the ways in which two key ideas of voice are manifest in a selected number of historical epochs and dramatic forms. One idea relates to the voice, the individual and performer identity. The other takes the instrument of voice as object and examines the ways in which it is shaped by social value and theatre form in its expressive context.

I piece together evidences of the sound of the voice within Western theatre history and consider how the actor's individual voice supports or parts company with prevailing theatre values in two key moments: ancient Greek theatre and the early modern period. At stake is a new regard for the voice in theatre history, as it both belongs to and yet is never fully controlled by the individual, owing to the impact of context and external evaluation.

On offer are a number of historiographical tools to help understand the phenomenon of voice and to provide insight into a number of social and cultural factors that inform the ways in which voice effects theatre meanings. A number of case studies provide evidence of the ways in which the voice is both characteristic of the individual and, at the same time, the property of theatre form and context; they illuminate the interrelationship between unshaped raw material and the culturally influenced sonic elements that collectively define the output and perceptions of an individual's voice in any one expressive instance.

Some might assume that the history of voice *is* the history of theatre. Theatre historian Allardyce Nicoll gives the date 490 BC as marking the beginning of Western theatre, with the 'first extant drama by Aeschylus, *The Suppliants*' (Nicoll 1949: 25). But what Nicoll misses by this is an opportunity to make a distinction between voice and drama. He is also at odds with a contemporary view that regards the search for origins as complex, fraught and ultimately fruitless (Wiles 2003: 20). Nicoll justifies the date on the basis that there are no other extant evidences by which to formulate an alternative view (Nicoll 1949: 25). This, however, is part of the problem. He fails to distinguish voice from the dramatic textual context in which it features and, as such, renders the voice unperceivable. It is possible to read similar accounts of the origins of Greek drama and yet not understand anything further about the constituent individuated qualities of the material voice (Goldhill 1986: 4) or of how it might have sounded.

The ubiquitous nature of voice is part of the problem for the theatre historian. By this I mean that voice is as much a part of ordinary human communication as it is of performance in theatre. Its expression in civic life is part of the function of 'everyday' communication. As a consequence, it is important that 'everyday' usage, with its own impact on the efficacy of voice as an aesthetic vehicle, gets teased apart from the aesthetic of the voice in its expressive mode within theatre. Of related importance is the attention paid to voice when it is linked to the 'eloquence' of dramatic thought within the craft of authorship. By so doing, it is possible to appreciate more about the preferred effects of one voice over another and the performance standards they correspond to. This chapter, therefore, considers voice both on a functional material level and on an aesthetic level in correspondence with theatre's written forms and prevailing social and cultural values.

Before I examine the specifics of the material dimensions of the voice in various historical moments, I want to consider an idea that pertains across all theatre epochs and links all performers. It is the idea that a major component of the actor's job is the effective utilization of a number of identifiable and adjustable components of voice; it is to work with the material realities of the voice as instrument and as revelatory of states of mind:

> In each situation the actor needs his or her voice to be fully responsive, with the appropriate level of loudness, range, emotion, and quality. An actor's job is to express every kind of emotion, in virtually every kind of environment imaginable, when he or she chooses.
>
> (Jones 1996: 17–18)

In this contemporary account, there are several interrelated themes that have relevance to the early ancient Greek period and beyond. The *first* theme relates to the functional capacity of the actor's voice within performance. The *second* relates to ideas about acting itself and the communication of emotion. In the first theme, the voice as object is regarded as an instrument, capable of the production of multiple notes, similar to any other musical instrument. In the second, voice is considered as an embedded manifestation of the actor's uniqueness. In Chuck Jones' twentieth-century account, there is a stronger bias towards the idea of voice as the embodiment of the individual than towards the voice as instrument. However, both themes are present in his idea that voice is inseparable from the actor yet also worth training in order to exhibit a flexibility of emotional response. In Jones, there is an extension of the idea that voice is an instrument, not just of sonic features but of psychological ones as well:

> An actor's voice, then, should never stand out as a separate part of the actor's performance. The purpose of training is to make the voice an expressive instrument.
>
> (Jones 1996: 18)

Whilst it is not my intention to further speculate about concepts of selfhood manifest in the theatre voice, it is suggested that a cosmology more attentive to the function of the gods than to the human ego has the effect of rendering the instrumental voice of more significance to the Greek actor than the self-expressive voice. This links with numerous twentieth-century accounts in which the physiological management of the instrumental voice is also a prominent feature, including pitch, volume, clarity, health, durational sustainability and so on. The thematic about the voice as an instrument, however, obscures the specificity of the individual actor's unique presence in the personality of the voice, which, as I will show, is more relevant to the actor in the twentieth and twenty-first centuries.

Links between voice and concepts of selfhood are the subject of considerable discussion and debate. Theorist Steven Connor, for instance, challenges the perception that voice is a consistent and recognizable part of an individual's identity and places voice in the context of a set of wider perceptual relations. His account, though, offers the possibility to read the vocal performance of both the ancient Greeks and the present-day actor as part of the phenomenon of acoustics in which an individual is presented with the 'felt' experience and consequences of forward-facing sound projection:

> [T]he voice is not merely orientated in space, it provides the dynamic grammar of orientation. First of all, the voice establishes relations of facing and frontality. More even than my gaze, my voice establishes me in front of things and things in front of me. It is not just that I aim my voice at the world ranged in front of me, typically in an arc of about 30 degrees; for my voice also pulls the world into frontality, and disposes it spatially in relation to this frontality … As a kind of projection, the voice allows me to withdraw or retract myself. This can make my voice a persona, a mask or sounding screen. At the same time, my voice is the advancement of a part of me, an uncovering by which I am exposed, exposed to the possibility of exposure.
>
> (Connor 2000: 5)

The ways in which voice orientates individual spatial perceptions and how they can also be linked to proscenium theatre design, for example, in which the vocal trajectory for the actor is forwards and out into the auditorium, are all interesting considerations. It is, however, also useful to hold on to the widely held premise that places voice close to interior matters of self-identity and core belief. In this way, it provides a baseline from which to consider voice as both part of actor personality and part of an acquired and culturally specific theatre aesthetic.

As I have shown, the voice of the individual subject and the voice as an objective instrument, responsive to the laws of physics and acoustics, are often undifferentiated in historical accounts of the voice. In what follows, I further separate the conceptual strands of voice in two historical case study accounts in order to better understand the constituent parts of the voice, what it answers to and, even, how it might have sounded.

THE ANCIENT GREEK VOICE

Greek theatre of the sixth century BC demanded resilient vocal function. So does the theatre of the twenty-first century. Without it, the drama falters and cannot be sustained. There is, then, in both, a common need for vocal dexterity and durational capacity. Outside the shared function, however, is a difference presented by the specific realities of the ancient Greek theatre context, both in the theatre spaces and in the dramatic forms. The following quote suggests it is ancient Greek theatre design that makes particular demands on the Greek actor's voice (examined further in Chapter 4):

> In these roughly carved theaters, thousands watched the great plays of the classical period of Greece. Because subtle gestures and facial expressions were lost in the vastness of the arenas, Greek actors therefore paid much attention to developing an expressive, well-trained voice.
>
> (Jones 1996: 27)

It is possible to accept the view that Greek actors had well-trained voices, but we can never know for sure and it is too simplistic to make assumptions about it. What the voice sounded like remains largely unknowable, and premature conclusions based upon the aesthetics of the 'well-trained' voice are loaded with cultural and social connotations and remain problematic. It is probable, though, that factors related to practical and sustainable vocalization helped to determine the vocal stylistics of the day. In which case, it is the voice as instrument that comes to the fore, and not its aesthetic outcome in the drama.

Because there is no actual evidence of the sound of the voice in Greek theatre history, and all that can be called upon are well-judged perceptual recreations, the voice, as noted, tends to remain locked in its textual 'home'. Again, it is the job of voice history to allow it to sound off the page. Voice historian Jacqueline Martin points to the possibility of vocal vibrations as they are affected by the rules and practice of rhetoric. Her premise is that rhetoric, 'a practical art based on concrete advice and rules together with a general theory about what really happens in the process of speech and how people react generally to different means of expression, intellectually, aesthetically and emotionally', plays just as important a part in shaping the voice as the architecture, the choric songs or the rhythm (Martin 1991: 1):

> Rhetoric's influence and the well-made voice were seen in many aspects of acting in ancient Greece, partly because of the enormity of the open-air theatre and the critical nature of the audiences and partly because of the poetic and operatic nature of the Greek tragedies, which demanded that the actor be able to recite as well as sing. The basic elements of rhetoric were present in the way the chorus used gesture and moved from place to place, and in the beauty of tone and adaptability to the personality or mood of the character presented …

> Actors did not attempt to reproduce the attributes of age or sex so much as
> to project the appropriate emotional tone. Brockett [O.C. Brockett, *History of the
> Theatre* (1982)] maintains that they were judged above all else for beauty of vocal
> tone and the ability to adapt manner of speaking to mood and character.
>
> (Martin 1991: 2)

Martin takes us further than most with consideration given to the 'tone' of the voice. Where she falls short, however, is in a persistent equation of voice with canonical textual values from which assumptions are derived about the manner in which they are spoken. I suggest that this view falls in with both a literary view of the Greek dramatic canon and assumptions about the voice based on the notions of the 'well-made'. Both ideas obscure the voice as it is also an individualistic and variable event in which expression is marked by myriad subtle shifts of volume, pitch, tone, pace and so on. Whilst instruction in rhetorical delivery provides an individual with a range of 'craft'-based options, it is the subjective interpretation of the rules, the internalization of instruction and the idiosyncrasies of expression that are the missing factors in many accounts. It is worth considering that the results may not always be associated with a 'beauty of tone'.

Voice theorist Anne Karpf, like Martin, pays attention to the ways in which a range of invitations are made to effect the eloquence of vocal expression on the public platform:

> So obsessed were the Athenians with the improvement of the voice that they
> employed three different classes of teachers for the purpose: the *vociferaii* to
> strengthen the voice, the *phonasci* to make it more sonorous, and the *vocales*,
> the finishing masters, in charge of intonation and inflection.
>
> (Karpf 2007: 214)

I suggest that whilst this supports the theory about Athenian interest in the aesthetics of the voice, it also points to the fact that the voice as material instrument requires work to keep it strong and flexible. It provides an important indicator about the occupational hazards of the public platform, including the vocal endurance and strength needed for choric work, and the 'clarity and projection' it required. This is a view that corresponds with an account given about Sophocles, who, it is said, had to give up acting in his own plays because of his weak voice (Karpf 2007: 215).

The prized nature of the aesthetics of the ancient Greek actor's voice is corroborated in the following extract. In addition, it also offers an important link between the stylistic of the spoken voice in Greek theatre and the operatic voice more generally. Whilst proof of the exact relationship is hard to find, there is value in the suggestion that both share a need for expert management of breath support, pitch range and sound duration. Not only does the size of the classical theatre space require it but so does work in opera that involves singing above a full orchestra. I suggest, then, that whilst the extract provides further instance of the importance given to the aesthetics of voice in Greek theatre, it also reinforces the idea that the functionality of the individual's instrumental voice is of equal importance:

> It is undeniable that ancient audiences valued and prized good voices in their actors. Indeed, a performer's voice must have mattered a good deal more in the ancient theater than it does on a modern stage, since Greek drama is in many respects comparable to our opera rather than to pieces whose text is spoken. Musical skill and expressiveness must therefore have been of very great importance and an eminent actor's voice must have attracted attention to itself no matter what mask or costume he (*sic*) was wearing.
>
> (Pavlovskis 1977: 113)

Nicoll, by way of contrast, puts specific emphasis on the cult of Dionysus as formational to the development of the Greek actor's role. Whilst still not prepared to address the voice explicitly, he hints at it in his discussion about the importance of the voice in relationship to new spoken forms such as the 'ancient dithyramb, a choral song chanted in honour of Dionysus' (Nicoll 1949: 26). He speaks, again, to the lack of evidence, but is convincing about the probability of the influence choral chanting had on the development and expression of dramatic form. The writer Pindar, a contemporary of Aeschylus, wrote a dithyramb for the Athenians, and on this evidence contemporary theatre historian David Wiles gives a degree of support to Nicoll:

> Pindar's text survives because an ancient critic thought it a good exemplar of the 'austere' poetic style, and we have to work hard to re-embody such poetry in the performance space that gave words their meaning. Our text survives because it was not only a piece of Dionysiac ritual but also an original poetic composition. Since the Greek gods liked to be honoured with new creations, it makes no sense to regard ritual and creative originality as polar opposites.
>
> (Wiles 2003: 27–28)

The relationships between formalized patterns of choric chanting, dance and the expression of the voice are ones, whilst clearly speculative, corroborated in both Nicoll and Wiles:

> Again, however, even although the way be clearer, certainties are lacking, and we can but guess at the probable line of development. At first the dithyramb was, in all probability, an improvised affair, words and music alike issuing from the excitement of the festival occasion. At first too, the dithyramb must have been largely or wholly narrative in form, telling some legend relating to the god. Gradually changes came. At least by the days of Arion of Methymna (between the seventh and sixth centuries B.C.) individual poets were composing lines for the celebrants; and at the same time the separation of a choral leader ... from the

crowd led to the possibility of genuine dramatic action – or, rather, for the transformation of narrative into direct representation.

(Nicoll 1949: 26)

The account given by Nicoll of the transformation of narrative form into
dramatic form, again, whilst not directly about the voice, is useful for the
ways in which it suggests factors about the actual voice in performance
and its relationship to formalized movement or dance. This is further
reinforced in the idea that there is 'a tension between the static individual,
who would often gravitate physically to the point of equilibrium at the
centre of the circle, and the collective, processional chorus' (Wiles 2003: 66).
It is possible to imagine, based on this observation, that when the leader is
separated from the chorus, opportunities arise for the individual actor to be
distinctive in all manner of ways, not least of which is through the voice.
Informed and framed by the traditions of rhythm and song and presented
with new solo opportunities, it is also possible to consider the idea that the
ancient Greek actor developed vocally in ways that were both functionally
relevant (as instrument) and individually distinctive (as subject); produced
in relation to requirements set by and for the collective harmonic cohesion
of the chorus, the Greek actor is also influenced by a unique capacity to
resonate and amplify the sound.

The ability of the actor's voice to blend with others, as well as to exhibit
distinctive qualities, features in the following interpretation of the messenger scene of the *Agamemnon*, part of the *Oresteia* trilogy by scholar Simon
Goldhill. His reading of the text identifies the importance of the 'drama of
logos' in which a 'general awareness of the possibilities and dangers of the
tricks and powers of words' is also demonstrated by the voice in action
(Goldhill 1986: 2). The dramatization of 'message sending' is shown to
represent an artful way for the author to expose the 'role of language in the
production of meaning' (Goldhill 1986: 2). His interpretation supports the
idea that the actor who plays the messenger would have need of specific
vocal instrumentation, particularly pitch and pace, in order to underscore
the identified gulf between words spoken and their comprehension and to
'draw further attention to the role of language itself in the process of the
communication on stage' (Goldhill 1986: 3). He suggests that authorial ideas
about the mechanisms of communication in Greek drama are illuminated
as much in live performance via individual vocal cues of pitch, emphasis,
intonation and pace as by the intention of 'logos'. In *the Oresteia*, the messenger is given words that indicate an 'unawareness of the foreboding his
words give rise to' and:

his apparent inability to understand the words spoken to him or to respond to them,
seems to stress the uncertainties in the process of communication, the gaps and
misunderstanding between a speaker and listener in the exchange of language.

(Goldhill 1986: 7)

So, whilst the voice in this account remains subsumed by the organization of the words spoken, it also offers a way to consider the contributions of meaning presented by an actor's vocalization. It suggests that the live voice plays a significant part in highlighting the duplicitous meanings generated by logos and that it is the voice that communicates the message to an audience, not simply the text.

Theatre historian Oliver Taplin is prepared to speculate more than most about the live voice in early Greek theatre performance. Because historical voice is an un-hearable phenomenon, it leads Taplin, like Goldhill, to make claims for the reimagining of its expressive presence *behind* or underneath the extant words of the dramatic text:

> Behind the words of Greek tragedy there is action, behind the action emotion: the abstract and concrete are made one, the emotion and the meaning are indivisible. The actual and felt play is my subject. Greek tragedy is often thought of as static, verbal, didactic and irretrievably alien: I hope to show, rather, how it is theatrical, emotional, absorbing – and so can still speak directly to us.
>
> (Taplin 1978: 1)

Taplin's view is a reminder that at the heart of all that is historically unrecoverable is a nevertheless *real*, and *felt*, experience of the voice. It suggests that whilst the voice cannot be recovered, corporeal tools are available to re-experience its possible effects; it is in the body that the sensations of voice are re-felt. There is a parallel, here, with the words of T.S. Eliot in an early essay, 'Seneca in Elizabethan Translations' (Taplin 1978: 1), quoted by Taplin as a preface to the chapter referenced above:

> Behind the drama of words is the drama of action, the timbre of voice and voice, the uplifted hand or tense muscle, and the particular emotion. The spoken play, the words which we read, are symbols, a shorthand, and often, as in the best of Shakespeare, a very abbreviated shorthand indeed, for the actual and felt play, which is always the real thing.
>
> (Taplin 1978: 1)

The tools available to recover the voice, then, include both sonic and textual reimaginings of the live expression within the written form. It is important to remember, though, that whilst the act of voicing makes the voice no more *real* than the lines in the text, individual perceptual function often behaves as if it does. Linguist and philosopher Don Ihde attributes this to the ways in which sociobiology immerses the infant in an environment of sound that is attached to the human voice. The awareness of sound contributes to early formational psychological and physiological processes that start in the womb and may, in part, explain why voice *feels* more real:

Our language … is itself perceptually situated, embodied in receptive and expressive senses and bound to this primordial attachment to the world. So, with language there is nothing without its concrete perceptual dimension. It is first heard, then spoken. The infant, even in the womb, hears the voices of language. Just as we – if we attend to it – feel our voices when we speak, resonate and cadence within our torso, so the infant feels the voice of language before it is thrust into the lighted world.

(Ihde 2007: 185)

An atmospheric recreation of a performance of *The Suppliants* by *Aeschylus* in the early Greek period provides another opportunity to break out of the stubborn historiographical binary that regards the voice as either an objective instrument on one hand, or an adjunct to the written word on the other. As the performance is both long in duration and more closely akin to a festival than to an environment that fostered reverential listening, it serves as a valuable reminder that the voice in action remains subject to countless muscular, spatial and acoustic challenges. In combination, they have as much impact on the stylistics of the actor's voice and the performance outcomes as any determined by the shape and form of the language. The account aligns more closely with Ihde's perceptual views referred to earlier:

The crowd is expectant and eager, though physically tired, already there have been days and nights of ecstatic festivity, beginning with a solemn procession during which the statue of Dionysus has been carried from its temple down towards the Academy on the road to Eleutheros, and including a tumultuous torch lit return, when the god's statue has been placed, where it is now visible, beside the great orchestral circle. There has been sacrifice and ritual, flute music and the chanting of hymns, solemnity and ribald laughter in the atmosphere of release and reverence.

(Nicoll 1949: 27)

In terms of historiography, Nicoll provides a reminder of the importance of factoring in as many environmental conditions as possible in the recreation of the voice so that it is not overshadowed by the dramatic text. To this end, contemporary historians increasingly offer views about embodied performance conditions that range from a relationship between the gesture and the word, the mask and acoustic vocal function, as well as the ways in which the text is indicative of the sound of the voice itself. The following extract critiques the work of historian Oliver Taplin and signals a shift of approach that holds a strong regard for the performance context, even as it also provides no definitive answers:

Even if Taplin is correct that 'there was no important action that was not signaled in the words,' the performance context of a historical theatrical event would influence the delivery, the reception and the significance of those words in ways that are especially difficult for the performance historian to determine.

(Powers 2014: 102)

This suggests, then, the importance of adopting an approach that considers the multiple ways in which festival revels, rituals and poetic chants give rise to different kinds of vocal embodiment. This allows for consideration of the actor's vocal expression in relation to a set of plural impulses that fall outside the text: in relation to the mood or energy of the crowd, in relation to the rapport generated between actors as a consequence of their vocal energy and in relation to eliciting audience response. The capacity to direct the voice in time and space, to target its vibratory trajectory and to judge when to rise above or go beneath the volume of the crowd, amongst other factors, are all crucial elements here. They form part of an individual's calibrated ability to make decisions based upon their own instrumental capacities as well as those instilled in training. Whilst there is a temptation to be drawn solely by the shape of the language on the page, since it provides the extant evidence, as I have shown, it is important to go further in imagining the voice as 'absent' performance (Powers 2014: 13), in order to ensure its distinction from the word itself:

> [A]s classicist Richard P. Martin has well stated, 'timing, gesture, voice inflection, tempo, proximity to the audience … the setting … are factors that determine the meaning of the actual words spoken by a performer as much if not more so than the literal meaning of the words themselves.'
>
> (Powers 2014: 13)

Attention paid to the individual sensations of the voice and its expressive options offers a valuable means of getting close to vivifying the situation on the ground. Where there is debate amongst historians as to the shape and purpose of the dithyramb or whether a circular or rectangular formation influences the hearing and seeing of the performance, for example, the felt sensations of voice exist as a tool of investigation. Sensation-based enquiry also informs discussion where it is suggested that circular formation acoustics 'may not have been best suited to the ancient conditions of masked frontal drama' (Powers 2014: 23). A range of other enactments, which include choric religious ritual performance, masked character representation, solo poetic chants and so on, are all usefully investigated via embodied means.

In all cases, where scholars have assumed that the voice is a subset of the dramatic text, closer examination shows that it is better understood as pluralistic, many layered and predominantly sensation-based. When subjective experiences, along with those of an aesthetic, social and political nature, get put together, classical Greek theatre voice is more fully illuminated. An inclusion of the 'felt' experiences of voice within the spectrum of historical knowledge also enables voice to move a little closer to the contemporary era, in which embodied sensations provide a valuable source of what is knowable.

EARLY MODERN VOICE

I have shown that the impact made by the instrumental voice and its perceptual evaluation is influenced by the specific context within which the theatre or theatre movement is situated. In terms of the ancient Greek voice, the textual analysis that has hitherto provided scholars with the main evidence to support an understanding of its performance characteristics is now additionally supported by embodied supposition and recreation. Moving into the early modern period, it is equally important to identify tools other than the textual that are available for the historiography of voice.

Theatre historian Barbara Hodgdon overcomes some of the shortcomings created by a reliance on dramatic textual analysis by an examination of a number of other performance evidences. One such example is provided in the status hierarchies amongst actors. In the early modern period, as the individual actor comes into prominence, Hodgdon pays attention to the ways in which the Shakespearean 'star' actor is constructed. She notes how it takes place in companies with a social and cultural investment in strong 'lead' actors where high-status behaviour is a feature. I suggest that the company reward for this behaviour helps to support the actor's mindset in positive ways. Together with a number of *given* vocal characteristics, it creates the 'star' performer. It is also worth saying that, since the actor is solely masculine in this period, the socially rewarded qualities of masculinity necessarily predominate in the vocal presence of the 'star'. The socially determined contours of pitch, volume and resonance of the ordinary man in the street are both present and enhanced in the Shakespearean 'star' voice.

There is early evidence of the impact of 'star' quality in a description of actor Edward Alleyn (1566–1626), a regular in the theatre company known as the Lord Admiral's Men. His acting abilities are reported to have influenced his contemporary Shakespeare:

> Alleyn was the real thing: a majestic physical presence, with a 'well-tuned', clear voice capable of seizing and holding the attention of enormous audiences. Achieving instant and enduring fame for his 'stalking and roaring' in the part, Alleyn went on to play Faustus, Barabas, and many other great roles …
>
> The actor in Shakespeare would have perceived what was powerful in Alleyn's interpretation of Tamburlaine, but the poet in him understood something else: the magic that was drawing audiences did not reside entirely in the actor's fine voice, nor even in the hero's daring vision of the blissful object at which he lunges, the earthy crown. The hushed crowd was already tasting Tamburlaine's power in the unprecedented energy and commanding eloquence of the play's blank verse – the dynamic flow of unrhymed five-stress, ten-syllable lines – that the author, Christopher Marlowe, had mastered for the stage.
>
> (Greenblatt 2004: 191)

In the description of Alleyn, not only is there a convergence of the 'star' qualities of 'physical presence' and the voice but also the ubiquitous, yet hard to pin down, capacity of an actor to convey the word where the reception given to the voice is also reliant on the successful conveyance of dramatic language structure (discussed further in Chapters 5 and 6). Whilst this description holds with an unexplained reliance on the superlative that describes Alleyn's voice as 'fine', thereby giving no reliable account of the voice itself, the interrelationship between the actor's ability to give voice to the spoken word structure comes to the fore as an important consideration. It suggests that the capacity to engage in semantic understanding and to exhibit vocal dexterity mark some of the key qualities in an emergent 'star' actor in the early modern period.

But what else of voice and the 'star' system? I propose that an actor's perception of their social status gets reflected in intentional vocal presence. This, in addition to the capacity to sound the voice as instrument and as linguistic communication, contributes to the 'star' outcome. The individual voice in the 'star' system, informed by the interiority of mental conviction, benefits from the reinforcement provided by external rewards from both company and audience. Such are the qualities exemplified in Burbage, one of the leading actors in the Chamberlain's/King's Men:

> Arguably, Richard Burbage (1568–1619), the leading actor in the Chamberlain's/ Kings Men was the first Shakespearean star: according to his eulogist, who mentions his performances of Hamlet and Lear in particular, he 'suit[ed] the person which he seemed to have … so lively' as to amaze spectators and fellow actors alike, even to evoke in them a kinesthetic response.
>
> (Hodgdon 2007: 47)

Hodgdon continues:

> Burbage achieves stardom as understood today only through a kind of back-formation, for the notion of stardom is alien to early modern thinking: when Shakespeare's company staged *Hamlet*, *Othello* or *King Lear*, those roles went to Burbage because he was their most celebrated performer. In the early modern universe, a performer's success depended on his status as a sharer payer who shared the proceeds equally with his fellows; even if financial arrangements were an ensemble affair, then as now 'show me the money' was the bottom line.
>
> (Hodgdon 2007: 48)

Whilst I argue that there is something beyond being gifted with money at stake in Burbage's 'lively' manner, particularly in the contrast it provides with the 'majesty' of Alleyn, the confidence it gives rise to contributes to vocal demeanour as pitch energy, durational capacity and intuitively modulated tone. In all senses, Burbage evidences a *tonal* vocal confidence that is capable of enlisting audience engagement in dramatic action and its meanings.

Shakespeare wrote with particular players in mind, and it is not hard to imagine that, as his leading man, Burbage's exceptional qualities enabled him to make an outstanding success of the roles of Richard III, Romeo and Hamlet. His 'persuasive' tones, modulated by inner conviction, distinguish him from the other leading actor in the company, Will Kempe, with specialisms that combine verbal wit, physical dexterity and the utterance of 'obscene songs' (Greenblatt 2004: 292). It is likely that the melodies, rhythms, rhymes and tempos of the London voice impacted on Kempe more than Burbage because the 'persuasive' tones of the latter suggest he is linked more closely with textual interpretation. I suggest, too, that Kempe's physical and improvisatory skills, particularly in dance and clowning, as well as crowd-pleasing song, best suited the jig, the afterpiece of many Elizabethan productions, and he inflected his voice accordingly:

> The undisputed master of the jig was, unsurprisingly, Will Kemp [sic] – who looked back on his career as one 'spent ... in mad jigs and merry jests'. His stage presence, his comic timing, and more than anything else his dancing skill and stamina made his jigs famous.
>
> (Shapiro 2005: 47)

I argue that Kempe's voice holds a mirror to the inflection, tone, rhythm and pace of the jibe, present in London's living spoken cultures. This is in contrast to the voice of Burbage, which falls under the more dominant influence of the form and content of the written verse. Their combined legacies, however, establish a template for future 'star' actors. The instrumental, psychological and stylistic elements present in their vernacular vocal energy and intuitive verse delivery are all features that distinguish the actor in the British interpretive traditions right into the twenty-first century.

Hodgdon detects just such a combination of qualities in the actor Thomas Betterton (1635–1710) more than a half century after Alleyn, Burbage and Kempe:

> Like Burbage before him, Thomas Betterton (1635–1710) was dubbed 'our English Roscius' – the period's honorary epithet for 'star quality': perhaps the first great actor-manager deeply associated in the public's mind with Shakespeare, he was not only the most popular but the most remarkable (and remarked upon) actor of his generation.
>
> (Hodgdon 2007: 48)

Hodgdon reports that audiences responded to more than the external appearance of his acting but also to 'actions, gestures, intonations, vocal colors, mannerisms, expressions, customs, protocols, inherited routines, [and] authenticated traditions' (Hodgdon 2007: 49). The integration of voice with

embodied intention is clearly a critical factor in the acclaim he receives, as is
the audience recognition of the actor's place in a long line of acting traditions:

> In an age when audiences were especially tuned to hearing an actor's performance,
> Betterton's vocal musicality invites comparison with Sir John Gielgud's incom-
> parable attention to elocution and phrasing. Waxing rhapsodic, Cibber [Colley
> Cibber (1671–1757), an English actor-manager and playwright] speaks of hearing
> Shakespeare's words 'rising into real Life, and charming [the] Beholders'; and in
> 'all his Soliloquies of moment,' he writes 'the strong Intelligence of his Attitude
> and Aspect, drew you into such an impatient Gaze and eager Expectation, that
> you almost imbib'd the Sentiment with your Eye, before the Ear could reach it.'
> (Hodgdon 2007: 49)

Hodgdon regards Betterton and others as 'prototypes of the "personality
performance", in which an actor's persona and idiosyncratic performing
style overwhelm the role' (p. 48). I suggest that Betterton and others like
him, in full command of their vocal effectiveness and communicative strategies, on stage and off, succeed because they also fulfil a cultural and social
need. The actor who is able to synthesize both the mental conviction, spoken
about earlier, and a fully developed voice sets a standard not just for voice
and acting but also for public life in which the qualities of demonstrative
individualism get favoured.

Theatre voice at the end of the early modern period, then, is not just a
matter of vocal stylistics, but also about the ways in which the construction
of actor identity underpins the expression of voice. I return to questions
asked at the outset of the chapter about voice in theatre history and its
indelible links to the knowing subjectivity of the actor and the effectiveness of the vocal instrument as object. Imbricated, too, are important factors
about the ways in which the expressive voice corresponds with the social
and aesthetic values of the day and has its impact on audience receptivity.

The voice as instrument, capable of manifesting pitch, volume and
nuance in any performance space, also comprises the acoustic characteristics
of timbre that arise out of and also reflect an individual's unique physiology
and experience. Success for Burbage, Betterton and others lay in their ability
to fuse 'logos', body, vocal amplitude, timbre and characterization such that
they could work with, challenge and also change the theatre of their day.
They learnt to speak the language of theatre and the 'street', and voiced
both with an effective and calibrated sound dynamic that had the capacity
to succeed both on stage and off. I leave the early modern period with the
idea that, yes, voice in the theatre is about the instrument and the individual,
but it is also about the voice that possesses the capacity to assert a position
in any given theatre company and to fulfil the requirements set by the age to
advance specific artistic standards.

In a metaphorical, as well as a practical, sense, whilst it is the improvisatory
banter of the actor's voice that falters in the face of the ascendency of the

playwright's voice in the middle of the seventeenth century, the voice of the interpretive actor gets ready to respond to the artistic and social challenges that lie ahead:

> Shakespeare's victory over Kempe (even if Kempe had left by choice) was so complete that it's hard in retrospect to see what all the fuss was about. In 1638 the dramatist Richard Brome included a scene in *The Antipodes* in which a clown is taken to task for improvising and for bantering with the audience. When the clown defends himself by appealing to the precedent established by the great comedians of the past, he is told that the days of Tarlton and Kempe are over, it's a playwright's theatre now, and the stage 'purged from barbarism,/ And brought to the perfection it now shines'.
>
> (Shapiro 2005: 48)

Chapter

3   Voice and Stylistics

Critic and journalist Thomas Barnes (1785–1841) commented that Edmund Kean (1787–1833) evoked genius on his debut performance as Shylock:

> It was this that gave fire to his eye, energy to his tones and such a variety and expressiveness to all his gestures, that one might almost say 'his body thought'.
>
> (Hodgdon 2007: 52)

His prescient commentary about the gestural and vocal congruency of Kean anticipates the physical theatre laboratory stylistic of Grotowski in the mid-twentieth century. The difference more than a century and a half earlier, however, is that the power of Kean's physical and vocal fusion is seen to lend him not only a professional advantage, but one that allows him, in the manner of a genius, to transcend all that is quotidian.

Generations of audiences frequently refer to the qualities in actors that evoke in them states of euphoria. It is part of the pleasure of theatre-going to become enraptured by performance. This surfaces or diminishes in keeping with prevailing social and cultural taste. The diary entries of theatre critic Henry Crabb Robinson in 1811, for example, are representative of rapturous nineteenth-century audience responses more widely. His passionate declaration about the actor Sarah Siddons is one such notable example: 'She is the only actor I ever saw with a conviction that there never was nor ever will be her equal' (Pascoe 2013: 114). Sarah Bernhardt (1844–1923), in a later period, is described by Lytton Strachey as having 'superhuman resonance' and the capacity to shake the 'spirit of the hearer like a leaf in the wind' (Pascoe 2013: 22). It shows, again, how audience pleasure in these instances becomes closely linked to an actor's capacity for transcendence.

The descriptions given of Edmund Kean, Sarah Siddons and Sarah Bernhardt in performance, however, make it no less easy to identify their vocal qualities. With 'fire' in his eyes and 'energy' in his tones, Kean is described in terms largely reserved to describe the physical bearing of masculine performers. Siddons, on the other hand, is described in terms that eulogize her as without 'equal' and Bernhardt as 'superhuman'. The gendered connotations about Kean's body, and the enraptured adoration reserved for Siddons, mask perceptions of their actual voices. And although the description of Bernhardt suggests something specific about her resonant capacity, it is her ability to be other than ordinary that is remarked upon.

Whilst the obfuscation of the actual voice occurs in any age of theatre, as I have shown, it is important to think, in addition, about the particular problem it raises for perceptions about the voice of women in theatre. As the hitherto 'unheard' voice of the female actor makes a remarkable debut in the Restoration period, it is worth considering the ways in which the 'new' frequencies from women make an impact:

> Returning from France, where he had passionately enjoyed plays and women, Charles II's Royal Warrant, licensing new theatres in London specified that only women should play women's parts … The advent of the actress (*sic*) marked revolutionary changes in the position women held in the theatre. For instance, female title roles and leading parts now became immensely fashionable.
>
> (Morgan 1981: ix)

The cadences, pitch movement and rhythmic stresses of the female actor, in tandem with audience interest in their actual physical presence, represent a significant set of 'new' sensory dimensions in the restored public theatres. When the sonic, the somatic and the psychological impact of these changes are taken together, I suggest that a new awareness about the voice in action is ushered in for both actor and audience.

In this chapter, then, I examine a number of key voice stylistics from the seventeenth to the end of the nineteenth century. I consider not only the elevated vocal and gestural capacities that pertain to all actors, exemplified in the description of Siddons and Kean, but also the specific impact generated by the female actor's expression in theatre more widely. It is *her* body and voice that are displayed in public for the first time in Western theatre history, and the story of voice, as it begins to include the timbre of women, breaks tradition with the exclusive sounds of the not-yet-broken adolescent male voices that 'played' women throughout the Elizabethan era.

GENDERED PERCEPTIONS

The tragedienne Elizabeth Barry (1658–1713) is described in performance by the actor and critic Colley Cibber (1671–1757) as having 'forced tears from the Eyes of the Auditory':

> Mrs. Barry, in Characters of Greatness, had a presence of elevated Dignity, her Mien and Motion superb and gracefully majestick; her Voice full, clear, and strong, so that no Violence of Passion could be too much for her: And when Distress or Tenderness possess'd her, she subsided into the most affecting Melody and Softness. In the Art of exciting Pity she had a Power beyond all the Actresses I have yet seen, or what your Imagination can conceive.
>
> (Cibber 2017: 160)

An unknown male actor, on the other hand, is described by Cibber, in terms that indicate purely instrumental problems:

> The unskilful Actor who imagin'd all the Merit of delivering those blazing Rants lay only in the Strength and strain'd Exertion of the Voice, began to tear his Lungs upon every false or slight Occasion to arrive at the same Applause.
>
> (Cibber 2017: 107)

In the account given about Barry, the description of her feminine sensibilities outshines that of her voice. In the second, the masculine ego of the actor is shown to impact negatively on his voice. In their different ways, both serve to show that gendered assumptions influence both the performance and the reception to voice as well as the ways of recovering them in history. In the first description, Barry is praised for the impact of her femininity and in the other the male actor, assumed to be strong and effective, is admonished for his instrumental failures.

It must be asked to what degree is Cibber's *effusive* response to Barry part of the effect of the relative 'newness' of the appearance of women on stage and, therefore, part of a gendered story, and how much is it simply a response to her voice in action? Whilst it is likely a mixture of both, it leads me to consider more about the detail of the ways in which both the female and the male voice are recalibrated in relation to the shift in the custom of male 'versions' of the female voice on stage after the Restoration. Do some male actors try too hard vocally, as Cibber indicates, in order to compensate in the face of the new competition from women? And do women gain fame for their sensibility and yet languish for want of actual technical experience?

Although not easy to substantiate, the suggestion is that in all probability the 'new' frequencies from women are given a mixed reception by the audience. The custom and practice in audience receptivity, perhaps more responsive to the familiar, undoubtedly influenced perceptions not just about the female actor's voice but also about the female playwright. The 'problem' of perception is exemplified in the example of Susannah Centlivre (b 1667 d 1723), one of the emergent women playwrights of this period and reputedly one of the most successful.

> Her comedy, *The Busy Body*, 'went on to become one of the most successful plays of the early eighteenth century. It was acted over 450 times before 1800, and became a stock piece through the nineteenth century.'
>
> But the play met with opposition from the actors when in rehearsal for the first production. The actor Robert Wilks 'in a passion threw [his script] off the stage into the pit and swore that nobody would bear to sit to hear such stuff … it was a silly thing wrote by a woman', and the players 'had no opinion of it'.
>
> (Morgan 1981: 56–57)

The voice of the female actor, similar to that of the female playwright, faces not just the technical challenge of an emergence onto the public stage, but also the psychological barrier represented by aspects of a *refusal* of recognition, as exemplified in the response from Robert Wilks. I argue that the physical voice that is not listened to either retreats or forces itself beyond capacity. In both senses it struggles to function effectively.

I suggest, therefore, that a combination of factors impact on the vocal effectiveness of the female actor on the Restoration stage. It is possible that the vocally experienced male actor makes a number of conscious steps to compensate for or supersede the voice of women on stage. On one hand, these are shifts made for artistic reasons in the interests of tonal relativity on stage. But on the other, they are also made in the interests of job protectionism since men are no longer in a position to play female parts themselves. It is important, therefore, to consider the implications of these interrelated conditions for the voice of both genders during this period with their challenges to the existing status quo. As the material and authorial voices become more gender diverse, so do the compensatory forces of exclusion and it is within this dynamic that the voices for both genders forge ahead.

CHARACTERIZED VOICES

I suggest that specific historiographical clues about the quality and impact of women's voices are found in contemporary writers' character archetypes. Although I argue elsewhere in the book that the spoken word obscures the uniqueness of the voice, it is notable that woman's arrival on the stage, as author and actor, provides a new imperative by which to consider aspects of the dramatic text as partial evidence about the voice in action. One example is provided in Centlivre's last comedy, *The Artifice*. Morgan describes it as one of her 'coarsest', due to its characters falling outside the parameters of polite, gendered 'refinement' (Morgan 1981: 59). The contemporary critic who writes that the play is 'scurrilous, impious', 'monstrous' and 'without any beauty' is similar in tone to other negative responses about the new writing by women (Morgan 1981: 59). There is, in this critique, further proof of a fear that women are setting themselves above the 'arbitrary power of their husbands to exert their natural rights for the preservation of their lusts' (Morgan 1981: 59), both as actors and as writers. In *The Artifice*, this position is exemplified in the comedic character of Widow Heedless, 'who stamps around, shouting and boxing people's ears, and is determined not to marry below a lord' (Morgan 1981: 59). In act III, scene I, she addresses her problematic servant, Fainwell:

'Why, you thick-skulled rascal! You unthinking dolt! You senseless idiot! Was ever a pair of dirty clogs brought upon a plate, sirrah? Ha! Was there? Was there? Was there? Hedgehog?' *She follows him about and beats him. Sir Phillip interposing.*
(Morgan 1981: 59–60)

The dialogue suggests that the physical voice of Widow Heedless is loud, harsh of tone and wide-ranging in pitch. This is implied not only in the exclamatory punctuation marks, but also in the words of emphatic remonstration: 'thick-skulled', 'unthinking', 'senseless' and so on. Depicted as one possessed of unwomanly, aggressive tendencies and class 'brutishness' in the relationship with all those around her, particularly her servants, the expectation is that she will *sound* pushy – the ideological thrust of her social estrangement thus evidenced in the voice itself.

The social outsider characteristics of the Widow provide a fulcrum for comedic action. They also provide clues about the vocal expression of the actor and its consequences. It is likely that the actor playing the Widow will exhibit pressed (as in pushed) or constricted tonal features due to the fact that the exercise of the female actor's voice in general is still relatively 'new' to public life. In addition, the Widow's disruptive volubility *and* emphatic pitch, part of the consequences experienced in setting right her wrongs (as woman and as actor), lead to piercing vocal crescendos, such as at the word 'Hedgehog?' It is important to consider, then, that the volume, range and tonality in the voice of the actor playing the Widow might easily falter under this kind of duress. Emphatic and harshly asserted qualities such as these often result in vocal strain. Unless expertly activated by the breath and safeguarded by other vocal health parameters, the voice can become permanently hoarse, creaky and inflexible in tone.

Against a backdrop of theatrical convention, social prejudice and artistic interpretation, it is possible to imagine that the expressive options available to the female actor presented a number of technical challenges. It is unlikely that they received any guidance about managing the voice over the course of a run. In the case of *The Artifice* it only had a three-day life (Morgan 1981: 59), and until formal training was more widely available in the nineteenth century it is likely that the actor had to live with the consequences of vocal fatigue caused by the 'extremes' of this type of delivery.

EPILOGUES AND PROLOGUES

The new vocal ground occupied by women is additionally evidenced in the prologues and epilogues to the texts. They provide an additional source in which to observe and speculate about the timbre, reach and message content of the voice more widely. In Centlivre's *A Bold Stroke for a Wife*, for example, the Prologue, spoken by a Mrs Thurmond, activates the patriotic attention of the audience, via the seductive guise of the female actor who speaks on behalf of the playwright using a comparison that likens Centlivre to a dazzling soldier:

> You'll think, by what we have of soldiers said,
> Our female wit was in the service bred;

But she is to the hardy toil a stranger,
She loves the cloth, indeed, but hates the danger;
Yet to this circle of the brave and gay,
She bid me for her good intentions say,
She hopes you'll not reduce her to half pay.
As for our play, 'tis English humor all;
Then will you let our manufacture fall?
Would you the honor of our nation raise,
Keep English credit up, and English plays.

(Prologue, *A Bold Stroke for a Wife*, Google edition)

Notable in this passage is the gendered nature of the appeal made to the audience with its request for women's pay entitlements: 'She hopes you'll not reduce her to half pay.' The speaker of the prologue expresses a controversial request for equal pay (potentially delivered in an open-toned and unforced voice) whilst, simultaneously, deploying the conventions of gender and pitch with the disarming endearments of tonal modulation: 'But she is to the hardy toil a stranger.' She also uses semantic flattery, aimed in particular at the men in the audience, 'brave and gay', in order to elicit their favour about the play. In combination, the writing voice of the author and the vocal enactments of the actor work to provide a socially 'palatable' yet coded message within a commercial theatrical package. It serves as an example of the ideological influence on the theatre voice where contextual relevance impacts on the actual sound of the voice as well as the content.

Responses to the 'new' voices of the seventeenth-century stage are varied and, as Fidelis Morgan argues, are linked, in part, to the rise of new theatregoers who come from a 'rising bourgeoisie, conscious of themselves as arrivistes, seeking to establish social credentials and so unsure of their own tastes that they settle for what they deem "polite" and "proper"' (Morgan 1981: x). Theatre critic and pamphleteer Jeremy Collier (1656–1726) leads the moral charge on their behalf in his forthright publication, *A Short View of the Immorality and Profaneness of the English Stage* (published 1698) (Nicoll 1949: 372). In this work, Collier condemns the 'Disorders of the Stage' (McCollum 1961 23). He is particularly exercised by the language given to women by playwrights and the ways in which this contributes to transgressions of social decorum:

In this respect the Stage is faulty to a scandalous Degree of Nauseousness and Aggravation. For 1. The Poets make Women speak Smuttily.

(McCollum 1961: 21)

The puritan values that had closed the theatre in the first place are shown to rear their head again in the work of late-seventeenth-century theatre critics such as Collier. Their ideological thrust proves detrimental to both the theatre and the social voice of women: the instrumental voice is repressed and the other marginalized:

> The notion of 'politeness' came to insist on much that Puritans protesting against the theatre had proclaimed, including Jeremy Collier's view that 'modesty … is the character of woman.'
>
> (Morgan 1981: x)

WOMEN'S PUBLIC ROLE IN THEATRE

The emergence of women on the stage in 1660 is a significant milestone not only for the sound and management of the voice, but also for the history of the reception exhibited to women on the public stage as they become incorporated into its economic value:

> The crucial shift in 1660 concerns the terms upon which performing women in England now appeared … women were to be part of that essentially commercial activity – not simply brought in for an occasional appearance but recruited as members of the company of players.
>
> (Bush-Bailey 2009: 12–13)

As I have shown, the Restoration is a hotly contested gendered moment with strong evidence of male and female competitiveness with regard to who gets heard and on what terms. Questions remain, however, about the types of instrumental voices that emerge as exemplary models and the other ways in which women impact on the theatre voice more widely.

There are a number of evidences available to answer questions about voice, including the play texts, as I have shown, the diary entries of the audience, the accounts of the producers and so on. Important, too, are evidences of the impact made by collective theatre cultures, in which, I suggest, collaborative strategies set new relational benchmarks for the voice in performance. What do I mean by this? I propose that new systemic theatre structures give rise to rehearsal processes that, at times, sidestep the autocratic pronouncements of the theatre manager and allow female actors to develop their voices in relation to each other. Historiographic evidence suggests that prominent actresses of the day, such as Elizabeth Barry and Anne Bracegirdle, influenced not just the commercial theatre but also the qualitative relationship within the theatre rehearsal process. Historiography, in this instance, provides a view about the operational frameworks of theatre production in order to better identify the impact on voice and authorship more widely. Of particular note is the evidence provided in The Player's Company in London between 1695 and 1705:

> The company was formed on the basis of a players' co-operative, creating a conspicuously alternative model to the dictatorial management practices of the Theatre Royal Drury Lane at a time in which that theatre had enjoyed a thirteen-year monopoly on the performance of plays on the London stage ... The Players' Company took few risks in its choice of revivals but, during the course of their ten-year run, it produced a number of new plays that have become part of the Restoration dramatic canon ... the company also premiered at least seventeen new plays written by five female playwrights, representing approximately one-quarter of all new dramatic works produced in London between 1695 and 1705.
>
> (Bush-Bailey 2009: 18–19)

The Player's Company is no proof that a correlation exists between collective structures and the healthy production of the voice. It does, however, offer the possibility that its progressive cooperative values helped to promote dialogical opportunities for the benefit of both writers and actors, especially women.

In conclusion, whilst Restoration voice cannot be reconstituted, there is sufficient evidence to deduce that the newly emergent vocal styles remained, as ever, subject to the vicissitudes of both commerce and social taste in the hands of the writers, the producers and the audience. The cultivation of distinctive individual vocal qualities, in which close attention is paid to their healthy function and durability, remains, by and large, some years away. The privileges afforded the author and the producer suggest that those involved in generating the textual narrative retain their theatrical dominance and it is not until the latter part of the eighteenth century that actual vocal training begins to attract more interest than was previously the case. The interesting questions are how did this come about, where did it first arise and who were its first exponents?

TRAININGS

Training of the voice, found in seventeenth-century accounts of the tutelage of women by male actors, evolves in a more sustained fashion late in the seventeenth and on into the early eighteenth century, sometimes in the hands of the female actors themselves. When:

> Ann Dancer first appeared on the York stage William Cooke records that 'her tones were so shrill and discordant' that even an experienced judge like Charles Macklin thought she would never succeed as an actress: it was only 'under the tuition of the *silver-toned Barry*' he adds, that she became an effective tragedienne.
>
> (Brooks 2015: 58)

The account about Dancer serves as a reminder of not only the important economic contribution that healthy vocal function makes to the theatre industry, but also the importance of training to career longevity. The memoirs of actress Anne Oldfield (1683–1730) suggest, additionally, that the 'active transmission of rhetorical skills amongst' female actors serves as one of the ways in which they resisted the 'discursive containment' of male-centred teaching (Brooks 2015: 58).

The rise of the actor manager in the early eighteenth century helped to disseminate performance standards for voice and acting. Inevitably, this also played a part in the reproduction of certain gender stereotyped stylistics, compounded by the use of 'imitation in the transmission of theatrical skills' (Brooks 2015: 56), increasingly regarded as a particular element in the training of the eighteenth-century female actor. To imitate is to create a sound of belonging and it is possible to conclude that female actors trained each other in their own styles of gendered voice in order to enable them to fit into dominant theatre models.

There is a historical problem, too, presented by the attempt to describe the sound of the voice in prose. Even when there are recording devices available, it remains an issue. It begs the question about the language that is most effective for this purpose. I suggest that the vocabulary of vocal perception, as it is linked to the social expectations of gender, provides a useful starting point. It offers an opportunity to better imagine a number of distinctive vocal features that are a consequence of the ways in which the tropes of gendered voice are retained in the cultural ear across time. The effect of the sound in the mind is a tool often utilized by poets and as a consequence is often equally as 'believable' as that which is uttered. Where the actual voice recedes, the structures (and sounds) of gender endure. And whilst this in no way reproduces the voice nor fully identifies the qualities in the voice that retain a stronger cultural hold over others, it points the way to an effective utilization of perception in order to activate the recreation of the voice in the mind.

GENDERED STYLISTICS IN THE EIGHTEENTH-CENTURY THEATRE VOICE

What follows gives consideration to some of the ways in which the combined impact of theatre designers, writers, producers, actors and, particularly, audiences fosters and perpetuates the 'heightened' vocal stylistics in the theatre of eighteenth-century England. It is of additional interest that, as ever, the actor able to occupy an exclusive position, by virtue of their vocal virtuosity, is the one most likely to corner the job market; the one who is able to make a virtue out of their singularity in this respect also impacts on public attitudes about the economic conditions of the acting profession in ways that are sometimes detrimental to the actor who is not able to make a mark. In other words, the public encourages and, in return, is encouraged to hunger after a singular 'star':

> A rare theatrical commodity – a singular commodity in other words – was valued in the market in its own right, according to how much it would bring a manager, and more importantly, independently of the performer's gender.
>
> (Brooks 2015: 25)

This provides evidence that even in the performance of underdog femininity a few 'select' women are able to gain a market advantage. The actress Mrs Jordan, otherwise known as Dora or Dorothy Jordan, for example, in common with many of her contemporaries, is shown to make a performance feature out of the recognizable and valued aspects of her own gender:

> She was not alone in doing so. Sarah Siddons, Jordan's contemporary and tragic counterpart mirrored Jordan both in the cultivation of an effect of sincerity – sincerity being defined by Jacob Golomb as the congruence of 'one's behaviour and one's innermost essence' – and in the techniques used to elicit it.
> …
> In doing so both these women transformed the way in which women's theatrical performance was understood, re-aligning it within the framework of bourgeois notions of femininity and cultivating in the process a relationship between the personal and the performed which still persists to this day.
>
> (Brooks 2015: 96)

The argument put forward by Brooks makes it possible to appreciate audience preference for vivid aural and physical evocations of gender in which the actors appear to utilize 'through the characters … their own authentic emotions and selves' (Brooks 2015: 97). I suggest, then, that gender is one of the key social factors to inform the vocal characteristics of the late eighteenth-century theatre. Interestingly, although the vocal aesthetics generated are unfashionable and virtually inaudible to the contemporary ear, exposure to the 'authentic' identity of the performer is still sought after and remains an abiding feature of audience reception more generally. I argue, for instance, that in the following 2016 review of Lorca's *Yerma* at the Young Vic Theatre in London, the reviewer's rapturous response to the performer Billie Piper is underpinned by his prior knowledge of the performer's age and life experience:

> The gutting brilliance of Piper's performance is that, even while it traces the protagonist's descent from witty charmer into crazed obsessive with unsparing honesty, it keeps offering aching reminders of the luminously winning young woman she once was.
>
> (Taylor 2016)

And a critique of Piper's delivery in the *Telegraph*, in the same play, provides clues about a prized vocal quality in her 'extraordinary spontaneity', which links to knowledge about the 'truth' of the actor herself':

> Appearing in all but one scene, she snares you – uttering each line with an extraordinary spontaneity which in turn brings an emotional truth.
>
> (Lawrence 2016)

In both instances, there is a reviewer response to the gendered emotional reflection in the voice. This provides parallels with the eighteenth-century appetite for heightened yet familiar vocalized gendered qualities. There is an important difference, however, in the eighteenth century. Here the terms for evaluating performance are set at a different end of the scale and expressions of 'truth' are indicated by extremes of pitch, volume and modulation:

> theatergoers not only enjoyed performances that we would find overwrought, they enjoyed watching these performances over and over and over again. In fact, the intensity of their pleasure seemed to stem partly from the repetition, which allowed for a deep familiarity with the lines and gestures associated with particular plays. We might regard the memories of romantic theatergoers as recording devices that were assisted by the repetition of a familiar repertoire. And serving as a further aide-memoire was the condensation of the romantic theatrical experience to a collection of emotionally, visually, or sonically intense scenes that helped to imprint these plays on the memory. The memorization of these 'points' made theatergoing more intensely pleasurable, as audience members anticipated these particular moments, watched them play out, and compared them to versions they had already experienced or even enacted themselves.
>
> (Pascoe 2013: 72)

The influence of intense and wildly embellished physical and vocal performance on eighteenth-century audience pleasure is noted in accounts that reference the work of actor-manager David Garrick (1717–1779). They provide further illustration of the ways in which audiences were acculturated to extravagant movements of voice that were distinctively set apart from the conversational norms of the day yet also still bore a relation to the gendered perceptions that gave rise to them. Again, there is evidence of audience desire for extremities of sensation, albeit based upon recognizable features:

> They had long been accustomed to an elevation of the voice … with a sudden mechanical depression of its tones, calculated to excite admiration, and to entrap applause. To the just modulation of the words, and concurring expression of the features from the genuine workings of nature, they had been strangers.
>
> (McIntyre 2001: 39)

Historian Pascoe concludes, likewise, that it is, in part, the vocal range itself that provides a key to the enduring success of actor Sarah Siddons:

> What audience members heard when they witnessed Sarah Siddons perform was, to a large extent, what made them quiver and burst into sobs, what made them succumb to hysteria and collapse in the aisles, and what led them to conjure her performances in conversation years after the fact.
>
> (Pascoe 2013: 109)

Where she cautions with later evidences about Siddons' capacity to interpret the word as the key to her success (thus raising the thorny question of whether it is the voice or the words uttered that hold sway), it is clear that her use of voice as a highly nuanced reflection of both thought (in language) and emotion is second to none. In the following account, she notes Thomas Campbell's description of Siddons' Queen Katherine performance in which he celebrates the:

> clear and intelligent harmony of unlaboured elocution, which unravels all the intricacies of language, illuminates obscurity, and points and unfolds the precise truth of meaning to every apprehension.
>
> (Campbell 1834 cited in Pascoe 2013: 109)

George Frederick Cooke's turn-of-the-century Shylock in the early 1800s mirrors some of the audience-pleasing vocal stylistics exercised by Siddons but, in his case, he successfully draws upon prevailing masculine tropes, as well as those that are distinctive to him personally. Several of them are idiosyncratic and a few of them less than vocally optimal:

> he seized and strongly kept your attention; but he was never pleasant … He loved too fondly his own caustic and rascally words; so that his voice, which was otherwise harsh, was in the habit of melting and dying away inwardly in secret satisfaction. He limited every character to its worst qualities; and had no idealism, no affections, no verse.
>
> (Gross 1994: 103)

It is very likely that Cooke's 'harsh' tone had a relationship to the heavy consumption of alcohol. (This causes the vocal folds to swell in a way that sets up the conditions for abrasive phonation.) He appears to have made good use of the situation, however, and was able to attach his own harsh tone and attendant vocal histrionics to existing aesthetics in which value is ascribed to extreme modulations of pitch and tone, as well as to the abrupt disappearance or dying away of the voice. He thus made a unique feature out of his condition and readily incorporated it as part of his singular and acclaimed stage signature. In ways not dissimilar to the female actors who called upon the vocal aesthetics of 'distressed' femininity, he was able to deploy the voice of dissolute masculinity to great acclaim:

> He was often drunk on stage, often so drunk he did not even show up at the theatre, and in 1809, having exhausted most of his credit with London audiences, he decided to accept an invitation to appear in New York. As the first established star of the English stage to visit America, he proved a major attraction. His sins were overlooked; his performances were extolled – and one of the parts that he played was naturally Shylock … Cooke offered something new. American playgoers thrilled to his sarcasm, his harsh exultant laughter, his rage, his rapid shifts of mood.
>
> (Gross 1992: 104)

VOCAL VIRTUOSITIES

Sarah Siddons (née Kemble), born on 5 July 1755 (d. 1831) to a leading theatrical family, and a member of Garrick's troop as a young woman, learnt her craft in the company cradle of extreme 'verbal orchestration' (Manvell 1970: 125). As stated earlier, the ways in which she adapted dominant vocal styles and made them her own had a huge impact on her audience. She deployed not only the tones of 'feminine sincerity', but also those that ranged across a scale of operatic musical virtuosity:

> she orchestrated the part by means of her high talent in the use of voice and gesture. The fustian verse, so inadequate or even ludicrous when set down in cold print, became unaccountably enriched when she gave her impassioned expression to it.
>
> (Manvell 1970: 125)

Siddons incorporated recognizable social tropes described by Pascoe as emergent in an era distinctive for its romantic nostalgia:

> Siddons's voice – unique, irreplaceable, transient – came into being at a moment when people were exceptionally preoccupied with ephemeral objects, and with sound, in particular, that most ephemeral of entities.
>
> (Pascoe 2013: 111)

So, not only was her sound evocative of the unrecoverable fact of voice in a prerecording era, it was a sound that stretched the spoken voice out of recognition by virtue of its operatic-like qualities. The result was a voice that went beyond the bounds of the ordinary. Actors like her became:

> intensified … human beings, still rhetorical by our standard, since every passion had to be given its outward, visible sign through the art of 'pantomime', the constant deployment of face and body to reflect and, when necessary, heighten, the expression of the voice.
>
> (Manvell 1970: 126)

CHARACTER VOICE

Siddons was keen to ensure that her voice was matched in the semantic content expressed. In a letter to an amateur writer that admonished him about his literary failings, Siddons underscores a requirement for a full emotional palette in her character portrayals. It gives further evidence of the expectations she had for her own performance, and clues about the ways in which dramatic character necessarily evoked the full gamut of emotional expression:

> the plot is very lame and the characters very, very ill-sustained in general, but more particularly the lady, for whom the author had me in his eye. This woman is one of those monsters (I think them) of perfection, who is an angel before her time, and is so entirely resigned to the will of heaven, that (to a very mortal like myself) she appears to be the most provoking piece of still life one ever had the misfortune to meet. Her struggles and conflicts are so weakly expressed, that we conclude they do not cost her much pain, and she is so pious that we are satisfied she looks upon her afflictions as so many convoys to heaven, and wish her there, or anywhere else but in the tragedy.
>
> (Manvell 1970: 127)

In this letter, Siddons expresses a commitment not just to the powerful and emotional acting choices associated with the period, but, again, to those that draw upon recognizable gendered emotional features. Audiences generally concurred, with inevitable costs for the actor at the heart of this highly wrought vocal and physical stagecraft. It is notable that as Siddons waited in the wings at Drury Lane on the night of 10 October 1782, she is described as having real concerns about the sustainability of her vocal instrument:

> Above everything else she feared the loss of her voice … Two days before, after the first of the two meagre rehearsals allowed her, she had found herself afflicted with a sudden hoarseness.
>
> (Manvell 1970: 2)

Siddons remained under pressure to ensure that her voice stayed in optimum condition. With expectations running high, she needed both her voice and her interpretation to work in harmony in order to affect the audience in the accustomed ways; the parting of craft from content was unwanted exposure and unduly tested audience acceptance and loyalty.

The actor who wished to remain high in an audience's esteem had to find ways to manage not just their vocal health, but also their emotional resilience. As in any era of acting, livelihoods depended upon an ability to work at optimal vocal capacity and to recreate affective emotional expression night after night:

> Actors and actresses were expected to cleave their way into the hearts of their audience, banishing all resistance, derision or would-be intellectual criticism by

appealing directly and irresistibly to their emotional susceptibilities. Men would weep when moved to do so; fashionable women would fall into hysterics, fainting in the hot crush of the theatre pit. What audiences above all resented, and resented vociferously, was the inability of an actor or actress to stir them.

(Manvell 1970: 2)

The play by Thomas Southerne, *Isabella, or, The Fatal Marriage*, in which Siddons appeared in October 1782, suited her abilities well. Her capacity to weave the nuances of pitch, tonal modulation and tempo with those of gestural synchrony chimed, as we have seen, with the expectations of her audience. Historian Roger Manvell writes lyrically about the fact that the plays themselves were often 'written precisely to achieve these ends' (Manvell 1970: 2):

The moment she took the stage at the beginning of the play and spoke the first familiar lines, using all her skill to hush and then to move her audience, Sarah knew she was carrying the audience with her. … Everything was in her favour: her voice had returned to her and she was using it with powerful effect.

(Manvell 1979: 3)

The relationship between Siddons' unique psychophysiological set-up and the roles that the writer Southerne wrote for her provides a key example of the ways in which dramatist and actor historically synthesize their frameworks. This is evidenced in work right into the twenty-first century, particularly in the close actor, writer and director relationships of Mike Leigh, Alan Bennett and Pedro Almodóvar, to name but a few. Such examples provide evidence of a mutuality of interest between the artistic and the commercial viability of the voice where it has an influence on the rise or fall of an audience's estimation with consequences for the box office. Positioned in this way, voice is one of the key 'meaning' systems not only in eighteenth-century theatre, but across theatre history. Where the play, or later the film, is deemed artistically or commercially ineffective, the voice, too, is seen as part of its failure. Conversely, where the play is a triumph, the voice is often regarded as a key factor in its success.

Theatre historian Manvell emphasizes an enduring belief in the profound impact of Siddons' voice on the development of English acting. Pascoe explains the impact on the ground that she 'broke with cultural memory, topping the settled accretion of past interpretations and causing audience members to hear familiar lines in new and disconcerting ways' (Pascoe 2013: 111). Manvell, similarly, cites her interpretive capacity. He gives particular reference to one of her most celebrated roles, Lady Macbeth. In the following account, she is described as showing respect for the conventions of gendered expression along with the more transgressive signatures of a mind under duress. Her interpretation is seen to rely on a fluid use of pitch range, constriction of the larynx – in order to give emphasis to the inexpressible – abdominal squeezing to punch out the breath, and sharp bursts of both modulated and unmodulated phrasing in order to complete a vocal extravaganza:

> Her audience on 2 February 1785 – her benefit night – included … Burke (who, in his *Reflections on the French Revolution*, was to speak of 'the tears that Garrick formerly, or that Siddons not long since, have extorted from me'). The tears were not for Lady Macbeth but for the line in characterization Sarah and her audiences most favoured: pathos, moral sentiment, and rhetorical fervour and disdain.
>
> (Manvell 1970: 122–123)

In this description, there is evidence of the ways in which Siddons places the voice at the epicentre of her interpretive ability, to render it one of the strongest and most effective elements of her stagecraft. In using voice to evoke powerful emotions in the audience, much as music does, Manvell also suggests it exploits prevailing ideology about the inequity of women's social role:

> She became the embodiment of all women who had been wronged, and the consciences of her self-willed, violent and sentimental audiences were stirred … on the stage she spoke with an impassioned energy felt by many to have never before been equaled in the English theatre.
>
> (Manvell 1970: 123)

VOICE AND REGIONALISMS

Manvell's account of Siddons' Lady Macbeth as the embodiment of 'all women who had been wronged' is clearly open to interpretation. What it does offer, however, is another example of the ways in which themes of social and cultural relevance are reflected in the voice. Included in these, in addition, are the class and regional differences that play a part in the reception given to Siddons. There is sufficient information provided in contemporary accounts to indicate that audience reception fluctuates once she is at a remove from her protected and elevated status in London and on tour in the provinces. Manvell draws on the account of a contemporary, the actor Charles Mathews, who describes a tricky encounter during a summer season in Leeds in which the audience is less than attentive to her status and feel perfectly comfortable about interrupting her performance. This anticipates discussion about the status of vocal regionalisms in relation to standard speech, but also about the voice as part of the ideals of social improvement that increasingly preoccupies trainers, educators and performers on both sides of the Atlantic from the mid-eighteenth century onwards:

> It was very painful to the admirers of Mrs Siddons to witness her involuntary submission to such brutal treatment. It was not surprising that the majestic and refined style of her performances should not be appreciated by such people; they

would have prized far higher the efforts of a good wear-and-tear pair of lungs, that could 'split the ears of the ground-lings', than the beautiful subdued tones, for which this accomplished mistress of her art was so celebrated in particular scenes, and which reached the heart by their tenderness.

(Mathews cited in Manvell 1970: 134–135)

The impact on voice not only of class and regional differences, but also of ethnicity, is another reminder of the importance of framing theatre voice in ways that allow it to be regarded within the simultaneous operation of pluralistic sociopolitical as well as individualistic frameworks. Twenty-first-century voice practitioner Tara McAllister-Viel, for example, makes conscious efforts to challenge the assumptions of Western voice praxis and work with 'an alternative way to think about, talk about, and train an actor's voice in relation to an actor's culture' (McAllister-Viel 2009: 427). And whilst matters of interculturalism are not likely to be at the forefront of the eighteenth- or nineteenth-century theatre mind, it is important to factor in notions of difference to the historical approach in order that assumptions are examined. Kemble family biographer Percy Fitzgerald, for example, by looking at a number of audience responses to Siddons' acting, usefully suggests that there was more than one way to respond to a particular performance and that not all audiences were of the same composition or inclination:

Fitzgerald tries to divide the response to parts in which she appeared during her London career into categories, 'those in which she overwhelmed her hearers with the grandeur and majesty of her impersonating' and those 'when she excited, pleased, and interested them. In comedy, in which she tried so hard to shine, he admits her to have been 'mediocre, or, at most, intelligent'.

(Manvell 1970: 123)

VOICE MENTORS

Siddons' impact overall serves as a benchmark of dramatic interpretation for a generation and, as such, leaves an indelible mark on the voice in the English theatre. Manvell, for example, argues that Ellen Terry, at the end of the nineteenth century, is much influenced by Siddons and uses her work as a template for her own interpretation of Lady Macbeth in Henry Irving's production in 1888 (Manvell 1970: 123). As an example of cross-generational mentorship within acting cultures, then, the model provided by Siddons offers a useful segue into subsequent theatre voice history. A note of caution is again, however, important. The narratives which frame actors such as Siddons, Garrick, Terry and others of their ilk are ones, in the main, created within white, bourgeois, metropolitan theatre cultures. Their story is part of, but certainly not all of, a full spectrum of performance life in which voices exist that are as notable for being unheard as those that are heard.

It is crucial, therefore, to give thought to the unheard and the undocumented in order to ensure that diversity sits at the heart of the history of voice in theatre.

The question of the diversity of representation is important, too, when it comes to a consideration of actor training. At the start of the nineteenth century, for example, as it was not yet a feature of mainstream British stage life, actors had to learn their trade within the companies in which they worked. The question of which actors were accepted into these companies (and from which communities drawn) needs to be factored in to any overall assessment of the impact training had on the profession, and consequently on the voice:

> actors in the 1830's who did not come from theatrical families, but who showed some aptitude for the stage, learned their craft by working in a company. They might need some tuition in elocution and fencing and would have to invest in the purchase of the appropriate 'props' (as the actor's wardrobe was called). By the end of the century definite moves had been made towards the establishment of a regular system of training.
>
> (Jackson 1994: 82)

Within the erratic context of actor training at the turn of the nineteenth century, there is evidence that voice is seen, on one hand, as an *objective* skill, like fencing, whilst, on the other, as part of a *subjective* capacity imperceptibly *acquired* within theatrical families and companies. The voice, as such, is deemed capable of response to technical instruction with regard to not only the clarity of textual expression, but also the subjective perceptions related to character emotion. These capacities are further shaped in the light of the social context, the plays themselves and the spoken language norms outside the theatre.

As I have shown in previous theatre epochs, the actual *sounded* qualities of the voice are formed from and created in reference to the cultural spoken norms of the general population. They are then either copied or exceeded to different degrees in the theatre. I suggest that the 'successful' nineteenth-century theatre voice, as with the voice in any era, is one, then, able to operate in relation to two main influences. One is made up of the baseline awareness of the rhythms and cadences of the conversational voice. These are then magnified and elaborated according to context. The other is the voice that is tied mysteriously to the emotional disposition of the actor in their character role – but not yet to themselves. An individual's subjective experience of their life per se is generally not seen to contribute to the psychophysical materiality of the expression of voice itself, although of course their gendered characteristics, in general, are. It is not until later in the twentieth century that an individual's subjective account of their lived life is acknowledged to constitute part of the synthesis of elements that make up vocal expression in its entirety.

More impactful on the operation of voice in nineteenth-century theatre than issues of an individual psychological nature are the conditions of class, as they affect the baseline norms of speech and shape of the voice itself. The theatre stylistics generated in both Pantomime and Circus spanned the class divide, but a move towards the creation of a theatre of 'respectability' in this period begins to further highlight a split between 'high' and 'low' theatre. In turn, this leads to divisions of the actual sound and manner of the voice into ever more precise delineations of class and social privilege:

> theatres began to accommodate themselves to social rituals familiar to middle- and upper-class playgoers – to the exclusion or at least marginalization of others.
>
> (Jackson 1994: 11)

VOICE AND CLASS

The discussion about voice and class necessarily also includes the geographical location and design of the theatres (discussed further in Chapter 4). These two factors offer additional ways in which to draw parallels between the social background of the actor and their audience and the ways in which accommodations were made for different audiences within theatre buildings themselves:

> The trend was emphatically towards smaller, more comfortably appointed and socially exclusive theatres. At the same time, music-halls were growing in number and capacity: as a venue for popular entertainment a good music-hall suffered none of the inhibitions of the newer theatres, and from the managers' point of view they were cheaper to run.
>
> (Jackson 1994: 11)

Social historian Michael Sanderson connects social mobility in the late Victorian period to a change in the selection of the dramatic canon for performance. He suggests that some of the ways in which art mirrors society can be traced to the fact that the plays in this period begin to be chosen for the ways in which they speak to and also represent a 'new' educated class:

> The change in the social origin of the actor was closely related to the nature of the plays in which he was called to perform. Irving, and before him Phelps, Macready and Kean, worked in the theatre of romantic costume drama and Shakespeare. The grand gesture, torrential rhetorical style, elaborate costume and disguise, characterization far remote from the experience of the audience, the very chiaroscuro of limelight and shadow distanced the players from the audience. The rise of naturalistic drama from the 1860s … began the subtle change. Now the

characters wore modern dress, inhabited recognizable interiors and spoke in the educated parlance of the day.

Actors from an upper-middle-class background were needed on the stage because most of the characters depicted in plays came from that milieu.

(Sanderson 1984: 18–19)

VOICE, SPEECH AND VERSE DRAMA

In contrast to the late Victorian acting tradition, personified by Henry Irving (1838–1905), stands the work of William Poel and the Little Theatre movement in the USA. Born William Pole, later known as Poel, on 22 July 1852, he is a key figure in both the promotion of poetic drama, including that by Shakespeare, and the means of speaking it (Webb 1979). The following account suggests he was someone highly dedicated to the process of fostering a specific voice and speech stylistic for the speaking of the Shakespearean canon:

> Although Poel's "Poetry in Drama" may be considered his most important single article on poetic drama, his article "On 'The Speaking of Poetry'" (Shakespeare League Journal, April, 1918) is interesting as a study of the Poelean approach to two disparate subjects: spoken poetry and textual criticism. Under a single title the article includes, first, a discussion of the speaking by actors of Shakespeare's blank verse and, second, minor arguments about scholars' treatment of Shakespeare drama, such as the interpretation of the prologue to Romeo and Juliet.
>
> (Webb 1979: 48)

Using an analogy with music, Poel articulates a wish for Shakespeare's blank verse to be heard, rather than read. At a stroke, he links British theatre to the values of the oral performance of dramatic composition, in which attention is principally paid to the organizing structure of the thoughts, rather than to their actual emotional impact in expression. It is this strand of the spoken tradition that begins to have a major impact on the early origins of voice training in the UK's drama schools (see the discussion in Chapter 6):

> Shakespeare is written to be spoken. Dramatic poetry, so long as it remains unspoken, may be compared with a composer's libretto; it is something that is incomplete. The music, which in this case is elocution, must be added. (Poel quoted in Scott in 'Bringing the theatre to the countryman', The World's Work, p. 614 [a partially identified clipping in the William Poel Collection in Watson Library, University of Kansas] cited in Webb 1979: 49)

William Poel puts great store by concepts of rhythm: the rhythm of speech, the rhythm of individual lines, the rhythm of sections and, if the poetry is in the form of verse drama, the rhythm of the play as a complete unit.

Furthermore, within the rhythmic lines, he draws attention to the necessity of a varied tempo:

> Surely the good reading of good poetry needs variety of time as well as tune [Poel 1913]. ... Because of Poel's preoccupation with 'time and tune,' his preliminary rehearsal of actors in a Shakespeare drama resembled the practice of a children's choir under a stern music master
>
>> He began his rehearsals by 'teaching the tunes' to the company. Every line was analysed as a series of musical notes. Then Poel would himself 'give the tune' with deliberate exaggeration. The actor had to repeat it with the same exaggeration over and over again until it was firmly fixed in his (sic) mind. Only then would Poel allow the actor to speak the lines without exaggeration.
>> (Norman Marshall 1957 cited in Webb 1979: 50)

Of particular note is the insistence on a 'natural' voice, on one hand, matched against the enforcement of its 'naturalness' in voice training systems marked by repetition and routine. It is of significance that the paradox implicit in the call for the use of 'natural' conditions of the voice, in order to support 'artificial' teaching regimes, is one that makes a regular appearance throughout the history of vocal training methodologies:

> Despite his disciplinarian attitude in enforcing memorization of the 'tune' of dialogue, Poel preached the effectiveness of an everyday quality in language. He favoured the rhythm of modern colloquial speech, he said, ruling, on one hand, against the artificial speaking of verse fashionable in the eighteenth century and, on the other hand, against a sing-song recitation ... Any sing-song cadence that occurs in speech, he argued, is a symptom of artificiality, of a situation in which the speaker's words do not reflect sincerity.
> (Webb 1979: 50)

Theatre historian Bernice Webb states that Poel was bolstered by other contemporary critics such as M.A. Bayfield in his work *Shakespeare's Versifications*. Both were of the view that a freer, more natural speech basis was implied in a loosening of metrical attention in Shakespeare's later plays in which, they argued, there was to be no overt stress on the end-of-line rhymes:

> [Poel] opposed rhyme. Any rhyme present in dramatic verse, he said, should be obscured in speaking. Aiming for naturalness, Elizabethan dramatists inserted no more than an occasional rhymed couplet.
> (Webb 1979: 51–52)

Poel's dramatic verse-speaking innovations begin to take their place against Irving's exaggerated vocal stylistics and the repressed 'underplayed' speech of the Bancrofts (Kennedy 1989: 34). (Marie and Squire Bancroft, both independently and in their partnership, were regarded as leading figures in the theatre in the mid-Victorian period.) Whilst this is evidence of a theatre industry capable of supporting a wide divergence of approaches, it is clear that Poel's day had come: 'Neither of these styles, which Barker called "the Irving idea and the Bancroft idea," would suit Shaw or the New Drama of the new century. Both had flourished from 1860 to about 1880, and were exhausted' (Kennedy 1989: 34):

> London acting in 1904 was at the end of two stylistic traditions, both reaching back deeply into the previous century. Irving's dark, kingly romanticism was atavistic, listening to the echoes of Edmund Kean … But it was Irving who was the architect of the late-Victorian stage. Though his manner was old-fashioned at the start of his career, and his mannerisms so egregious as to inspire cartoonists to absurdity, Irving remained at the turn of the century the unmistakable genius of the London theatre. In the teeth of realism, he could play magnificently to the Victorian fondness for strong passion and astounding shows.
>
> (Kennedy 1989: 34)

OVERLAPPING VOCAL TRADITIONS

At the start of the twentieth century, then, we can appreciate the coexistence of a number of overlapping vocal traditions. It is, however, Harley Granville Barker's work at London's Court Theatre that offers a clear aesthetic step forward, and significantly impacts on the development of vocal stylistics in the early twentieth century. His work is markedly different to the extravagant vocal antecedents represented by Irving, as noted above, and picks up on the 'new' work of William Poel. Interestingly, we see that the emergence of a particular 'natural' vocal stylistic is also made possible at the Court due to a company ensemble context, as against the actor-manager-led production in which 'control of performance shifted away from text to the interpreter' (Kennedy 1989: 33):

> whether the work required passionate elocution like *The Trojan Women* or understated realism like *The Silver Box*, acting at the Court was known from the start for its natural quality.
>
> It is important to understand that the 'naturalness' associated with the Court company does not mean Naturalism in its nineteenth-century deterministic sense … Barker's aim … was 'truth as opposed to effect'.
>
> (Kennedy 1989: 30–31)

Kennedy continues with further detail about the quality of the speech and voice of the actors at the Court in London:

> Two noteworthy characteristics further distinguished the quality of the acting. The first, the diction of the speakers, was a matter of technique. A large number of

Vedrenne–Barker plays depended on eloquence for their chief support. The long rhythmic lines of Murray's Euripides, the musical passages in *Prunella*, the rhetorical brilliance of Shaw, the public speeches of *Votes for Women!* – all required technical excellence of diction and great vocal control. Lewis Casson says that Barker and Shaw could not have accomplished what they did without a stock of actors who had been rigorously trained in stage elocution. They were

> speakers who had grown up in a tradition that there is an art of stage speech as definite and distinct from the speech of the street and drawing room as the art of opera or ballet is from everyday life … It included a much wider range of pitch, much more use of melody in conveying significance and meaning, and definite unwritten rules on phrasing (rhetorical punctuation one might call it) … There were good and bad actors of this tradition, but they were all audible, and the good ones could, under it, give the illusion of 'natural' speaking, though with far more significance.
>
> (Casson cited in Kennedy 1989: 32)

The following extract from Sanderson (1984) provides a useful summary about the many layered factors that pertain to theatre voice in this period, including the social developments in relation to class in the UK, the characteristics and locations of the theatres at the turn of the twentieth century and the emergent emphasis placed upon a physical training of the voice so that audiences are assured of hearing the play. He anticipates the move into an era increasingly preoccupied with the values of speech, of accent, the shape and sound of the vowels and the tunes and cadences of class, region and race. The voice itself, however, has to wait several decades for its place as an expressive vehicle on its own terms within the theatre practices of later in the twentieth century:

> One of the most important developments in the professionalization of the actor in the 1900s was the creation of new, better organized forms of drama education … Various factors gave greater urgency to the need for more formal training. For example, upper class, public school and university men who were coming on to the stage spoke the language of their social class. It was complained that 'they don't pronounce half their words at all', pronounced 'hyah' for 'here', 'thah' for 'there' and, adequate as this may have been in the drawing room, it did not project in the theatre. This problem was exacerbated by the increasing size of theatres … Mrs Campbell had to go into a nursing home in 1897 with fatigue and overstrain. She reflected that if she had had a proper training, 'I would have known how to spare my emotional temperament and to depend a little on skill technique'.
>
> (Sanderson 1984: 32–33)

Part III
Theatre Spaces

4 The Voice Performs Theatre Spaces

INTRODUCTION

An understanding of the design and rationale of theatre space helps in the reconstruction of the distinctive subjective performance of the voice within its environs. Picture a temporary theatre space made of scaffolding, wood and canvas situated in a performance enclosure in the middle of the Brighton (UK) Arts Festival in May 2016. The sound of pedestrians in the street, heavy traffic and distant construction penetrate the performance. As a consequence, the performers are required to enact a number of fine-tunings to breath intensity, volume, sound placement and pace in order to counteract the intrusion and mitigate its negative effects for both player and audience. It takes several runs in order for these to be successfully incorporated in the performance and is representative of a number of ways in which the material voice responds to the unpredictability of acoustic environments.

On the other side of town, but at the same festival, in the Grade II listed Theatre Royal Brighton (built in 1807 and one of the oldest theatres in the UK), performances take place in an auditorium designed to shut out external noise and to provide actors with an acoustic environment directly suited to focusing audience attention. The challenge faced by the actor on its proscenium stage as they look out to its four-tiered auditorium is less about the management of external noise and more about the directional angle of sound, volume control and the management of relational energy in order to cross the arch and reach the audience. Although the two environments could not be further apart, they share in common the fact that theatre design impacts on both an audience's capacity to listen and an actor's ability to effectively vocalize.

This chapter examines a range of themes about performance and audience reception in relation to voice within the material environment of the theatre, whether in impromptu builds such as at the Brighton Festival or the permanent environs of buildings such as Brighton's Theatre Royal. The way in which the materials of building design and set construction, such as wood, glass, stone, concrete and so on, impact on voice production forms part of my thematic concerns. Questions, too, are raised about the ways in which design is also influenced and shaped by the artistic needs of the theatre makers themselves for whom vocal stylistics play a significant role in the transmission of theatre meanings.

Finally, the discussion on voice in Western theatre spaces is one that also needs to acknowledge the anomalous fact that, as I have shown, it is only the male voice that is heard in theatre up until the first appearances of the female actor in the Restoration period post-1660. As a consequence, it is a story in which representation of the female voice by male actors leads to a number of theatre conventions about pitch, pace and the movement of pitch. Some of these contribute to a number of persistent stereotypes that continue to present challenges for the actualization of women's voices in the acting profession up to and including the contemporary period.

Professor Bruce Smith provides a key framework for this examination by making vivid the relationship between the external material space of the theatre, the internal physical spaces of the vocalist and the acoustic phenomenon they both give rise to. His seminal work, *The Acoustic World of Early Modern England*, begins not with voice itself but with the variables involved in the reception of the voice as listeners get affected by the cultural and material conditions of the theatre:

> First of all, there is the intractable individual listener, with his distinctive knowledge and experience, her own particular goals and intentions. To understand these factors, we need a psychology of listening. Since knowledge and intentions are shaped by culture, we need to attend also to cultural differences in the construction of aural experience … We need a *cultural poetics* of listening. We must take into account, finally, the subjective experience of sound. We need a phenomenology of listening, which we can expect to be an amalgam of biological constants and cultural variables.
>
> (Smith 1999: 8)

In Smith's account, social and cultural listening norms affect the reception of voice and its expression. In its utilization of a sociocultural lens, and one that is psychophysical as well as transhistorical, his account opens up views about theatre space that indicate a complex range of interrelated influences. His approach goes beyond design and building materials and gives consideration to the psychosocial phenomena involved in the creation of theatre structures. In some cases the spaces themselves usher in problematic conditions for optimal vocal expression and, in other instances, promote viable and notable vocal qualities.

In order to better analyse the ways in which the voice functions within theatre spaces, at the level of both expression and reception, Smith starts with an assessment of the impact of immersive auditory perceptions on the individual listener:

> Sound immerses me in the world; it is there and here, in front of me and behind me, above me and below me. Sound moves into presence and moves out of presence: it gives me reference points for situating myself in space and time. Sound subsumes

me: it is continuously present, pulsing within my body, penetrating my body from without, filling my perceptual world to the very horizons of hearing.

(Smith 1999: 9–10)

Smith concludes that the immersive and *spherical* shape of the auditory field, in contrast with the linear and 'objective' line of the visual field, has an influence on the ways in which vocal qualities are both received and expressed. This, in turn, bears on a discussion about the Western theatre voice in which a philosophical predisposition for the ocular works with, but also sometimes works against, auditory sense fields. He goes on:

'Listening is centripetal; it pulls you into the world. Looking is centrifugal; it separates you from the world' [Stephen Handel 1989: xi]. It is this sense of separation, perhaps, that explains why Western ways of knowing are grounded in metaphors of seeing.

(Smith 1999: 10)

The expressive voice in relation to these philosophical and perceptual concepts forms part of a wider thematic about the importance of the meeting points between the material conditions that affect the voice (physical body, architectural givens in building and set) and the immaterial (psychology and physics). I suggest that it is important not only to know more about the production of voice in both the individual's body and the theatre structures as part of sensory and material experience, but also to further understand the voice as an immaterial signal within the constructed theatre environment that is subject to the law of physics.

What are the implications of this for the discussion about voice in the theatre space? When the voice emanates from a mobile individual actor, and the sound is moved in multiple ways around a performance space, it is possible to consider that the space may or may not be conducive to enhancing and/or amplifying the signal. Back to Smith again, and I am reminded that a layered and sophisticated notion of multidimensional oral expression and auditory perception is invariably, but not always, dominated at design level by sight-centred or linear preoccupations. As a consequence, the optimal functioning of the voice in the space is left to chance and individual skill rather than to deliberate design. Factors relating to architectural aesthetics, choice of building materials, social need, finance, patronage and so on tend, instead, to take priority – a matter of the *ocular*-led fixtures and fittings of the building trumping the mobile and transient *orality* of the voice.

Contemporary architects variously address questions about the ways in which traditional construction values impact on the activities generated within the confines of their structures. Whilst a wider discussion about architects and the ways in which they articulate a relationship with the activities they give rise to is not the focus of this chapter, the ways in which the voice is invited (or not) to perform in a number of architectural givens are central.

In her book *Theatre and Architecture*, Juliet Rufford suggests that theatre architecture frames both the event and the reception of the voice and is indelibly obliged to the politics of its construction (Rufford 2015: 48). It is possible, once again, to see the impact of both material and immaterial forces on the shape and possibilities for the voice and the ways in which auditory perception is adversely affected when the build is designed with other priorities in mind. On the one hand is the actor on a stage where the acoustics and proportions of the auditorium invite the audience to experience the voice at the level of an unforced spoken register. On the other is the actor whose voice is destabilized by factors in the design that are there to satisfy a range of other stakeholders, including civic authorities, sponsors, architects, set designers and so on, with their sometimes *ocular* preoccupations.

In the countless ways in which contemporary theatre spaces are configured, the voice, as I have shown, is invariably subjugated to the wider conceptual fulfilment of the building design as a whole. Voice itself is rarely central to the acoustic design of the space or considered in terms of its easeful proximity to the audience. Rarely are the optimal conditions of temperature, air humidity and flow considered, and seldom is the impact of intrusive environmental noise mitigated. Theatre craft does not move 'beyond building types and topography to include discursive sites and social contexts' or spark interest 'in the sensate and in the body's experience of space, form and location' (Rufford 2015: 69). These have seldom been the primary concerns of historical theatre builds.

That said, it is important to examine a select number of theatre design exemplars in which the dialectical relationship between design and voice impacts positively on the output of voice. I examine, therefore, three different theatre structures across the historical spectrum in which there are general principles that pertain to optimal and/or exceptional vocal expression.

VOICE AND THE THEATRE BUILD

There is no doubt that the different perceptual processes of listening and looking influence the expression of the voice, and they are significant considerations in the following examination of three theatre spaces: the open-air Greek amphitheatre, the early modern theatre in the round and the proscenium. The way voice performs in these iconic theatre structures also offers a suggestion about its expression in a range of other performance spaces.

In the three models, I consider the spatial invitations made to the voice and examine the ways in which their visual, stylistic and perspectival strategies both enable and compete with those of the voice. I also consider how certain spatial structures better foster the needs of easeful, durational, healthy vocal expression whilst others enhance vocal expression that falls outside conversational, speakable norms.

I turn the discussion, then, towards the problems presented by the *fluid* voice juxtaposed against the *static* building structure. On one hand is the unfixed, dynamic voice capable of expressive responsiveness to the vagaries of individual interpretation, technical skill and durational capacity. On the other hand are the principles that underpin the spaces that 'house' the voice, and the ways in which they correspond to values about unity, consistency, technical certainty and durational presence. In other words, the building itself invariably provides the fixed starting point as opposed to the variability of the voice. Taking this further, we consider the voice as symbolic of the actuality of inhabitation whilst the building is symbolic of collective and idealized inhabitation. Both architecture and voice, however, also share a notion of *transcendence* that has an afterlife over and above its material life. This suggests that both have the potential to *become* more than the sum total of their construction or technique.

The ideal of 'transcendence' stems from a debate at the heart of architectural history, and is one I fruitfully reference in this discussion about the expressive voice. It invites consideration about the degree to which the theatre build gives rise to the particularities of vocal qualities and the degree to which the voice actuates itself in spite of the material and aesthetics of the build, and remains the sole provenance of the individual. It raises questions, overall, about the usefulness of parallels drawn between voice and architecture. As with architecture, I ask, does voice 'possess poetic and aspirational qualities that transcend the pragmatism of building and imbue built form with meaning … [suggesting] a synthesis between architecture as real thing and architecture as representation' (Rufford 2015: 16). In other words, is voice more than the sum of its parts? Does the assemblage of the components of writer's input, aesthetics, acoustics, individual physiology, skill and so on comprise something closer to the transcendence referenced in the ancient Hebrew philosophies? Its importance as a question, whilst not fully answerable in this chapter, lies in the fact that it draws attention to the ways in which the impact of both build and concept poses an identifiable influence on the outcome of the expressive and healthy voice and on its reception.

EPIDAURUS

I start by testing the question at Epidaurus, the ancient Greek theatre designed in the fourth century BC. It is renowned for an acoustic environment in which voice is invited to express without force. It likewise offers optimal auditory reception for the audience. In terms relevant to the discussion about the relationship between architecture and voice, Epidaurus sets both a transcendent and a pragmatic template for the voice. The phenomenon of the design, combined with specific building materials, in particular the use of limestone seats, found to filter out low-frequency sounds and, conversely, amplify the higher frequencies from the stage, is of specific interest here because it gives ideal voice conditions:

> The seats, which constitute a corrugated surface, serve as an acoustic filter that passes sound coming from the stage at the expense of surrounding acoustic noise. Whether a coincidence or not, the theater of Epidaurus was built with optimized shape and dimensions.
>
> (Declercq and Dekeyser 2007: 2011)

The uniqueness of the design at Epidaurus, however, also raises questions about subsequent theatre construction post-Epidaurus. Why, when the intrinsic value of the human voice in the build gets effectively recognized at Epidaurus, is it not replicated in all subsequent theatre designs? Additionally, what is it about the Greek theatre in the fourth century BC that provides the aesthetic culture for the voice in theatre out of which this design emerges but which isn't necessarily continued?

It is clear that at Epidaurus, with its unique potential to both support and dispel theatre's illusory properties, invitation is made for an expression of voice that provides a seminal, if expensive and complex, reference. On the one hand, the sophisticated design invites the voice to be complicit in the 'trick' that continues to draw contemporary tourists to marvel at how 14,000 audience members can hear the simple scratch of a match or the drop of a coin from the centre of the stage. On the other hand, Epidaurus also works in *sympathy* with the voice by enabling it to function within the parameters of socially recognized easeful usage. (The debate about the use of masks and their potential to enhance [or not] the harmonics of the voice is one that is live in theatre history. For the sake of this discussion, I refer to the actor who appears without a mask and who makes use of 'naked' acoustics.) Whilst the answer to questions about the durability and viability of Epidaurus as a theatre template cannot be dealt with in depth, its endurance as an acoustic model with strong vocal sympathies is significant:

> In the theatre at Epidavros, still despite increasing wear from myriads of tourists the best preserved of the classical Greek theatres, the guide who accompanies parties will willingly demonstrate the acoustics by sending his group to the top of the *theatron* and then dropping a coin on the stone base at the centre of the *orchestra*. The sound is clearly heard: he then drops the coin a metre or two metres off, with greatly diminished effect. All amateur reciters, of which there are many, German or Japanese, hold their audience from the centre of the orchestra.
>
> The acoustics are demonstrably at their best at this central point, and in the absence of any stage, certainly of any substantial raised or extended platform, play comes forward: to the chorus in the orchestra, and to the audience.

The architectural proportions at Epidaurus clearly both foster the phenomenon of theatre as illusion, where the voice appears simultaneously to speak individually and effortlessly to each and every member of the audience, and reinforce a theatre stylistics based upon human vocal proportions that approaches a version of 'naturalism' at one and the same time. It is important that an interpretation of the conditions for the voice at Epidaurus moves away from the literary attention given by theatre historians to the voice of the single actor in Greek lyric tragedy as one that is 'highly conventionalized, not in the least naturalistic' (Kitto 1986: 28). It needs to include, instead, more about the materiality of voice as it performs within specific acoustic conditions.

The theatre at Epidaurus, as I have shown, draws upon and subsequently encourages a vocal expressivity that asserts a complex paradox of the 'miracle' within the 'ordinary'. The themes of illusion and realism are ones that are familiar as they appear and disappear throughout the history of theatre. Whilst the template undoubtedly retains a value into the twenty-first century, it is instructive that its priorities get overshadowed by design values that intentionally or unintentionally put the voice into a marginal position. When faced with competition from *logos*, the ocular preoccupations of the scenographers, the finances of the engineering and so on, the voice has to work harder to be heard.

It is important, however, to attempt to consider why, in the light of a legacy of the optimal vocal conditions at Epidaurus, the voice is forced to work harder in the twenty-first century. In his *Short History of Western Theatre Performance Space*, David Wiles reinforces the view above when he says that modern theatre has 'become predominantly ocular. Spectacular sets, reinforced by stage lighting, air-conditioning, protective arm-rest and an architectural emphasis on sightlines, makes the experience of theatre-going a pre-eminently visual experience' (Wiles 2003: 12). He reinforces this with discussion about a marked change from auditory to ocular acculturation:

> Vitruvius' account of the Roman theatre illustrates how times have changed: in a theatrical culture centred on oratory and music, it was the acoustic properties of the theatre that demanded almost all the architect's attention. Good acoustics mean that the actors can hear the audience, not only laughter and applause but tiny rustlings and shufflings that demonstrate the quality of attention, so that communication becomes a two-way process.
>
> (Wiles 2003: 12)

The ways in which ocularity underpins an ideology linked to the erosion of socially consenting space, as represented by Greek theatre, offer a useful thread by which to begin to better understand the relationship between space and voice. Although the reasons for the cultural shift of balance towards ocularity are complex and are not examined in depth here, an important aspect is the ways in which the 'monumentality' of certain theatre builds enhances or constrains the actor's expression and how, in turn, this relates to and mirrors wider social hierarchies.

With reference to the 'monumental' Epidaurus, I agree with Wiles' interpretation of the cultural geographer Henri Lefebvre when he says that 'architectural volumes generate rhythms, processional movements and musical resonances that allow bodies to find each other at the level of the non-visible' (Wiles 2003: 12). This gets closer to offering an understanding of the ways in which certain forms of Greek theatre provide the actor and the audience with multisensory meeting places where the ocular does not dominate but jostles as just one among the many senses exhibited in dance, music and theatre. It also shows how public assembly and performance spaces derive from the same source in the circular dithyrambic dance (Wiles 2003: 168), with a relationship also to the spherical shape of the acoustic field described by Smith:

> The circular auditoria of the Hellenistic world were not only intended for tragedy and comedy, but were in most instances also places of political assembly, and thus embodiments of the social structure.
>
> (Wiles 2003: 168)

Wiles continues with an important note about the significance of ritualistic singing and the dithyrambic dance that provides further clues about the qualities of the voice required for these projects. Its capacity to blend with other voices, to exhibit flexibility of pitch movement and sustainability of note duration, suggests a theatre voice that is musical and capable of sustainability and of inflecting in ways that allow it to blend with fellow actors:

> Epidaurus … is located in a shrine to the god of healing. Here there was no city to assemble, only visitors from across the Greek world. The stage building is set further back, and the dancing circle fixed by a stone border and a *thymele* (sacred stone) in the centre. The architecture is governed by Pythagorean mathematics to create a space of perfect geometric harmony. The singing of paeans to Apollo was probably a more important ritual in this space, with its emphatic focus on the orchestra, than the performance of tragedy and comedy.
>
> (Wiles 2003: 169)

Of relevance is the probability that the acoustics were designed not just for the efficacy of vocal expression but for the communication of a ritualized voice necessary to express 'the healing that stems from harmony of mind, body and environment' (Wiles 2003: 169). This indicates not only that recognition was given in the design to fostering the harmonics of the singing but that the build, in turn also helped to redefine the aesthetics of theatre voice. Wiles, again, argues persuasively that certain structural design realities encouraged the emergence of an unforced and harmonic vocal aesthetic that sat at the heart of the Greek theatre:

> The Greek theatre is wrapped around a central point defined by the sacred *thymele*, which creates the feeling of repose … and reflects the idea that the earth, the matter at the centre of the universe, is inherently stable.
>
> (Wiles 2003: 184)

I suggest that whilst Epidaurus provides an exemplary template for a vocal aesthetic that reaches towards both the 'Gods' of healing and an 'earthly' listenership, it is not one required in all contexts. I show that as theatre voice begins to move closer to answering secular 'human' concerns in the early English theatre of the Middle Ages, it is the church rather than the theatre that gains a closer correspondence with the voice that is modelled at Epidaurus.

THE EARLY MODERN PLAYHOUSE

The phenomenon of civic stability – wished for or real – which under-pins specific classical Greek theatre builds, provides a reoccurring theme throughout the history of theatre spaces. The story of the early modern play-house on London's South Bank, my second model, is a case in point. Here the presenting cultural need for communicative proximity stands quite apart from the formal visual distance built in at the 'monumental' Epidaurus, even though it, paradoxically, also allowed the voice to be 'close' to the listener.

In the early modern theatre, the proxemics are such that the audience is able to get physically close to the action. The players, in turn, play with the reverberations of sound. Their sound waves meet both receiving bodies and built surfaces and air, and make the theatre voice experience palpably different to that on offer at the multitiered amphitheatre at Epidaurus. Kate Godfrey, voice trainer at the Royal Shakespeare Company (RSC), for example, observes that in both the RSC's Swan theatre and in London's reconstructed Globe, the drying oak timbers of the wooden structures afford the actor more vocal resonance (Workshop comment, Stratford Upon Avon, 10 June 2017).

Professor Joe Kelleher, in his chapter 'Human Stuff: Presence, Proximity and Pretend', suggests that since the theatre 'tends to privilege the represen-tation of human life' (Kelleher 2006: 21), the construction of relative closeness between player and audience in the early modern playhouse comes as no surprise. On the theatre and its human dimensions he continues:

> It tends to be enjoyed – when it is enjoyed – by human beings, so much so that a general account of theatre as a mechanism of human interaction, or more elabo-rately a means of representing reality from – and to – a human point of view, hardly seems worth elaborating.
>
> (Kelleher 2006: 21)

I suggest, likewise, that the proximity of player to audience in the early modern playhouse enables both sides to better participate in the visceral realities of sound waves. This, in turn, influences the use of the voice in ways that correspond to, though do not necessarily mimic, voice use and reception outside the walls of the theatre. A contemporary actor at the reconstructed Globe speaks to an engagement with this experience as it is part of the 'generation of energy in the circle within the building' (Wiles 2003: 193). Bruce Smith takes up the case to suggest some of the historical reasons behind the centrality of acoustic focus:

> The South Bank theatres … were built not to display but to contain. Inside, not outside, provided their very reason for being. What they contained, most obviously, was spectacle: many-sided galleries, surrounding the thrust stage as a focal point, gave much better sight-lines than a square structure would for viewing not only the play but other members of the audience. Extrapolating from the Fortune contract, no one in the Fortune or the 1599 Globe was more than fifty feet from an actor standing downstage, at the focal center of the space. That same actor, standing at the center of the visual space, stood also at the center of an aural space … The South Bank amphitheaters were, in fact, instruments for producing, shaping, and propagating sound.
>
> (Smith 1999: 206)

Taking Smith's view, then, I suggest that the material structure of the playhouse provides a key source of amplification and magnification for the voice in which the sound waves are also able to behave in ways that correspond to conversational modes of delivery. At the Globe, there is the additional phenomenon of sound becoming 'broad' as it disperses amongst the audience and the players, whilst at the Blackfriars, the theatre has a 'round' sound as a result of its more rectangular shape (Smith 1999: 216–217).

What does this mean for the types of qualities of vocal expression evidenced? In the open-air Globe, Smith contends that the 'broad' effect means that sound is perceived first on one side and then the next, but that this also fosters a consistent reference point at the centre of the stage. The 'broad' effect of the sound spread also creates the need for the use of well-supported (in terms of breath) directional voicing that can efficiently target specific sections of the audience:

> In a cylindrical structure like the Globe, open at the top with nothing for soundwaves to strike against and closed at the bottom with highly absorbent material in the form of human bodies, sound waves would have been reflected mainly from side to side, not from top to bottom.
>
> (Smith 1999: 213)

Whilst there is debate about the actual dimensions of the canopy known to have stretched over the stage at the original Globe, it remains useful to speculate about the ways in which an actor might have used it as a sounding board for the voice:

> Experience in the reconstructed Globe in London has offered opportunities to consider that the position of greatest dramatic power is not all the way down-stage, where some theater historians imagine soliloquies to have been spoken, but several feet back, somewhere in between the two pillars holding up the canopy. An actor may occupy the position of greatest visual presence at the geometric center of the playhouse, but he commands the greatest acoustical power near the geometric center of the space beneath the canopy.
>
> (Smith 1999: 213–214)

An actor at the original Globe, no doubt, was able to utilize this spatial and acoustical knowledge to their 'playing' advantage where possible. Historian James Shapiro provides additional evidence to support this claim in his account of the actor's active involvement and 'use' of building proportions in the Globe's first incarnation in 1599 under the watchful eye of master carpenter Peter Street:

> The Globe was the first London theatre built by actors for actors, and Shakespeare and his fellow player-sharers would have worked with Street closely during the setting up, especially on last-minute decisions about the tiring house and stage … They brought a good deal of practical experience to the task – and they knew the strengths and weaknesses of each of London's playhouses, having performed in all of them.
>
> (Shapiro 2005: 131)

The reconstructed Globe of the 1990s provides modern audiences and actors with a first-hand opportunity to witness the interactive and inclusive conditions of the original Globe. But questions remain inconclusive about how to account for the material impact on the audience perception of the individual historical voice – of that actual impact of the 'sound in the larynx, in the mouth, in the bones, tissues, and cavities of the skull. Of sound in the ear and in the gut' (Smith 1999: 29).

Wiles makes a case for the easier appraisal of the actor's *physical* impact in both the original and the 1990s Globe in contrast with the more complex appraisal of the impact made by the voice. He suggests that the reconstruction of the role and function of the late sixteenth-century voice is harder to achieve due to the fact that a replication of its actual impact on an audience remains entirely speculative. It is a complex point but one that leads to observations about important differences of perception that involve not just presence but the meanings generated by that presence.

In other words, he suggests that the voice remains subject to the reception conditions of its own historical moment in ways that are different to the body. Whilst this is not a matter that I will pursue in any depth here, it is noteworthy that the sixteenth-century audience who heard Cleopatra's description of Antony's voice as 'propertied As all the tunéd spheres' (Wiles 2003: 194) may have been convinced of the truth of the statement due to the exceptional pitch and timbre range of the actor who played Antony, which was remarkable for its standout qualities in a quieter unamplified world. It is possible, too, that the central focus of the Globe stage provided the prerequisite physical prominence necessary to support a belief in his transcendental vocal qualities and abilities:

> We can feel how the Globe stage ... was a tool for creating dominance, and allowed the actor to command the pit in a way that neither medieval theatre in the round nor Roman theatre architecture permitted.
>
> (Wiles 2003: 194)

The modern audience, on the other hand, accustomed to amplification, powerful orchestration and digital animation, might not be so convinced by the transcendental aspects. Whilst the actor shares common characteristics across history through skeletal and physiological actualities, creating 'circumstances that are set in place by the human body' (Smith 1999: 28), the conditions that define the perceptual judgements of the listener are less tangible.

It is hard to isolate just one factor that has shifted the relationship to the voice in the twenty-first century, although clearly electronic amplification has played its part. The listener has come to expect the 'real' sound of a chainsaw, a bell, a cry, and not its mock-up. Whilst we know that attitudes to the body have also changed over time, there is something notable about the shift in audience reception to sound in general. Contemporary audiences are less likely, for example, to suspend their 'belief' in relation to manually produced sound landscapes on stage (coconut shells as representative of the hooves of horses do not stand muster in most theatre in which realism is a guiding ethos, for example). This corresponds with the contemporary reception to the voice in which it is judged to correspond with communication standards valued in civil society or with those that are distant and 'other' in the aesthetic stakes and therefore deemed 'outside' the terms of realism expected by that audience. Reception, too, is historically influenced by the fact that the male voice has spoken on behalf, and as representative, of the voice of women. The example of Cleopatra above, spoken by a man on behalf of a woman about another man, shows the complexity of perceptual matters about the voice when gender is also added into the equation.

It is possible that audiences at the Blackfriars theatre in the seventeenth century shared a similar capacity to suspend belief as did listeners at the Globe. It is possible, too, that both audiences may have been willing to 'believe' in the power of the great king Antony as a consequence of the signal set by pitch extremes in ways that has no correspondence in the contemporary audience. Again, both views are speculative. However, evidence in the building structures themselves indicates the probability of different acoustical impact on audiences. At the Blackfriars (occupied by the King's Men from 1609 to 1642 [Smith 1999: 214], Smith observes the importance of structural shape:

> In its shape the Blackfriars theater fostered a very different kind of sound than the Globe … it dispersed sound waves throughout the room rather than focusing them in the center. Standing in the rear of the stage, a speaker commanded a 140-degree broadcast area that covered much more of the available listening space than it would have for an actor in the same position in the Globe.
>
> (Smith 1999: 216)

How does this support a better understanding of the voice in action at both the Globe and the Blackfriars? First, the Globe. An actor in full command of the acoustic environment on centre stage at the Globe had opportunities to develop intimate relationships with the audience via the medium of a conversationally relational voice. The actor could, similarly, activate thrilling qualities of the voice at close quarters in order to involve an audience in a visceral experience of the 'fireworks' of extreme pitch usage. I think, here, of the example suggested in the power and presence of actor Will Kempe, one of the Chamberlain's Men, to better imagine this in action. His performance skills in the Elizabethan post-play 'jig', noted in Chapter 2, are likely to have had an immediate and potent impact on the audience. Although the jig has perhaps more in common with the fairground or the circus, it is worth considering that its presence as the afterpiece of a play contained vocal values that were worthy of importation into the main drama – that is, they incorporated an active voice that landed on and communicated directly with an audience:

> Jigs were basically semi-improvisational; one-act plays, running to a few hundred lines, usually performed by four actors. They were rich in clowning, repartee and high-spirited dancing and song, and written in traditional ballad form. Though nominally independent of the plays that preceded them, they were an extension of the clown's part. If the comedies were about love, jigs were about what happened after marriage … Jigs – anarchic and libidinal – were wildly popular because they tapped into parts of everyday experience usually left untouched in the world of the play.
>
> (Shapiro 2005: 47)

The actor in a jig who succeeded in wooing an audience was, in all likelihood, able to take advantage of the same acoustic values and audience proximity as the actor in the main play. It is also possible to make parallels between the ways in which the two sorts of performances utilized vocal register (colloquial or formal), proxemics and pitch range to exploit the closeness to the audience with its visceral consequences for their engagement.

In either a jig or the main play, the successful actor at the Globe was one able to exploit acoustic environments that favoured a position at the centre of the stage. At the Blackfriars, with its 'round' sound, the audience required a different kind of attention to the one at the Globe. The reverberations of its sound delay suggest that the actor needed to utilize an intimate understanding of the effects of the 'dispersal' of the voice in the space in order to manage the auditory perceptions of the audience:

> [T]he sound the speaker sent out into the hall would not immediately have been returned to the center. This dispersal effect would have been enhanced by the multiple planes of the galleries. However deep they may have been, whether or not they ran the full perimeter of the room, the galleries provided a series of differently angled, resonant wood surfaces that contributed to the dispersal of sound in its full range of frequencies.
>
> (Smith 1999: 217)

PERSPECTIVE AND THE PROSCENIUM ARCH

The recreation of Elizabethan playhouse acoustics and the instruments sounded within them, however, does not in itself answer specific questions about the kinds of vocal qualities that were deployed. 'The hautboys, and cornets are much easier to specify than the sounds of human voices' (Smith 1999: 222). Smith identifies in this a reoccurring problem about defining the actual qualities of the individual voice in action when it is shrouded not only in discussions about acoustics but also in the cerebral utterances of speech, amongst other factors. Whilst this is still some distance away from defining the full specifics of an individual actor's vocal output in both the classical and the early modern period, consideration given to factors such as architectural perspective helps to get closer to some of the general ways in which the voice is designed to move in a space.

Wiles puts forwards a theory that considers, on one hand, the:

> 'word-based collectivist mode associated with the public playhouse' ... in which the 'culture of the Protestant word, at least in the short term, triumphed over the cult of the royal image'.
>
> (Wiles 2003: 219)

And, on the other, the *theatre a l'italienne*, 'which came to be regarded as the natural architectural form of theatre within western culture' (Wiles 2003: 214):

> We can define the 'Italian' form as a conjunction of two things: an encircling auditorium alluding to the *cavea* of Roman antiquity, and a perspectival stage laid along a central axis. The latter found its validation not in Roman archaeology

but in Roman writings, notably Vitruvius' account of perspectival scene painting and Servius' reference in his commentary on Virgil to a *scaena versilis* (revolving façade) and *scaena ductilis* (sliding façade). The strength of this arrangement lies in the way the circle makes the audience function as a single organism, whilst perspective allows this audience to see the same face and the same action at the same moment.

(Wiles 2003: 214–215)

The shift of focus provided in the 'Italian' theatre auditorium has a critical effect on the voice. I suggest that, as a result of the shift of perspective afforded by the proscenium, the actor at the front of the stage, framed by the arch, takes up a position that asks somewhat less for audience *engagement* and more for signs of successful audience *approval* and consumption as witnessed by their applause; one that promotes a one-way journey for the voice that is larger than life and less relational in tone. What does this sound like? Loud, unidirectional and with less adherence to conversational modulations of tone. Juliet Rufford confirms that such effects are a necessary by-product of the cultivation of the suspension of belief in an audience so that it is 'seduced into accepting its fictions' (Rufford 2015: 48). Like Wiles, she highlights the importance of a move from the early modern playhouse to a perspective-led theatre interior in fulfilling the promise of 'dramatic illusionism' (Rufford 2015: 48):

The stage type most commonly associated with illusionistic theatre – the proscenium-arch stage – developed around the taste for perspectival staging, or the playing of scenes against an illusion of deep space created through the use of artificial perspective … The stunning perspectival effects, which were measured from a central vanishing point behind the scene and were fully revealed only to the princely seat positioned directly opposite, set up a relationship between theatrical illusion, architecture, eye-point and authority. Theatre architecture not only forms and manipulates audiences' perspectives on events but also upholds social hierarchies and ideologically laden visions of the world.

(Rufford 2015: 48–49)

The voice, in turn, becomes imbricated in the principles of perspective. Whilst general rules about healthy and effective voicing also pertain, as voice specialist Patsy Rodenberg says, 'projection itself is really quite natural and not at all a mystery' (Rodenberg 1992: 224), the adaptation required for voice in a proscenium theatre implies an actual shift of mindset. It is a shift that involves accommodation to the spatial dynamics that favour the eye and requires that additional work is done to ensure that the qualitative aspects of vocal timbre are rendered effective for auditory reception.

The strong visual lines of proscenium-arch design get repudiated and reconfigured in many quarters of nineteenth-century theatre experimentation. One such theatre experiment sought a return to the playing conditions of

the Elizabethan playhouse, in part through the reinvention and adaptation of the proscenium stage. Harley Granville Barker's radically restaged
Shakespeare involved a realignment of the actor with the audience in order
to fulfil his vision of more 'authentic' Shakespeare, and he took the alteration
of the actual space as his starting point:

> Barker's work aimed at reestablishing a non-illusionist relationship between actor
> and audience that characterized Shakespeare's theatre. The modified stage alone
> could not do it, of course, but could aid actor and audience alike, give them an
> imaginative shove in the right direction ... taking the audience back to an older
> sense of the theatre and its purpose. The foots and the arch, the crutches of the
> drama of illusion, had trapped Shakespearian actors for more than two centuries
> in a box that, whatever its size, was always constricting. In an interview in *The
> Observer* (29 September, 1912: 9), Shaw noted that Barker's additional apron,
> actually quite small in dimension, had 'apparently trebled the spaciousness of
> the stage ... To the imagination it looks as if he had invented a new heaven and
> a new earth.'
>
> (Kennedy 1985: 125)

In Kennedy's extract about Barker there is a reoccurrence of a familiar theatre binary: theatre as illusion on one hand and theatre as maker of 'truths'
in 'authentic' theatre on the other. Whilst it is not the aim of this chapter
to examine this in any great depth, it is important to consider the ways in
which Barker's challenge to the domination of perspectival staging gives
new licence to the expression of the voice, especially in staging Shakespeare.
I consider that this challenge to the proscenium arch initiates the disman-
tling of a 'straitjacket' framework around the player that is both literal and
metaphorical. It also reinforces an interest in a stripped-back playing space
so that more attention is given to the text:

> The power of the soliloquy in Shakespeare came from the actor's intimacy with
> the audience, just as the speed of action derived from the bare platform stage ...
> the overall effect was disturbing because it provided a swiftness and intimacy that
> violated the accepted conventions of the Victorian and Edwardian theatre.
>
> (Kennedy 1985: 131)

In Barker's experiments it is possible to discern several layers of vocal function in operation, some of which are reactive to convention and some of
which reinforce it. There is the unidirectional declamatory voice, for example,
as it contributes to the illusion of stage fictions and the rhetoric-inflected
voice as it shapes and directs recognizable meanings. There is also the voice
that gives rise to humanly proportioned communicative intimacy, craved in
theatre as much as in life, wherever relational communication is a key factor.
Finally, there is the voice that wittingly (or unwittingly) absorbs and reflects
social hierarchies and influence. These dominant social factors include the

challenge posed by the reinventions of the playing space, the material content of the New Drama, and the existing working practices of the early Edwardian period, including the 'star' system. The voice, as a consequence, formed within values that pay closer attention to 'distinct speech [and] over-whelming service to the play' (Kennedy 1985: 310), also has to contend with the hierarchical conventions of the actor-manager-dominated theatre:

> The actors of the New Drama recognized that 'to make others feel you must feel yourself, and to feel yourself you must be *natural*.' It was not possible to be natural … under the normal conditions of the Edwardian stage, when a play was usually chosen because 'a prominent actor' saw in it an opportunity to exploit his talent.
> (Kennedy 1985: 31)

In London, April 1904, Barker took the opportunity to put some of his theatre experiments to the test over a three-year period at the Court Theatre. Barker's theatre ethos at the Court, in its adoption of some of the proximal characteristics of the early modern playhouse, anticipates aspects of the twentieth-century experimental work by Jerzy Grotowski, Peter Brook, Eugenio Barber and others. Their desire to return to the essence of an immersive type of theatre, deploying both actor to actor intensity and actor to audience intimacy, has a direct correspondence with the work at the Court, where actors in the 1890s and early 1900s were influenced by Frank Benson, 'who [was] strenuously opposed both to the star system and the long run' (Kennedy 1985: 31–32) and promoted the acting ensemble (Kennedy 1985: 31). Barker's theatre, in its rhetoric-inflected intimacy, also retains aspects of the vocally ritualistic work from the classical period in which highly shaped oral figures are directed towards an audience assumed to possess fine auditory discrimination.

In September 1907, Barker's Court Theatre moved location to the Savoy Theatre in the heart of the West End. Here, the large dimensions of the auditorium, and the geographical location of the theatre, amongst other factors, all played their part in ending an era of important theatre experimentation. I suggest the conditions put the voice under strain and it struggled, as a consequence, to adjust to the proxemics of the 'new' theatre:

> The Savoy, only some 350 seats larger than the Court, nonetheless made intimate playing difficult, and the pioneer audience felt uncomfortable in the heart of theatre land … the Savoy was run like a commercial theatre, and the old audience – that precarious amalgam of Shavians, Fabians, feminists, lovers of the Court idea, theatrical pioneers – was repudiating its leader for invading the West End.
> (Kennedy 1985: 28–30)

The voice at the Court Theatre, supported by a distinctive acting ethos, a loyal audience and a sympathetic theatre space, was part of a system that celebrated the individual as subject and anticipated, as I have suggested, similar theatre experiments later in the twentieth century. It set a template for the voice in Western humanistic theatre practice in which the synthesis of acting, design and production utilizes individual actor qualities to the extent that they are indispensable to the inception and reception of the performance. This use of a flexible vocal dialectic, with reference both to the classical past and a humanistic future, serves as a formational aesthetic for a theatre edging away from the domination of single authorship towards the collective authorship of the ensemble practices of the mid-twentieth century and beyond.

Part IV
Theatre Speaks

Chapter

5   Voice and Logos

In this chapter, I examine some of the ways in which voice remains 'silent' within the order set by speech forms within linguistic signification and the problem this sets for the historiography of the theatre voice. In the order of written signs, where the alphabet itself is part of the reason for the domination of the word, the voice becomes sidelined (Harris 1986: 29) and its presence harder to qualify. In order, then, to better distinguish voice within the registers of meaning performed in theatre, I examine in brief a number of key philosophical and linguistic theories that reveal how an inheritance from the Greco-Roman philosophers and the early medieval and Renaissance period in England has helped to perpetuate speech values over those of voice. Such traditions have influenced many significant mainstream trends in theatre voice and have also been overturned in several notable radical theatre experiments examined elsewhere in the book. For immediate purposes, however, I examine the ways in which several of the theoretical assumptions underpinning speech have led to the problem of voice as 'unacknowledged, unrecognized and uncredited' (Kennedy 2009: 407).

The organization of the *written* word depends on historically specific social and cultural communicative norms that relate to but are also distinct from those that pertain to the voice as carrier of the *spoken* word. The live act of *speech* formation, with its counterpart in print, often obscures the perceptions about and sensations of voice in the expressive process. In other words, a preoccupation with logos, more often than not, distracts from the subjective sensations of voice and leads to 'misconceptions' (Kennedy 2009: 406) that make it hard to identify and recover the material sensations of voice. The historiography that turns, instead, to imaginative reconstruction within wider, newly positioned 'interpretive frameworks' testifies to the importance of finding new ways to retrieve and reflect on the voice. Judith Pascoe's study of the voice of Sarah Siddons is an excellent example of this process in action. She reports on her own work as it is influenced by a new generation of theatre historians:

> Wanting to distance themselves from the field's antiquarian tendencies, they strive to unite old-school archival work with new-school performance theory, to pay their respects to both material specificity and epistemological uncertainty. My study contributes to this effort by resurrecting the surviving traces of Sarah Siddons's voice and considering them with the help of interpretive frameworks

devised by sound historians and media theorists … By trying to hear voices that
predate the advent of sound recording technology, we recover something of what
it was like to sit in a theater and viscerally experience, not just see, a particular
performance.

(Pascoe 2013: xi)

Perceptual recall of the voice, though, is a difficult task and it is important to
remember that in an attempt to retrieve it, the dominant presence of logos,
and the ways in which logos refers not just to the word but to systems of
reasons and discourse, also needs factoring in. Audience perception of voice
when it is part of tune, timbre and emphasis is closely linked to comprehension of the word itself and so it is often hard for the ear to distinguish the
boundaries between voice and speech. The difficulty of retrieval, however,
is no reason to doubt its existence:

The voice is not visible; yet its invisibility does not negate its substance or its
tangibility. As vocal sound is shaped by language, it retains its identity as the
sound of the speaker, and the sound is contingent upon and informed by the
'sensible world or history … the present and the past, as a pell-mell ensemble of
bodies and minds.'

(Kennedy 2009: 416)

Several mainstream theatre lineages play their part in the determination
of expectations about voice due to the fact that distinctive ways with
words are embedded in a majority of acting stylistics. In contemporary
interpretative theatre, the voice is regarded as inseparable from textual
language because its melodic pattern carries the semantic content to the
listener. In other words, voice participates in interpretive theatre meaning
by serving the word.

A tuneful and sometimes 'extravagant' stylistic (in terms of duration of
the vowels, management of the pause, volume range and pace shifts) has
a long legacy in UK acting traditions. Actors such as Ian McKellen, Judi
Dench and Patrick Stewart offer versions of this inheritance in which traces
of heightened voice and speech characteristics are detectable. In a review
of a production of Harold Pinter's *No Man's Land* at the Theatre Royal in
Brighton, McKellen and Stewart pay homage to the vocal traditions they
inherited from the original actors in the same roles:

The original production starred Sir John Gielgud as Spooner and Sir Ralph
Richardson as Hirst. Stewart was there on opening night and returned to see it
twice in the same week. He said: 'I worship both of those actors, and they had
very distinctive styles and voices. I can hear Sir Ralph's voice in my head now,
and there's one line that I say exactly as I remember him saying it.' McKellen
found it daunting to follow in Gielgud's footsteps. He said: 'I thought it was

impossible for me. That's why I didn't want to do the play. It's taken an awfully long time to forget those intonations.'

(Sleigh 2016: 13)

It is of note that McKellen and Stewart testify to the influence of vocal traditions in which characteristics such as intonation and tonal colour both support speech meanings and also supersede them. They pay homage to a long line of acting in which vocal stylistics include the adoption of notable sound features of the past as well as those of the contemporary moment. The voice of Edith Evans is part of this tradition and it is of particular interest that its capture on film has ensured it remains a vocal benchmark for the future:

Evans's Lady Bracknell in *The Importance of Being Earnest*, with its almost self-parodying haughtiness and deadly swoop on 'a hand-bag', bedevils any actress, thanks to its notoriety from the 1952 Anthony Asquith movie.

(Coveney 2015: 4–5)

Maggie Smith's BBC recording of *The Country Wife* in 1985, in turn, is characterized by 'inflexional idiosyncrasies and gestural extravagances' (Coveney 2015: 144) and by technical peculiarities that involve 'the insertion of an intake of breath, even a tiny "d'you know", as a missing beat in a line that might not otherwise stand up and be funny' (Coveney 2015: 7). Judi Dench's performances of Lady Macbeth, Cleopatra, Viola, Portia and others, as observed by the critic Michael Coveney, are described as, likewise, having elusive but memorable vocal qualities that are refracted through the words themselves: 'The release of feeling, a sort of glorious shiver with an instantly recognizable crack in her voice, characterizes all these Dench performances' (Coveney 2015: 5).

In the main, though, whilst the voice is occasionally aptly vivified in prose, the complex integration of elements that shape the development and production of speech and voice in theatre performance renders the voice notoriously hard to describe and reveal. The historical retrieval of the variable and unrepeatable voice in theatre practice in which the 'someone' (Kennedy 2009: 407) is present, often gets lost in the mix:

Since the days of ancient Greece, Western voice and speech training has evolved in response to theatrical convention and venue, acting and oratorical styles, a knowledge of the physical instrument, technological advancements, and the fashions and predilections of the day.

(Saklad 2011: 1)

It is notable that many such descriptions stick to the familiar coupling of 'voice and speech'. Again, the persistence of this yoke in the historical account suggests that finer degrees of discernment need to be applied in order to properly excavate voice as a physical, individualized, variable act of sound making in its own right.

VOICE IN SONOROUS SYSTEMS

As stated throughout this book, it is important to view voice as distinct from speech utterance and written language structure in order to counter the now familiar obfuscations that contribute to the invisibility of voice itself. The issue of the word and the ways in which it has come to overshadow the voice is one that regularly surfaces in the history of not just theatre but also Western civilization. The Hebrew tradition provides a partial explanation of why this is so. According to contemporary philosopher Adriana Cavarero, evidence in the fusion of the Greek and Hebrew traditions provides an important source of understanding about how cultural theories, present in the history of voice, have embedded meanings that give voice both its agency and, paradoxically, its silence, because it is regarded as part of a bigger range of sacred meanings that predate speech:

> Both refer to the mouth of God, and both evoke the essential bond between voice and breath, a bond that in the Hebrew Bible is at once pneumatic, sonorous self-revelation and creation. Ruah and Qol – which are sources of an inspiring and vocal communication between God and the world, and human beings – belong in the Hebrew tradition to a fundamental sphere of meaning that comes *before* speech.
>
> (Cavarero 2005: 20)

The position of voice within transcendent (sacred) sonorous systems, as noted above, prior to its role as a carrier of speech and language systems, is examined elsewhere in the chapter. For now, I suggest that the ways in which both breath and voice are imbricated in religious ideas about the *sacred* help to explain the hierarchies between voice and speech in a secular theatre context and the subsequent binary this has fostered in which voice is associated with the unknowable and speech with the known.

PRINT–ORAL BINARY

I turn for clues about this binary persistence to a discussion in Walter J. Ong's seminal work *Orality and Literacy* (1982) in which he distinguishes the word in print and the word in an oral/auditory culture of expression and reception. In this influential work, he signals some of the reasons for the dominance of print over orality in Western culture, as they pertain well into the twenty-first century:

Texts have clamoured for attention so peremptorily that oral creations have tended to be regarded generally as variants of written productions or, if not this, as beneath serious scholarly attention.

(Ong 1982: 8)

Ong's work invites subtle and graduated observation about the differences between the types of words that are uttered, and helps to identify what it is that voice does on its own. It is particularly useful in making the distinction between the written word when it is part of poetic language structures that are spoken to an audience, and when it is evidence of the character who speaks within a dramatic text. These distinctions enable appreciation of the fact that when formalized poetry is taken from the page and spoken to an audience with specific intention, the *voice* itself forms part of the difference made to its reception where it is less obscured by the word. In this action, the voice becomes a co-creator with the writer and a creative *second text* is formed, one generated by the liveness of the embodied voice in relation to the words spoken. This has parallels, too, with the 'second text' referred to in Chapter 6 that arises when the actor responds to the training manual (and trainer) in the rehearsal studio and expresses their own embodied vocal trajectory in relation to the proposed exercises.

Under the conditions of the formation of a creative *second text* in an expressive context there are at least three ways in which this functions. The first is where a reader or actor voices an extant poetic text and the voice mediates the language. The second is where an actor speaks the words of an author within a dramatic performance and the voice is obscured somewhat by the effects of the author's intentions as characterized speech. The third is where the poet delivers her own poetic text to an audience and the voice animates both the individuated literary text and the unique expressive moment.

I argue that there is a qualitative difference between the vocal expression of *character* in a dramatic textual context and the vocal expression of the word in a poetic structure that sits outside a dramatic context. When intentional vocalizations actively engage with a range of sensory possibilities that arise from a poem, the listener is offered a choice that allows them to make more direct experiential *sense* of what they are hearing. In this case, the authorial mask is stripped away and, in the immediate sound exchange that takes place between the poetic word, the speaker and the listener, a range of sensory perceptions are ushered in that are closer to those of oral-based cultural practices than they are to those of textual dramatic practices:

In a primary oral culture, where the word has its existence only in sound, with no reference whatsoever to any visually perceptible text, and no awareness of even the possibility of such a text, the phenomenology of sound enters deeply into human beings' feel for existence, as processed by the spoken word. For the way in which the word is experienced is always momentous in psychic life.

(Ong 1982: 73)

Even though I write here about the oral communication of the poetic word as it is underpinned by a written text (and not the purely oral cultural text referred to by Ong), I argue that it is also possible for the phenomenon of oral cultural expression to be evoked even in a print-dominated culture. In order that this phenomenon is activated, it is important that the heightened sensory perceptions of the physical embodiment of the word are engaged. Ong takes as his key signature, the body – and the voice, of course, is situated in the body:

> The oral word ... never exists in a simply verbal context, as a written word does. Spoken words are always modifications of a total, existential situation, which always engages the body.
>
> (Ong 1982: 67)

True, not all poets embrace writing that evokes the traditions of orality. Many focus more on the literary, on-the-page merits of their work. Some, however, embrace the economy of communication I refer to here: a multidimensional spoken economy of orality and embodied receptivity. When Ong's notion of orality is transferred to voice in a theatrical/dramatic context, in which the words of the playwright 'become' those of the individual actor, it highlights, again, the ways in which the voice of the individual becomes obscured by the structured word on the page when it is already characterized by the author.

AUTHORIAL PRIVILEGE IN WESTERN CULTURE

Contemporary philosopher Michel Foucault explains that some of the differences between the impact of written narratives and the impact of orally transmitted ones are due to the fact that both are part of the operation of social and cultural privileges afforded to those in charge of language structures. How does this impact on voice in theatre? The link is provided by the fact that whilst both feature in the communicative strategies within theatre, it is the written dramatic text that predominates. Of particular interest here is Foucault's suggestion that both oral and written narratives, in their celebration of the immortality of the Greek hero in the early Greek epics, relate to and reproduce powerful 'invisible' cultural assumptions. He goes so far as to say that the formational impulses for the creation of narrative become a way of refuting mortality itself and that its production counters 'this accepted death' (Foucault and Rabinow 1984: 102). Whilst a detailed philosophical discussion about the power constructions imbricated in narrative structures is not relevant here, the ways in which they participate in the obfuscation of the materiality of voice remains noteworthy.

The work of contemporary poet Alice Oswald, as poet and performer, provides a case in point that illustrates one of the ways in which the written word, when combined with an impactful vocal presence in performance, offers an alternative to the sometime obfuscation of the voice. I suggest that in the way she voiced the epic poem *Tithonus 46 Minutes in the Life of the Dawn* at the Purcell Rooms in London, on 9 October 2014, both text and voice worked together to produce an effect that rendered both recognizable. How? I suggest that it rests with her voicing of the poem. Performed in the real time of its title, she deploys a mix of devices that include the ordinary speech value of words, the poetic device of repetition and the accumulated power of its effects, along with the qualities of her spatially relational voice. In combination, it provides a performance in which the living orality of the poet, for that once-only moment, exceeds and yet still refers to the authority of the word on the page.

The issue of narrative, and its power in general, despite the exceptions noted in the work of Oswald, provides a useful theoretical and artistic reference point in relation to better understanding the structures that define voice, the text and the authorial position in both oral and literary traditions. Foucault offers consideration of the ways in which writing as a material act becomes masked and the author elevated into a potent 'transcendental anonymity' (Foucault and Rabinow 1984: 104). This, again, draws attention to the complex issue of the privileges afforded to the writer and the ways in which the speech and language systems they command can shore up the privilege of an omnipotent author. Whilst this is not necessarily useful to the task of answering the reasons why voice gets obscured, it draws attention to ways in which language systems play their part in the process. This points to a need to make further extrapolations from linguistics and philosophy in order to better retrieve voice from its sometimes *secondary* place.

Foucault's position is useful for the way in which it allows for the location of voice and its practices within philosophical debate. In showing how Aristotle and other classical philosophers initiate a tradition that plays a part in allowing the printed word to gain authority over the orally transmitted word, he adds to an understanding of the marginal position of voice. In his trajectory, the processes of orality are regarded as less than important and in some senses are excluded from consideration under the mantle of Western philosophy (until possibly the theorization of phenomenology in the nineteenth century).

It is important, too, as I have shown, to extrapolate from Foucault's view and to read across to theatre, where the attention and respect associated with certain authors and texts works alongside, but also competes with, the oral traditions associated with the voice. This suggests a new problem, not yet raised, about the ways in which power and status are invested in those who speak certain *significant* words in a range of cultural contexts, regardless of their vocal qualities and abilities. In certain circumstances, the speaker becomes invested with power in such a way that their status and the words they speak deflect attention away from the voice itself. This returns me to Foucault's notion of the writer's elevated pregiven status, in which the social privileging of the written word itself has the potential to mask and supersede the actual events of the voice.

ORAL COMPOSITION

The problem of the voice, then, apart from where it is obscured by the cultural status of the author when words are spoken, also lies in the ways it gets confused and sometimes lost within different traditions of orality. American folklorist Albert B. Lord discusses the reasons why the art of oral composition is widely misunderstood. He draws particular attention to the problems of *terminology* in his examination of the work of another leading orality specialist, Milman Parry. Lord notes the importance of distinguishing the spoken word based upon a written text from one that involves the spoken word that is composed and activated without text. The act of noting these distinctions allows the effects of the voice in both forms of orality to become more tangible and thus clears the way for closer study:

> The need for clarification of the oral process of composition is reflected in the many terms that are used for oral narrative poetry. To no small degree difficulties have arisen because of the ambiguity of terminology and because each school has chosen a different facet of this poetry as distinctive. The term 'oral' empha- sizes, I believe, the basic distinction between oral narrative poetry and that which we term literary epic. But it too carries some ambiguity. Certain of the misunder- standings of Parry's oral theory arise from the failure to recognize his special use of the word 'oral'. For example, one often hears the definition that oral poetry is poetry written so that it can be recited. Oral, however, does not mean merely oral presentation. Oral epics are performed orally. What is important is not the oral performance but rather the composition *during* oral performance.
>
> (Lord 2000: p. 5)

Whilst Lord usefully underlines the importance of attention paid to the definitions of orality, he also raises questions about oral performance with- out making mention of the role of the voice in the process. At the level of micro-observances about oral performance, it is imperative that distinctions are also made about an individual's voice. Also important are the lines drawn between the act of the communication of an author's word on the page and the entirely distinct category of oral epic song as it represents the art of 'live' composition and its relationship to the Homeric compositor:

> We realize that what is called oral tradition is as intricate and meaningful an art form as its derivative 'literary tradition'. In the extended sense of the word, oral tradition is as 'literary' as literary tradition. It is not simply a less polished, more haphazard, or cruder second cousin twice removed to literature. By the time the written techniques come onto the stage, the art forms have been long set and are already highly developed and ancient.
>
> There is now no doubt that the composer of the Homeric poems was an oral poet.
>
> (Lord 2000: 141)

ANXIETIES ABOUT VOICE

Lord's theory, as it champions the complex compositional elements in orality that place them on a level with 'literary' intelligence, takes me back to the work of Alice Oswald, referred to earlier. Oswald's radical poetic platform in itself challenges assumptions about the 'deified' authority presumed to reside within the constructions of the written word on the page. Her active interest in the spoken word, demonstrated when she performs her own work from memory, also opens the possibility that as a writer, she is both able to anticipate and also *inscribe* the differences effected when the voice activates the spoken word. Her embodiment of the voice as a reader of her own work provides a view that simultaneously challenges the under-theorized and often invisible position of the voice and also suggests why it might be feared because of its powerful unpredictability in live expression.

In the following quote, Jacques Derrida cites the unpredictability of voice as a problem, although, again, he still fails to actually name the voice itself, preferring to name it speech:

> Speaking frightens me because by never saying enough, I also say too much. And if the necessity of becoming breath or speech restricts meaning – and our responsibility for it – writing restricts and constrains speech further still. Writing is the anguish of the Hebraic *ruah*, experienced in solitude by human responsibility; experienced by Jeremiah subjected to God's dictation ('Take thee a roll of a book, and write therein all the words that I have spoken unto thee'), or by Baruch transcribing Jeremiah's dictation (Jeremiah 36: 2.4) or further, within the properly human moment of *pneumatology*, the science of *pneuma*, *spiritus*, or *logos* which was divided into three parts: the divine, the angelical and the human. It is the moment at which we must decide whether we will engrave what we hear. And whether engraving preserves or betrays speech.
>
> (Derrida 2010: 9)

In the extract, Derrida links to significant philosophical discussion about the voice and the footnote explanation in the same edition offers further insight into the depth and complexity of the discussion that goes back to the Hebrew traditions noted by Cavarero earlier:

> The Hebrew *ruah*, like the Greek *pneuma*, means both wind or breath and soul or spirit. Only in God are breath and spirit, speech and thought, absolutely identical; man can always be duplicitous, his speech can be other than his thought.
>
> (Derrida 2002: 384)

Derrida raises three problems about the voice that remain persistent. First is the voice as it is associated with the unsayable qualities of the sacred; second is the voice as it is associated with transcendent thought as speech;

and third is the voice as it is linked to the sometimes duplicitous human capacity to separate thought from intention. How does theatre practice answer this? It is addressed, if not resolved, in a number of theatre voice methodologies in which 'truthful' expression is a desired aesthetic. Such approaches aim to ensure that authored dramatic speech aligns both with the individual actor's vocal instrument and with a capacity to reactivate congruent thought impulses when performed. The vocal instrument of the actor, then, in combination with the authorial voice spoken afresh, out loud, aims to give both voice and speech positions of equal importance in the expressive communicative act. It thereby moves it closer to the position taken by Alice Oswald in the voicing of her own poetic text spoken about earlier. Interpretive theatre, thereby, seeks to resolve the problem of voice in its reframing of several philosophical elements in such a way that the sacred *and* the profane are both incorporated.

VOICE AND SILENCE

But what about the problem of voice when it presents as a cultural metaphor for the unsayable? Dramatist Samuel Beckett suggests that he, too, as in the sacred traditions, regards the voice as symbolic of the way it exemplifies all that cannot be *said*. This complex paradox is part of a profile in those dramatic writers for whom voice is an acknowledged presence. Beckett's early search for form looked to the ways in which its dramatic 'voice' was neither exactly transcendent in a sacred sense, nor exactly prosaic in a theatrical sense. Literary critic Harold Bloom uses a quote from Beckett to show the ways in which the playwright reached almost mockingly towards the voice and away from words but also, paradoxically, towards an end to or absence of voice:

> At first it can only be a matter of somehow finding a method by which we can represent this mocking attitude towards the word, through words. In this disso-nance between the means and their use it will perhaps become possible to feel a whisper of that final music or that silence that underlies All.
>
> (Bloom 2005: 230)

Performance theorist Peggy Phelan, too, looks for the cracks between the word by her regard for voice as it is at some remove from the semantic function of the word and closer to the 'other' paralinguistic effects of melody, scat, moans and the acoustic worlds they open out (including silence). In this sonorous system, whilst voice is able to carry meaning in individuated qualitative and paralinguistic ways, it does not *think* in the same way that language thinks. The discrete functions of voice as formed out of 'silent' thought, individuated instrumental qualities, scripted speech and paralinguistic elements are all, thereby, better clarified.

VOICE AND SPEECH

The distinctions made between voice and speech are perhaps more frequently articulated in voice training pedagogies. Here, the voice is regarded as the instrument of a body–mind synthesis, and speech represents the semantic function in which words are carried on the sound waves of voice. However, the notions raised about voice at a philosophical level rarely enter the training studio. Whilst this has been long discussed within poststructuralist circles (Jacques Derrida, Roland Barthes and so on, as indicated), the vocal training context itself has taken as its focus matters of instrumental management and expressive outcomes. Conversely, theoreticians have hitherto rarely engaged with the material properties of voice in the transmission of meaning and its reception. I suggest that each has the potential to inform the other in ways that are productive for the individual voice and the development of conceptual abstract thought.

Phelan's observation about voice at a point prior to its expression (when it is present in intent but not yet voiced) provides a useful example of one of the ways in which philosophy helps to inform the outcomes of the voice. Her belief that voice is only nameable as voice when it leaves the speaker and re-enters the ear of the listener invites the speaker to think afresh about the moment of expressive delivery and of what it is comprised (Queen Mary University, London, Public Lecture, 22 March 2012). In this process, perception of voice, as constituted from sound waves, is distinguished from linguistic perceptions formed out of an awareness of pre-existing language structures that are not yet sounded. Knowledge of this gives the speaker more potential ownership over their vocal expression.

Voice as pure signal, and its potential masking by an already pre-known word, marks the return to a now familiar theme about the meaning conveyed by the voice as distinct from the meaning conveyed in language. A salutary reminder about the physics of the voice reminds me again of the important function of voice as an instrument of sound making:

> The sound produced by the vibrating vocal folds, called the voice source signal, is a complex tone containing a fundamental frequency and many overtones, or higher harmonic partials … Voice and speech together convey semantic meanings. The voice on its own communicates meaning that falls outside the conventions of linguistic structure but is never the less meaningful and of perceptual relevance to the listener.
>
> (Sataloff cited in Linklater 2006: 379)

The intractability of the distinction is always present, however. Whilst it is assumed that the date given to the origin of the human capacity to develop speech is 'forever hidden in the mists of time' (Harris 1986: 3), and the history of voice likewise, it is notable that the history of writing holds a prominent position precisely because it offers existential solutions that the voice appears only to unsettle. I refer, again, to the fears triggered by the instabilities of the voice in comparison with the certainties provided by the visual trace in the orthographic record, even as they also remove the speaker from the face-to-face consequences of their communication and create other levels of uncertainty:

> Writing set human communication free from the limitations imposed by the impermanence of speech, and dispensed with the live presence of a speaker. It made verbal communication independent of the individual communicator, by providing an autonomous text that could survive transmission over time and distance ... It divorced verbal communication from the original efforts and intentions implicit in face-to face speech.
>
> (Harris 1986: 24)

Linguist Roy Harris describes a symbiotic relationship between speech and the word in religious communication frameworks that date back to the medieval and Renaissance period and beyond (Harris 1986: 45). In these formations the written word was given more cultural significance than the speech act to the extent that it was idealized at the expense of the voice:

> The tyranny of the alphabet is part of that scriptist bias which is deeply rooted in European education. It fosters respect for the written word over the spoken, and respect for the book above all as a repository of both the language and the wisdom of former ages. At first sight, the insistence that writing is only a representation of speech may appear to run quite counter to the prevailing scriptism of European culture. But that appearance is deceptive. The doctrine that writing represents speech becomes a cornerstone of scriptism once the written representation is held to be not a slavish or imperfect copy but, on the contrary, an idealization which captures those essential features often blurred or distorted in the rough and tumble of everyday utterance. Thus it is possible for the written representation to be held up as a model of what the spoken reality ought to be.
>
> (Harris 1986: 46)

Of importance here is the fact that not only is it speech that gets sublimated to the 'ideal' of the printed script, but a double obfuscation occurs in which the voice within utterance is also obscured.

Historian Janette Dillon helps to explain the development of the idealization of written forms due to their links with specific theological and secular functions of Latin in early English drama. A case in point is provided by the medieval morality play where the high-status signification of Latin is ably appreciated by a barely literate audience who don't necessarily understand its literal sense but who certainly understand its presence. Latin, in this way, serves as a marked contrast to the signification of the spoken English vernacular. Dillon provides examples of the multiple ways in which a mix of word value, song, jest and the musicality of sound provides an acoustic key to the mood and status of the narrative line or character dilemma in the drama. Of particular relevance is the fact that spoken Latin denotes key revelations or climaxes of meaning:

> Not only do they mock Mercy with Latinate English, translate obscenities into Latin and mingle Latin with English in a kind of macaronic carnival; they also make up pseudo-Latin words from English roots, utter mock prayers and blessings, trivialise some of the most sacred moments of Christian history in the Latin of the Gospels, construct a prolonged pseudo-trial (suggesting the Last Judgement) in a mixture of English, Latin and pseudo-Latin and play with the sheer sound of Latin until it is reduced to nonsense.
>
> (Dillon 1998: 67)

The actual task of recreating the voice of Latin utterance is assisted by a kinaesthetic approach that provides the feel and sensation of Latin in the mouth and on the lips and tongue. In this way, it is possible to consider that the actual movement of the syllables, with their multisyllabic weight and pace differences, as distinct from the Anglo-Saxon branch of English with its singular pace and heaviness, had an impact on both the muscular processes of sound making and audience reception. The distinctive movement of Latin as pure sound, based on kinaesthetic evidence, had the potential to provoke sensations of deep resonant sound making in an individual speaker disposed to reflect and magnify the musicality of the sounds: 'sound can clearly create meanings other than through sense, and meaning is only one of the pleasures available from sound ... Plays always offer pleasure beyond the meaning of their words' (Dillon 1998: 154).

With this in mind, it is possible to imagine, then, that the voice differed in quality when it voiced Latin, as opposed to the vernacular, and that these qualitative sonic differences carried over into the material life of the players' voices:

> Latin, in these plays as elsewhere, is also the language of the clergy, God's representatives on earth ... exchanges between clerical, virtuous characters and non-clerical sinners thus create the context for explicit discussion of language choices and make clear that the expression of moral opposition between the church and its enemies through an opposition of linguistic registers is a deliberate project. Characters identify one another's moral status via their dialects, and in doing so teach the audience the linguistic equation the plays seek to endorse: Latin or elevated English is the discourse of holiness, while aggressively vernacular speech is a rival discourse which wickedly (if also delightfully) seeks to challenge the discourse of Christian truth.
>
> (Dillon 1998: 51–52)

The importance, here, is in the fact that Dillon draws attention to the effects of different language structures not only within medieval drama settings but also within the wider social and political circumstances of Elizabethan political projects of colonial expansion. It is also in this febrile environment that spoken English fights for its place, not only within religious settings but on the stages of early modern England:

> The kingdom ... was increasingly seeking to consolidate the status of empire, in the primary sense of owning no allegiance to any power beyond itself ... Empires, of course, traditionally need to keep the barbarians and their languages at bay; but the problem for England ... was defining the barbarians. Traditionally, Western Europe as a whole looked to the Latin of classical empire as a model of eloquence; but the debate on translating the bible highlighted the extent to which specific aesthetics implied specific religious affiliations. Where secular translations were concerned, and aesthetic considerations were paramount to the texts in question, English was regularly accused of being too 'rude' and 'barbarous' to render the great classical texts adequately.
>
> (Dillon 1998: 141)

This raises questions not just about the power battle between church and state and between elevated Latin and the vernacular languages, but also about the word uttered live and the word in print, and who has access to its expression overall. It is of particular interest that there is evidence of a strong Puritan resistance to the use of vernacular English and attendant 'rhetorical handbooks' (Dillon 1998: 143). As the handbooks spread and widespread English is brought closer to the elevated status of Latin in its proud and elegant state (Dillon 1998: 143), those in power feared that their privileged access to eloquent language would be eroded:

> What really bothers the Puritans about rhetorical handbooks is not their recognition that language can be eloquent, but their humanist implication that eloquence is to be achieved by individual study and endeavour. For the Puritan eloquence is an expression of inspiration and grace; the notion that human beings can or should wilfully cultivate it is misguided and presumptuous, even idolatrous.
>
> (Dillon 1998: 144)

On this evidence, it is not hard to appreciate the reasons why some within the Puritan movements turned against theatre itself as an act of idolatry. This is due to the fact that dramatic representations of faith as enacted by human speakers are not the actual communications of the prophecy of the Holy Spirit itself. Put another way, when words begin to describe and stand in for the word of God, a challenge is posed to the notion of faith itself:

> The performance of plays threatens the very root of a faith that is grounded on a continued and spontaneous witnessing to the truth. The act of representation is by definition at a remove from truth and therefore, for the most literal-minded Puritans, a lie.
>
> (Dillon 1998: 145)

Those able to speak and understand Latin and those unable to do so are inscribed in the extant play texts and provide crucial indications for an audience about social positions and status. It is assumed that the players who knew the effects of Latin and English, and were able to command both, gained credibility – in time – to equal the audience-winning antics of the clown. Dillon argues that whilst it is never possible to fully determine the wheres and wherefores of audience attention, it is reasonable to assume, based on the fact that not all plays are comedic, that audiences began to acculturate themselves to the art of listening to the more complex and ornate ideas and references contained in a Latinate-heavy play text.

The actor who could not only command Latin on the tongue, but also manage the jig, the sword fight and much more, it is assumed, set a standard well into the early modern period. Although the acting is largely 'demon-strative, gestural, explicit and focused on stage picture to a degree that is unfamiliar now' (Dillon 2006: 92), it is also possible to assume that certain players developed a capacity for speech dexterity, and sonority, based upon the Latin sounds, that was sufficient to render the work comprehensible to audiences beyond the pulpit. Dillon suggests that the theatre of this period prioritizes a 'direct relationship with the audience through direct address and physical proximity' (Dillon 2006: 90). It is conceivable that the player who engaged with this was also able, in time, to develop a style of delivery suitable for the soliloquy.

I imagine that the audience eventually begins to anticipate a clear and immediate line of sound in the soliloquy and to expect a certain standard of auditory and conceptual stylistics. The following extract shows how an audience might have attended to a variety of volume and pitch levels in a production of *King Lear* in the sixteenth century. The implication is that the actors involved used the practical challenge as a template for the enhance-ment of their own playing styles:

> The change in focus is visual, spatial and aural; and the aural register includes not only voices, differently pitched speaking publicly or aside, but also the presence or absence of music, background noise or silence. And audiences feel the texture of each moment not only against other moments in the same play, but against their experience of other plays.
>
> (Dillon 2006: 95)

'Playscripts show certain kinds of performance and certain modes of acting and occupying space, persisting over the whole period' (Dillon 2006: 95). A description of the 'scenical strutting, and furious vociferation' (Dillon 2006: 95) of sixteenth-century star actor Edward Alleyn indicates that his was a style of acting marked by demonstrative vocalization that was already becoming outmoded to some degree by the beginning of the seventeenth century. Although a version of passionate and vociferous acting styles makes a return in the eighteenth and nineteenth centuries, as shown in

Chapter 3, evidence reveals that Elizabethan audiences began to appreciate the nuanced understanding that is effected by a modulation of vocal stylistics. Dillon suggests that if the writer wished to indicate a loud playing style, it would feature in the playscripts, sometimes marked in by the actors themselves. Evidence in the dramatic text itself also indicates the ways in which contrasts of vocal expression became part of audience expectation in the early modern period. In the following quote from *Troilus and Cressida*, Shakespeare takes a 'jibe at the strutting player' from the mouths of both Hamlet and Ulysses (Dillon 2006: 96):

> 'Strutting,' both Hamlet and Ulysses make clear, was linked to noise, to a resounding step and a 'bellowing' voice. Heightened physical movement and heightened speech went together; and we can see 'strutting' scripted across a range of parts … Richard Burbage, by contrast, was praised for making audiences feel that they were seeing, not theatre, but real life.
>
> (Dillon 2006: 97)

Two centuries on, in the nineteenth century, as the craft of the actor expands to consist of far more than reckless or furious voice making and gesture, it starts to mirror, instead, the artistry of the word. The nuance, modulation and variation of tone, more closely associated with the composed gradations of rhetorical expression in the classical period, become part of the ways in which the actor's voice works to synchronize with the playwright's written task. The standards set by organized linguistic structure in rhetoric are never far from centre stage and are referenced in the actor's ability to persuade or dissuade an audience of any given position:

> From Greek antiquity on, the dominance of rhetoric in the academic background produced throughout the literate world an impression, real if often vague, that oratory was the paradigm of all verbal expression, and kept the agonistic pitch of discourse exceedingly high by present-day standards.
>
> (Ong 1982: 111)

As the actor takes on the fashions of spoken eloquence and dramatic authorship becomes concerned as much with argument as with entertainment, so the audience comes to expect, understand and appreciate the art of verbal position making. It is to rhetoric, again, that the nineteenth-century actor on both sides of the Atlantic returns:

> In the mid-nineteenth century, American actors learned their craft through apprenticeship, observation, and elocution training, which dictated the use of gesture as well as inflection patterns, range, 'appropriate' tempos, 'force', and even breathing. While perhaps foreign to a modern-day audience's ear, elocution excluded subtlety, and was synonymous with the imitative acting style of

the day. This form of voice and speech training was not typically concerned with the actor's vocal or gestural authenticity. Instead, elocution invited the listener to enjoy the 'correctness' and 'beauty' of the speaker's tone, pronunciation, style, and gesture ... The nineteenth-century listener's ear was discerning and so prized 'good' sounds and 'appropriate' sounds. In the American Elocutionist, author and orthophonist William Russell, who also worked with Rush and Murdoch, states that nasal tones were bad and guttural tones inappropriate, but when combined, the two were considered 'doubly injurious'.

(Saklad 2011: 2–3)

A coda to the discussion about rhetoric and the craft of the actor is provided in an account given by Gwynneth Thurburn – principal of the Central School in London between 1942 and 1967 – in a 1978 lecture towards the end of her life. It offers insight not only into the status given to elocution within UK actor training in the early to mid part of the twentieth century, but also to the ways in which it changed over her lifetime. In it she speaks about Elsie Fogerty – first principal of the Central School – who was forced to give up ideas of becoming an actor, due to family pressures, and to take up the more practical option of teaching elocution:

The demand in those days existed for teachers of so-called elocution. She set to meet these demands but she didn't really like the elocutionists and what they were doing. She thought they were too pre-occupied with Manner rather than Matter. Now I am going to take a moment off just to illustrate what elocution was when I was a small child. But let me stress this isn't what Elsie Fogerty taught me, it's what I was taught by somebody else long before I met her. You had to place your feet so – you put those two fingers together, and then dropped your hands in front of you and there you were in a graceful position.

(Transcript from the Elsie Fogerty Lecture, 1978, by Gwynneth Thurburn, The Royal Central School Archives, London)

The ways in which speech and gesture are codified under the rules of elocution, described as effecting more manner than matter in this account, provide yet more evidence of how voice is obscured in the late nineteenth and early twentieth centuries, even as a 'yearning for the old orality' makes an appearance (Ong 1982: 115). As a consequence, 'the nineteenth century developed "elocution" contests, which tried to repristinate printed texts, using careful artistry to memorize the text and recite them so that they would sound like extempore oral productions' (Ong 1982: 115).

Catherine Lambert (b. 1918) – Professor of Speech and Diction at the Royal College of Music and a student at the Central School in the 1930s – states that Fogerty's teaching had an immense influence on her subsequent career (Lecture, 9 March 2011, Royal College of Music). Fogerty's suggestion to keep the voice direct and forward by 'rolling it along the floor' towards the audience, thus matching the movement of the phrase and the shape of the thought in a gestural and vocal harmonization, is an excellent example of how early spoken voice techniques utilized both the structured thought of rhetoric and the sound-making capacities of the voice.

In 1942, in the USA, Edith Skinner added her own version of an inheritance from classical rhetoric in her book *Speak with Distinction*. Skinner was descended from a formidable speech-training line led by William Tilly (1860–1935) who, in addition to developing World English, was especially regarded for his fervent promotion of the International Phonetic Alphabet (IPA); Tilly advocated that certain phonemes were superior to others. At that time, classical plays in the USA were performed with the accent prescribed by Skinner. Actors who studied her method were said to possess exquisite skill in articulation and were said to have sounded, not surprisingly, very much alike (Saklad 2011: 7–8).

By way of a sharp contrast, the contemporary period into the twenty-first century is marked by a strong distaste for all prescriptive rules of speech. Even though the rules have lost much of their regulatory potency, their ghosts still haunt theatre and training platforms where audience expectations, as well as actor ability, strive for agreement about what constitutes a congruent relationship between voice and speech and what exactly informs standards of contemporary public eloquence.

AN INTERVIEW WITH KRISTIN LINKLATER, 1 SEPTEMBER 2015

KL – Kristin Linklater

JB – Jane Boston

JB: Why is voice important in theatre? Why has it got its place in our imagination and in theatre practice?

KL: Surely it is because theatre started off as storytelling and storytelling is done through the voice, going back to probably Homer and the bards of Europe and Wales – there is a whole bardic storytelling rootedness and then, of course, the church, music and again stories and stories that have to be told.

Theatre came out of a time when people were not reading – they certainly didn't have iPhones and their computers and so on – that is at the *heart* of the origins of theatre. Yes, the body – but, I imagine the troubadours travelling in medieval times from castle to castle, sitting by the fire and telling the stories of what had happened at the previous castle, or wherever, or village they had just come through – and that was how people knew what was going on in the world so the content would be: where – where am *I* in my world; and the language in which it was conveyed would be *vividly* vital in the event – and then singing is obviously part of that too.

I am certainly prejudiced in favour of the voice, to the point where I would say I think the voice was probably much more dominant in the *earliest* manifestations of what we now call theatre than the body was – yes, you have mime and jugglers and entertainments through the body, but as we now understand, body and voice come together in performance – I don't think probably that was so in the earliest days, so I am quite clear in my mind that it was voice that was the central element; and if you come through to Shakespeare's day, look at the dense and wonderful texts that you've got – the poetic texts – where the voices had to be … and you're in big outdoor theatres seating hundreds of people … the voices really had to be the crucial part of delivering the story – with an enormous amount of variety and richness and expressivity.

JB: It is interesting that the voice, for some people, became an expert craft – became something that could be developed and enhanced and how that eventually became slightly apart from…

KL: When – when are you talking about?

JB: I don't know … I am thinking about a time when an individual began to stand apart as a storyteller, to tell the story of their community, and how they managed it and what the signs were that they had the skills to do it. Did it simply evolve that people thought they had something in their storytelling voice that would be worth listening to and retaining? You know, when did we really start noticing these 'expert' abilities?

KL: I don't know when you'd say people started noticing; I was just thinking of who would it be – quite possibly the people who didn't want to go out in the fields and do all that hard work that everybody else was doing [laughter]. I'd rather – 'oh, people want to hear stories, well, I'll tell them stories while they work, but I don't want to have to lift that!'

JB: Because on the other side, we have got Frankie Armstrong's archetypal work – and the work song – so you get people finding something as a community in the fields through rhythm – and then there evolves this person who is slightly apart that you're suggesting, who didn't necessarily want to go down to the fields.

KL: Well, I don't know – I am just making that up as an idea. But when we get the separating out of somebody who has a particular talent for telling the stories and he [*sic*] is the one who tells the stories rather than the communal thing, which is the singing for work so that you could work with pleasure …

JB: I suppose we have to think, too, about memory and people who had the capacity to retain words?

KL: But I think everybody had it. I think we have just lost it. Whoever invented the first writing – or came up with and brought it to the ruler of the time – probably in Greece or Rome – saying 'look at this extraordinary invention of writing', and he replied, ' this will be the end of humanity – the end of civilization – we will no longer have to remember what we are and what we say, it is now out of our minds and on a tablet' – the idea that writing actually was in lieu of memory – I think memory was an integral part of everybody's existence.

JB: Some people must have developed a greater capacity somehow?

KL: Well, if you think about it, yes – Homer … those great massive epic poems and so on. And the other bit that I come back to is – I'm sure I've told this story before – the Greek actors and the harnessing of the harmonics of the voice?

JB: Go on …

KL: Apparently they not only had to come on the stage and tell the story at Epidaurus [built around the third century BC Epidaurus is one of the best preserved of the ancient Greek theatres] to thousands of people – telling the story out *horizontally* through the persona – though the masks – but the harmonics of their voices were picked up by bronze urns of different shapes which were built into the aisles of the seats and those different-shaped bronze urns reinforced the harmonics of the voice and took them *up* to reinforce the music of the spheres – to keep the cosmos together. You know I *love* that story – how important is the voice there? It is keeping the whole cosmos together!

JB: That must have been informing the work you first did in Boston [the women's festival in Boston, USA, c. 1984] when you had the planetary sounds coming into the diagonal body shapes …

KL: Into the vowels.

JB: I always remember that … so you have somebody who emerges as capable of managing the resonant frequencies – a specialist with those kinds of capacities …

KL: Yes.

JB: … who can handle the resonant frequencies. And then I guess it sets you apart – closer to the gods – if you could do that for an audience; if you could feel that?

KL: I suspect it was a powerful position.

JB: A powerful, peaceful tool. Against the realities of war, famine and death you then have somebody capable of harnessing these transcendent matters – it is quite potent.

KL: Maybe it is just a residue of that – that now we say that you have to have a voice in the theatre because, in a way, you don't have to have a voice in theatre – sadly, you can do it all with electronics.

JB: Well, yes, that is partly what I am curious about – what are we going to say to twenty-first-century students about voice in the contemporary theatre? My next question moves towards that and is about what made you locate yourself in theatre and in voice?

KL: Oh, that is nothing to do with it – happenstance.

JB: There was no one specific moment in theatre?

KL: No.

JB: So how did you get to LAMDA [London Academy of Music and Dramatic Art] then?

KL: I think I was seventeen or eighteen. I auditioned for LAMDA, that's all – to act – and I remember auditioning with Imogen's speech waking up to the headless Cloten beside her – an impossible speech – so I decided to do that.

JB: Do you not, then, have any recollection of anything that made you think, I want to develop this?

KL: No.

JB: So when did it happen?

KL: Michael MacOwen sent me a letter when I was acting at the theatre in St Andrews, when I was twenty-one, saying would I like to come and apprentice with Iris Warren – so to speak – because she was ill, actually, and she hadn't trained anybody to do her work and I was flattered, that is all, I was flattered.

JB: Quite right though.

KL: But I had no vocation or calling. *No* – I just turned in the direction that beckoned and I was – I was beckoned there – and there we are.

JB: Just pressing you one more time, in your upbringing there was story-telling …

KL: Ah, yes – there was a lot of voice in my upbringing.

JB: Anything you care to drop in – if it wasn't theatre, the voice was in – in what …?

KL: I cannot with honesty put any of these things together – there was a family voice – a speaking voice – a speaking voice in Orkney initially – but mostly during my teenage years, I remember, my father was always shouting at us – my mother – we all shouted at each other a lot

JB: In love, hate and war?

KL: Anger, yes, and so on.

JB: Did you spout songs – any expressions other than animosity?

KL: I suppose; we'd sing around the table after dinner sometimes – yes, my father would sing old Victorian Music Hall songs when he was in a good mood, but it was nothing uplifting. I'm sorry I can't come up with anything inspiring at that level.

JB: But that is interesting though …

KL: What happened was it *gradually* grew in me; the whole thing. And it was one of those things when you discover something because somebody else tells you about it. So when people started telling me that these strange exercises that I was doing that I'd learnt from Iris Warren were *really* helping them, then I had to pay attention and think more about what it was. It wasn't until I went to America that I had any idea about the anatomy of voice or anything.

JB: Something had been kindled by this flattering invitation to work with Iris and you said yes – you didn't say no, you said yes.

KL: And then I had to figure out what to do – I was a pupil teacher and I was teaching within probably two to three months without knowing anything about what it was; I was just doing these noises; it was just by gradually doing it that I found something out.

JB: So you found something out and you found something out that served theatre?

KL: Absolutely nothing but theatre – and it wasn't particularly open. Iris had this sense of a centre and that that was truthful and that's what we were looking for, but there wasn't the kind of psychological and emotional climate – I am talking about 1959/1961.

JB: So there was *Look Back in Anger*?

KL: Just, but how long does this take to feed in? And *Waiting for Godot*, but that was not particularly emotional – but *Look Back in Anger* was the watershed in terms of something real and it was a bit of a shock. But we were not emulating that for our students at LAMDA; we were still doing rather polite Shakespeare – nice strong voices, good-sounding voices, truthful but not particularly exciting.

JB: Was truth important to Iris's idea of the centre?

KL: Yes, definitely – not pushing and shouting or overacting.

JB: Did you perceive a difference in her approach? Were you already aware of what other people were doing around London, say, such as the work of Clifford Turner, for example?

KL: No idea.

JB: My impression is that the voice was taught in the upright position, most of the time, and the men had their shirts done up – so we could say it was buttoned-up teaching, and whoever got down on the floor has got a lot to answer for?

KL: I know – I don't know who first said let's lie down on the floor.

JB: It is an interesting phenomenon – maybe it came from dance? Dance is surely a huge influence?

KL: No, not in those days in London – that was in New York.

JB: They were doing fancy 'new' stuff in Dartington.

KL: Oh, yes, in Dartington, and of course we had William Elmhurst (connected to Dartington) who was a student at LAMDA.

JB: It strikes me there were pockets of places that brought over the Laban work and experimented with new work in the summer schools and some of it must have percolated through? So, when did you feel you had an idea of the kind of voice (process) that would work for the theatre – when did you really cohere that? Or was it evolving?

KL: Evolution. The big thing was going to America and beginning to understand the psychological and emotional life that lay behind and underneath the voice – that's where it all came from and it was the whole time of the human growth movement and consciousness raising and I began to do group therapy and psychotherapy. And I began to find out about all these other things that were going on … that contributed – the mind–body connection, the psychophysical connection – and I did an enormous amount of workshops and that then started to deepen it all – and of course I was working, to begin with, with a lot of actors from the Actors Studio and Lee Strasberg was still functioning then and *their* vocabulary was all emotional truth and Iris's vocab meant that; but then it started to go deeper – a give and take – between those actors that I was working with.

JB: You deepened it?

KL: Yes, I deepened it and took it into the body more and developed sound and movement and all that kind of stuff.

JB: But if you had not been in the States do you think it would have happened?

KL: No.

JB: It was the zeitgeist?

KL: Absolutely – it was what was needed there.

JB: They needed you, you needed them?

KL: It was a perfect time – culturally – for me to be there.

JB: Yes, you have often said that … so, in moving forward, how do you listen to voice in theatre now – what is your criteria for a successful voice in theatre performance?

KL: One that is communicating the character and the story, which may not necessarily be in beautifully rounded tones. It is not the beauty of the voice that counts; it is the truthfulness and very often the voice has to express dangerous and complex internal situations and must crack, break, hiss, spit – and the voice that is exciting is picking up all those elements of the human being.

JB: Will this voice endure in theatre?

KL: I think that voice will endure if it is true to its emotional source – voice is very strong. I think a lot of voice people are a bit oversensitive about it – they talk about vocal hygiene.

JB: And it is a health and safety era – a lot of things can dampen our curiosity.

KL: It is the emotional side that is the healer – the power of the voice; the powerhouse of the voice is the emotional life – and it is also the healer. If the voice gets harmed then the emotions need to come through. It is the inhibiting of an emotional state that causes the damage. I don't know if you know an actor called Bobby Cannavale who was in a play on in London called *The Mother F**ker with the Hat* – oh, a fantastically good play – raw beyond belief … and to begin with I couldn't bear it because his voice was hoarse. I thought he's never going to get through but that was the character's voice – as a drug addict – crazy and marvellous and magnificent – and he did eight shows a week and he made it through the entire run.

JB: American?

KL: Yes – it has had pretty good reviews. I thought okay, that's his voice and that's why they cast him but then I heard him do something else and his voice was perfectly smooth and normal.

JB: It came from the right place?

KL: Yes.

JB: So, I wonder what you think about the voice in theatre in the future? Training the voice has been your life's career – do you have any idea where things might go in terms of theatre and voice?

KL: Oh, you know – don't get me started, as they say. I go off on an absolutely dystopian route when I think about it, because things are moving so fast towards etherized existence – and this whole thing of developing the mind and having what they call a non-biological body to support the mind …

JB: Oh, yes…

KL: And talking about, 'oh, we don't need our voices, we are going to have microchips and we'll just have to go thought to thought through the microchips' – who knows whether that's true; I've talked to some clever young people who say, yes, that's where it's going to go and that we certainly won't need our voices – voices are a terribly inefficient way of communicating. And then there is the other side to this, with something called the human being, and certainly in my lifetime the voice is not going to be sidelined and told that it is no longer necessary in theatre – not in my lifetime. I feel in one way totally pessimistic about where theatre can go – but people have been feeling pessimistic about live theatre for ever.

JB: Ever since theatre began? It is a fundamental issue of what happens to us as human beings, I suppose, that presses on us?

KL: Yes … And the other possibility is that there will become such a need for something real in terms of communication that the voice will become more important than ever and that is the one that obviously I will have to focus on and invest in.

JB: But it is interesting that in a lot of contemporary theatre environments – particularly in universities – you will have subjects based on conceptual versions of the sound or the technical stuff such as the lighting– that are all taking off as subjects – and the voice sometimes feels as if it is left out?

KL: Oh, yes, it is a really bad time, I think, from that point of view.

JB: Sort of at the bottom of the pile in a sense …

KL: And you can almost see it even in the ways voice teachers are treated in training academies – they should be at the centre; we have talked about this before – as at the Central School under Thurburn – and Elsie (Fogerty). That was all you did – voice and poetry and the acting – then you go and rehearse a scene.

JB: The voice teaching was all of that!

KL: Everything came out of that – a little bit of movement to try and support – that was how it was up until a very short time ago, really.

JB: It was how it was when I was a student at Central.

KL: But now – the voice faculty – they are kind of the maids of all work who are meant to dust behind the larynx – but it is a very bad time in that way. And yet there is more being discovered about the voice and actually more scientific interest and more psycho- and neuroscientific and philosophical stuff coming out – so it is conceivable theatre will swing back again.

JB: There is a lot of pressure on the cerebral subjects – on the subjects that come out of the mind within, say, the Royal Central School of Speech and Drama, for example – if you can conceptualize it then that is where you can run with your subject. But those that are involved in getting down to the doing, can quite quickly get marginalized in university environs.

KL: It is funny because the shows that work in the actual theatre are the visceral ones – the ones that viscerally connect people to what is going on on stage – and so there is some disconnect – I think – between the Academy, so to speak, and the voice.

JB: Oh, for sure. I do worry about the career status – if you like – of the voice teacher in these university environs.

KL: That is why we have to be clever and we have to write and we have to publish.

JB: You are right, but I sometimes think we can't get too wrapped up in following the arguments – although it is tempting to follow the philosophers, for example, who hold their seminars and imagine that voice people will not be at the table, and I just want to say, yes – we can be at the table.

KL: Have you read the Santorini stories?

JB: Yes – published in Mosaic?

KL: That is where we joined with the philosophers – one of them had done a whole philosophical treatise on the Mouth and had never looked inside her own mouth.

JB: They don't.

KL: But they were so thrilled when they did.

JB: And it is that simple invitation that doesn't often happen in the Academy. It is so profound. One of the big discussions in the Academy is, does theatre think? I think voice is part of thought but has not been considered as such. The route of all thought is philosophical – philosophy claims to be the omnipotent source of all knowledge; you can't escape it according to philosophers.

KL: I think philosophers in the world at large are more marginalized than voice teachers.

JB: I think they are, but they also have a long history to call upon. Quite a lot of famous names to quote … Finally, though, to my last question – is there anything in your mind about a legacy – one key feature of your legacy for theatre?

KL: I am most proud of the numbers of teachers that I have trained – and trained very rigorously – and on the professional level that is what I am most proud of and they are my legacy, and what they are teaching is something that is very much to do with the depth of human communication that is possible and probably necessary for any real kind of civilization.

JB: Thank you.

Part V
Contested Trainings

Chapter

6   The Theatre Voice Manual

This chapter examines several key extracts from twentieth- and twenty-first-century theatre voice training manuals that exemplify a range of approaches to voice in theatre practice in the UK and the USA. The selected extracts represent a hybridity of style, including both pedagogical ethos and vocal exercise sequence, much of it, but not all, on the how-to spectrum. During the course of the chapter, I discuss how sequences of voice exercises, as set out in the form of the manual, raise particular problems for the field of voice, most obviously in the area of student usage and practical application, and in the fact that they are often ignored as repositories of cultural meaning.

There are problems for the student reader of the manual where they are instructed to follow and learn from exercises that are, by and large, immersive in nature and hard to experience fully with a book in hand. As I will go on to discuss, authors present a number of means to best activate the reader in such circumstances. These include the use of highlighted tips for the teacher who accompanies the exercise sequences with the student. By these means, there is an appeal to live engagement with the practice. This is the approach taken in David Carey and Rebecca Clark Carey's *Verbal Arts Workbook*. In Jeanette Nelson's *The Voice Exercises Book*, she uses a direct approach to the reader to suggest that they use the exercises to 'build a relationship' with the voice in whatever context they find themselves (Nelson 2015: 8). In *Singing and the Actor* by Gillyanne Kayes, both the student and the teacher are instructed not only about content but also about the importance of building 'a language for talking about singing that is not purely subjective' (Kayes 2000: xii). As a genre, however, whilst such manuals undoubtedly contain valuable practical strategies, they only offer partial solutions in relation to the experiences they prompt. Fundamental questions remain, then, not only about the ways in which voice exercise sequences can be read on their own terms but also as part of a wider conceptualization of voice practice as knowledge within theatre practice.

I suggest that the voice manual is best considered alongside a 'second text' that arises out of the practice itself. What I mean by this is that where the manual provides the exercise protocols, the 'second text' is evidenced in the individuated live vocal outcome in the studio as it arises out of the immersive studio process of which the exercises are a part. I argue, then, that by itself the manual, when it is read as part of solitary experience, is limited in its usefulness and only becomes fully realized when used in conjunction with and through the live and lived in voice. It is, nevertheless, important that the manual is interrogated as part of its inclusion within the field of voice knowledge.

Voice practitioners, historically, have taken the view that the physical voice, as an object under the governance of the mind, is suggestible to improvement. The Cartesian division of mind and body (voice) that this represents is challenged, however, by a mid-twentieth-century paradigm shift championed by theorist Maurice Merleau-Ponty. His claim for the importance of the phenomenon of the voice suggests that a deeper aware-ness and understanding are found through the embodied experience in which value is placed on the sensations inside the voice of the individual, as well as those that are perceived at the level of its reception. This validates the sensations of voice that lie outside the descriptive capacities of textual instruction and raises problems for the ways in which the manual maintains a relationship to experience. Contemporary performance theorist Phillip Zarrilli speaks to this paradigm change and the impact it has on the actor:

> When Merleau-Ponty shifted from an examination of 'I think' to the 'I can' of the body, he laid the philosophical foundation for a more processual account of how our relationship to the worlds we inhabit is constituted by our inter-sensory and inter-subjective engagement with those worlds. The actor, like other skilled prac-titioners, ideally gains the ability to inhabit a particular world of the 'I can'.
>
> (Zarrilli 2009: 46)

It is important, then, to add to this a consideration of the way this paradig-matic shift offers a useful lens through which to interrogate the genre of how-to voice manuals. It puts the manuals on a wider spectrum of intersen-sory awareness that includes, at one end, an embodied synthesis of body, mind and voice and, at the other, the descriptive and sometime prescriptive voice manual that sets out to tell the reader what is right or wrong about their vocal production. The elements on the spectrum impact and shape each other and, together, form a more inclusive body of praxis about voice in theatre.

FRAMING TWENTIETH-CENTURY VOICE PEDAGOGUES: THEIR PEDAGOGY AND TEXTS

Voice for theatre performance is, in the main, determined within the training studio or rehearsal. It consists of conscious and unconscious choices about breath, vibration, pitch and volume. In other words, taking Elsie Fogerty's shorthand definition for the voice:

> Four factors are recognisable in the voice:
>
> 1. Breath   3. Tone
> 2. Note   4. Vowel
>
> (Fogerty 1937: 108)

These elements form part of a dialectical contract at the heart of actor-centred theatre-making in which the individual voice is negotiated. The voice manual often suggests, or even echoes, these choices, but their complete manifestations are only fulfilled in the act of expression. In this way, it is important to observe that voice is both formed within the individual and shaped in relation to context.

One of the ways in which an actor's manifestations of the four factors of voice can be best understood is by a scrutiny of the documentation in the voice manual. As the repositories of voice practice, these manuals provide useful evidence about the preparation and outcome of the voice in performance, even when there are no available live recordings to prove or disprove the validity of their instructions. Even though the voice they instruct cannot be heard, it is reasonable to assume that the manuals relate the sound of the voice in theatre performance to the baseline tones and rhythms found in ordinary conversational reality that are all around and within earshot.

In the following reference about voice applied to Shakespeare, there surfaces yet another problem for the writer of the manual. Not only are the effects of voice hard to describe, but so is the degree to which the speaker's 'felt' experience of sound impacts on the perceived outcome:

> Commentary on minutiae of vocal performance is bound to be clumsy because sound cannot be translated into words and can only with great difficulty be described. Yet an attempt to do this is necessary to show how Shakespeare's texts are continually open to alternative ways of delivery and how choice of these will affect the speaker's involvement in the action of a play and, in turn, affect an audience's experience of its drama.
>
> (Brown 2002: 71)

I suggest that voice applied to Shakespeare in the late nineteenth century, for example, is supported by the instructional values contained in numerous manuals with their clearly stated rules about 'good articulation' (Anon. 1894). This shifts by the end of the twentieth century where there is a stronger emphasis on physical embodiment in actor training. For example, Patsy Rodenburg, a leading contemporary voice practitioner, identifies body, breath, voice and speech as equal factors in determining the success of vocal production where earlier generations of practitioners put more emphasis on articulation:

> What you are trying to do here is join up body, breath, voice and speech into one efficient chain reaction. One element needs and depends on the others for support. These exercises address some of our most nagging voice and speech habits.
>
> (Rodenburg 1993: 89)

Having established studio practice and the manual as mutually related determinants for the scope of expectations about the voice in action, it is useful to return to the examination of the 'second text', outlined at the beginning of the chapter, formed as a consequence of voice practitioner presence and actor immersion. Many distinguished theatre laboratories of the twentieth century share in this adherence to the optimization of the psychophysical input of performers. This is exemplified, for example, in the training mission of European theatre practitioner Jacques Copeau. In 1913, along with Charles Dullin and Louis Jouvet, they all 'retired to the French countryside to train and prepare a company and repertoire':

> For Copeau, training must take place prior to whatever leads to performance. It is a period during which the actor should discover an optimal, psychophysical condition or state of readiness, that is, a state of 'repose, calm, relaxation, detente, silence or simplicity'.
>
> (Cole and Chinoy 1970 cited in Zarrilli 2009: 25)

This reminds me of the importance of distinguishing between the aims set out in the voice manual and the actual circumstances of the trainer's espousal of them. Added to this is the student's own 'felt' experience of the work. The governing ideals in the manual, and their expression and reception in the studio, with its many variables, work together to ensure that voice is both an effective experience and a viable sign in theatre performance.

It is important to also consider how these elements combine to set evaluative benchmarks for the voice in performance. The standards set for the voice sometimes part company with the terms set by the actual experience and this thereby creates a tension. This is seen in the gap between the training ideals and the actuality of the actor experience described by Copeau. He pursued a training ideal in which the actor could understand 'calm' and yet still remain responsive with regard to invitation and opportunity – 'ready for what comes next' (Zarrilli 2009: 25). He was, however, continually frustrated by his attempts to develop this for the actor:

> Despite his continuous experiments, Copeau remained dissatisfied with the result: 'I do not know how to describe, much less obtain in someone else, that state of good faith, submission, humility, which … depends upon … proper training.'
>
> (Cole and Chinoy 1970 in Zarrilli 2009: 25)

Pedagogical authority in the studio is one thing, and the effective influence of that model on individual vocal output another. To this end it is necessary to consider the anecdotes about UK voice teacher Clifford Turner at RADA in the middle of the twentieth century with reference to the impact of his voice. Verse speaker Betty Mulcahy recalled Turner's mesmeric tone of voice and its overwhelming mellifluous properties; and, in a private conversation with another of his contemporaries, I heard of enduring memories about Turner's 'party piece' recitations for students at the RADA (personal conversation with Betty Mulcahy 2011). But, whilst his vocal demonstration was perceived as an exemplary model, it had a varying impact. On the one hand, Turner's voice inspired adoring vocal mimesis from a pupil and, on the other, served as the barometer for a vocal style that was, because at times 'overwhelming', ultimately repudiated.

The day-to-day physical presence of the 'master' tutor raises problems for student learning, particularly when expert modelling and powerful exhortation are deployed. This is evidenced in both the Copeau and the Turner examples and has parallels in several other theatre practices. In Nancy Saklad's preface to a collection of essays about voice and speech teachers in the USA, she celebrates her engagement with a number of inspirational teachers:

> I have been fortunate to study with exceptional master voice and speech teachers. Several of them I studied with intensively to experience the shifts in voice, body, and awareness that can accompany total immersion. These teachers were magicians of the genuine sort, who waved their magic 'voice and speech wands' and brought about essential transformation. They shed light on the work, not surprisingly, with their brilliant thinking.
>
> (Saklad 2011: ix)

Her glowing tribute to the 'magicians' of voice not only reveals a highly prized investment in the immersive teacher and student relationship, but also in the idea of the voice practitioner as a conduit for studio transformation. She identifies the immersive experience as fundamental to her vocal development. Where some students cite Clifford Turner's voice as an influence on their vocal development, as I have shown, others, such as Saklad, cite the value of the trainer who is able to impart physical intelligence via their psychophysical processes in the studio.

All of the elements in this complex relationship underlie the voice manual as a textual object and they need to be borne in mind when the manuals are closely examined as representative of both the ethos and the active presence of studio voice teachers in relation to vocal pedagogy and theatre practice in the late twentieth and early twenty-first centuries. This exploration may in some cases be supplemented by all too rare recordings or, more productively, by recollections and written commentary on the work. The main evidence resides, however, in the voice teacher's own published texts. It is their capacity to shape, define and express the subject of voice in writing that forms the main body of the discussion.

THE VOICE MANUAL: A HYBRIDITY OF INFLUENCE

Many of the most renowned voice teachers have produced manuals that codify their work. The impact and influence of these texts relies not only upon the author's capacity to successfully organize and sequence the work on the page but also in the engagement of a readership who may or may not have first-hand experience of the author's practice in the studio space. Whilst the presence of the practitioner remains important to the individual voice student, it is their reputation in reproducing the work on the page that sells the book. The combined factors of textual influence, including dissemination, and the active presence of the writer in the studio, serve as useful indicators with regard to the likely historical prominence of key vocal practices.

Before I look closely at a sample of voice manuals, it is important to remember that an actor's preparation for vocalization in the theatre occurs within a wide triangulation of voice praxis. This includes the optimal working of voice through solo exercise and repetition within rehearsal and performance and the enhancement of its perceptual understanding, as highlighted earlier in Saklad's account. The physical and vocal exercises on the page act as a prompt to sensitize an individual's awareness about voice. But whilst the manual effects vocal awareness, as I have shown, it is likely that the actual vocal experience it engenders will also exceed an author's ability to describe or direct it and the partially indescribable second 'text' is the outcome.

The combination of elements that bear on the effective function of the technical manual are usefully summarized by the voice practitioner Kristin Linklater. In the following excerpt from her book *Freeing the Natural Voice*, she raises problems about the use of the stand-alone text where the benchmarks of student progress are harder to determine than those made under the guidance of a teacher:

> How do you induce a new use of the voice? By moving the body in new directions that break conditioned, habitual movements. How can the student know that a new experience is a constructive one without feedback from some external and trustworthy guide? To this last question I have no good answer, and do believe that a book is a poor substitute for a class.
>
> It is also important to keep in mind that this book may be difficult to use because it requires dealing with cause rather than effect. The exercises are concerned more with re-thinking usage than with re-doing sounds. This is a book to be engaged in slowly. It is a practical book for practical use, not one to be skimmed for new ideas.
>
> (Linklater 2006: 11)

Linklater's comments about rethinking 'usage' invite thought about the ways in which the voice manual relates to and influences the voice. The task is to evaluate and reflect upon the manual's success or failure in its representation of exercises that generate the felt experience of the 'second text' and evoke 'the subtleties of the practitioners' promptings as raw sound on the page, muscle memory in action, or the workings of the psyche in relation to the processes of utterance' (Boston 1997: 250).

WRITING THE STYLISTICS OF VOICE

In common with the rest of the performing arts, the processual nature of work undertaken in the voice studio counts as one of its dominant qualities. This is the feature of a range of late twentieth-century voice studios in which the ideal of an individual's vocal discovery and development at the level of heightened sensory awareness outweighs other kinds of responses. This has strong parallels in those contemporary theatre practices that require a veracity of actor presence over style.

In early twentieth-century voice practice, the voice manual and their theatre contexts were less congruent with the idea of individual discovery than with the necessity for instruction about effective 'heightened' vocal expression. The spectrum of influence affecting the ways in which the voice was trained in the early twentieth-century period was shaped by and geared towards the particular acoustics of contemporary theatre spaces, the style of the writers, and the cultural values and tastes of the audience rather than the needs of the individual speaker. This stands in contrast to the no less culturally acquired but seemingly more 'natural' approach adopted when the intrinsic function of an individual's *personal* voice is valued in the performance over an apparently more stylized voice.

In a general sense the fulfilment of heightened stylistic demands in the early twentieth century held more sway than the nuanced expressive desires of the individual voice. This remained the case until at least the mid-twentieth century when, as I will show, theatre and its audiences demanded more social range and flexibility of vocal expression under the influence of the intimacy afforded by radio broadcasting and the close-up of the TV and film.

EARLY TWENTIETH-CENTURY THEATRE VOICE MANUALS

The account of technical voice manuals begins with the early to mid-twentieth-century work of Elsie Fogerty, Gwynneth Thurburn, Clifford Turner and Cicely Berry. Their writing lays down some of the foundational exercises and values that shaped voice training for actors at a number of the UK's leading drama schools including the Royal Central School of Speech and Drama, Rose Bruford College, Webber Douglas Academy and RADA. Forms of that pedagogy persist to this day.

An examination of relevant passages provides wider social and theatrical contextualization, raises important questions about style and content, demonstrates authorial influence on vocal production in the theatre and reveals the impact other theatre artists had on the formation of their vocal ethos.

ELSIE FOGERTY AND THE CENTRAL SCHOOL

In 1904 the influential theatre manager Frank Benson (1858–1939) opened a London branch of his Shakespearean touring school. In 1906, in collaboration with Elsie Fogerty, one of London's pre-eminent voice and actor trainers, they established the founding ethos of the Central School of Speech-Training and Dramatic Art. Fogerty was the principal and Benson the president (Susi 2006: 17).

Fogerty's impact on the development of voice training in twentieth-century theatre in the UK, underpinned both by her publications and by her leadership, cannot be overstated. In a public lecture given in 1978, Gwynneth Thurburn (Central's principal from 1942 to 1967) notes how Fogerty contributed to the culture of debate that led to the eventual formation of the National Theatre in 1962: 'She was a founder member of the first committee they instituted to propose that a National Theatre should come into existence' (Lecture transcript, 1978, The Royal Central School Archives, London). This testimony, supported in many letters in the public domain about her work, also makes it clear that Fogerty's influence as a specialist in the field of the science and art of voice in theatre was important in the early formation of voice training for actors in the UK (Susi 2006: 69). She not only championed voice at the level of actor training, but also enhanced its position as a discrete subject at the highest levels of theatre and educational leadership:

> She had worked with some of the most well-known and respected actors and directors of the first half of the 20th century and been involved with some of the most innovative movements in theatre of her time. She had worked most of her life towards establishing a National Theatre, and had fought for academic recognition of speech and drama, and was a pioneer in both speech therapy and voice and drama teacher training. She was a world-renowned expert on voice and speech training. As her legacy, she left not only the Central School of Speech Training and Dramatic Art, but also the students she taught and the training they would pass on to others.
>
> (Susi 2006: 80)

VOICE, SCIENCE, ART AND CLASS

It was Fogerty, too, as shown above, who made links between multiple elements drawn from science, arts, education, acting and poetics, in order to forge one ethos for training the voice in theatre. Her book, *The Speaking of English Verse* (first published in 1927), is informed by a rich confluence of disciplines, evident in the book's acknowledgements. Thanks is given to, amongst many others, the speech scientists Dr W.A. Aiken, Dr William Pasteur, and Dr H. Hulbert; the phonetician Professor Daniel Jones; the musician Miss Kathleen Salmon; and the writers Siegfried Sassoon and Hilaire Belloc, for permission to quote their science, phonetics, music, poetry and prose. This specialist interdisciplinary knowledge echoes the tastes and interests of the UK's scientific and cultural leaders. It also reveals Fogerty's shared interest in widely held cultural beliefs about the socially improving function of speech and voice in which educated middle-class values for 'good' speech are held up as a model for the 'common' good:

> In all countries educated and refined people perform the movements of speech with greater accuracy and a stronger sense of rhythmic values than uneducated people. Just as they perform the movements of games, or of ordinary life, with a greater natural ease and sense of style.
>
> (Fogerty 1929: 230)

These paternalistic beliefs formed part of the governing principles behind the Pivot Club entertainments, an early fundraising activity at Central, known as the 'Slum Party':

> One of the Club's major tenets was to give 'pleasure, beauty and laughter to those poor and sick who have but little opportunity of such things in their lives,' so to fulfil this remit, Pivots would give an annual entertainment for children at a Mission in Notting Dale, which became known as a 'Slum Party.'
>
> (Susi 2006: 26)

The views behind the 'Slum Party', laden with the assumptions of an early twentieth-century ruling elite, though well meaning, provide further evidence of the complex mix of social, cultural and artistic values that are brought to bear on the formation of an individual's vocal expression in any era.

It is significant that the art of verse speaking and the related regulatory discipline of elocution were skills in which women could make a living wage at a time when employment opportunities for middle-class women were extremely limited. Fogerty's own work as an actress and teacher, under the influence of the legendary actor and producer William Poel (1852–1934), enabled her to develop an effective poetry reading style that aided her employability. Her stylistics are described below in the 1945 Memorial issue of *Viva Voce* by leading early twentieth-century actress Lillah McCarthy:

> Elsie had a fine voice and spoke the exquisite poetry beautifully; even then her rhythm and diction were a fine example to us all. Later, when we had become great friends, she told me she had attended the rehearsal of all of Poel's productions, making notes on emphasis, speed, rhythm which he insisted on, and giving her excellent groundwork for her own teaching.
>
> (Susi 2006: 14)

This background in theatre practice led her to assert that the vocal interpretation of verse was at the structural core of dramatic art itself, and formed
the heart of 'a play':

> Whatever may be the view held about the value of verse speaking in the case of
> lyric or narrative poems, it must be recognised that dramatic verse is meant to
> be spoken ...
>   ... the great dramas of the world have been written with no other end in view
> than dramatic representation; if the poetic expression they employ is of such a
> character that it fails to move us when we hear it spoken with a sense of dramatic
> fitness and with conviction, then the work is not in the true sense a play.
>   (Fogerty 1937: 190)

It is a view that identifies three components in the art of verse speaking: the
speaker's voice, the word of the author and its articulation as speech:

> The appeal of dramatic poetry when it forms part of the art of the theatre, is as
> wide as its appeal in life.
>   It is used to give lyric beauty to passion, to give points and delicacy to the
> merry banter of comedy, to give epic grandeur to a Lear or a Volumnia, but always
> it must speak through the lips of a human being, or it will become something
> different from drama. Very beautiful, possibly, in itself, but lacking harmony with
> character or circumstance.
>   (Fogerty 1937: 192–193)

In this, she singles out the potential of verse speaking as it adds something
to the theatre performance that is much harder to define – the 'lyric beauty
to passion'; 'points and delicacy' to comedy; and 'epic grandeur to a Lear or
a Volumnia' (Fogerty 1937: 193).

What does this signify, then, about Fogerty's place in the development of
an enduring ethos for the voice in theatre? It suggests that she placed the
art of voice and speech at the centre of textual interpretation and asserted
the value of this via several key structural elements familiar to the elocutionists, including the perfection of tone, pace, and diction, and, principally,
rhythm. She is both didactic and discursive in her account and combines
alignment, breath and oral postural instruction along with principles based
upon a mix of credible and less than credible assertions and 'laws'. In the
following quote we see an example of the way in which she constructed a
convincing method based upon her ability to attach the 'essential meaning
of rhythm as a law of audible movement' (Fogerty 1929: 5) to the art of textual interpretation:

> Every movement must pass through some portion of space, must occupy some
> interval of time, must be accomplished by some degree of force. The right meas-
> ure of these things depends entirely on the intention of the movement. When

space, time and force are automatically measured under the exact guidance of intention the action which results is said to be rhythmical.

(Fogerty 1929: 4–5)

Fogerty's combination of opinion, experience and natural scientific knowledge ensured that subsequent generations of voice practitioners could benefit from the close attention she paid to a rich synthesis of elements beyond simple instruction. It is possible to see in work such as this the seeds of a discipline that, in its complexity, refers not only to specific societal norms, dramatic authorship, individual vocal tone and interpretative choices, but also to some of the general principles of vocal health acoustics and physics that inform the voice wherever it is expressed.

AESTHETICS AND THE VOICE

For the sake of argument, I make the assumption that audiences in the twenty-first century are less preoccupied with the aesthetic function of voice in drama and verse speaking than audiences in the early part of the twentieth century. This does not mean that an interest in or concern for vocal aesthetics has gone away – far from it; and the competitive elements of verse speaking still hold cultural sway. The Speak a Poem competition in London between 1980 and 2002 and the contemporary LAMDA Communication examinations, for example, serve as evidence of the public's continuing interest in competitive public speaking. I suggest, though, that an insistence upon specifically designated aesthetics of vocal delivery has taken a different place in the hierarchy of cultural indicators that comprise theatre values.

It is possible to appreciate that the actor at the start of the twentieth century, as in previous centuries, was acculturated to and able to absorb the aesthetic values of mainstream theatre. Prior to the broadcasting values set by the BBC in the UK from 1922 onwards, with their 'authoritative' standards of speech that were 'armed with propriety' (McKibbin 1998: 459), I suggest that, apart from family background and class, the teachers and their manuals, it was the theatre-going audiences, the theatre managers and the theatre producers who held the most significant sway over the determining stylistics for the actor's voice.

In order to succeed and to be employed (not always the same thing, of course), actors would reflect and duplicate the prevailing vocal stylistics of the stage. In so doing, they enacted a double function. First was in the reproduction of the dominant social 'tone' through their expression of the authorial voice, and second was as agents for their own social mobility. By giving voice to the 'prestigious' words of the play, the jobbing actor accessed culturally privileged levels of articulacy not assumed available to either themselves or the audience outside the walls of the theatre.

In many ways to act – and to give voice – was tantamount to occupying a socially advanced position typically only available to the rich and privileged.

Contemporary accounts of actor shortcomings in the earlier Victorian era, when the profession laboured under a 'legacy of low esteem' (Sanderson 1984: 7), suggest that matching vocal sound and diction to the look and manner of the socially privileged was no simple task: 'Sir Squire Bancroft ... reflected that around the 1860s most of his fellow-actors were 'deficient in tone ... unhappily lacking the marks of breeding and education' (Sanderson 1984: 7).

Late Victorian actor manager George Alexander (1858–1918) insisted on the fashionable look and behaviour of his actors in order to match that found in 'polite society' (Sanderson 1984: 136) at various 'gentleman's clubs', including the leading London club for actors, the Garrick Club, founded in 1831. The Garrick provided actors with networking opportunities, as well as, less obviously, the opportunity to learn what it was to be accepted into Society, including the adoption of vocal tone appropriate to men of 'education and refinement' (Sanderson 1984: 136):

> Election to and acceptance into a club of this nature suggested not only the social status of a gentleman but also certain standards of gentlemanly behaviour.
> (Sanderson 1984: 138)

In the twenty-first century the aesthetics of voice, speech and spoken verse has become a more prominent feature within philosophical discourse. An example of a shift in its artistic and social behavioural provenance is found in the introduction to a book on interpretation, *The Acting Interpreter: Embodied Stylistics in an Experientialist Perspective*, by contemporary performance theorist Maria Grazia Guido:

> The central claim of this book is, therefore, that to achieve a total experience of poetic drama interpreters need to engage their own schemata in their experiential entirety ... The basic assumption of this claim thus, is that to be conceptually receptive to poetic language in general – and to poetic drama in particular – the interpreters need to be physically prepared to be receptive to it. For this purpose, they have to free themselves from their customary passive and silent position by giving poetry new, multidimensional semiotic contexts in space and 'inhabiting' them physically as well as vocally, through an interplay of form, body and mind. In this way, they would become Acting Interpreters. In other words, poetry interpreters do not have to limit themselves to the mentalistic practice of the 'sounding' of the 'voices' they achieve from the text just within their 'inward' ear, but they have to 'embody' such voices, 'inhabit' them within a 'physical space of representation'.
> (Guido 2013: 13)

This introduction lays claim to a 'new' twenty-first-century configuration of aesthetics that references the value of an individual's multifaceted vocal embodiment. It speaks to expectations about the actor's capacity to bring something of their own psychophysical experience to the task. This represents a subtle but significant departure from Fogerty's earlier essentialist assertions about the actor's primary task to voice with 'dramatic fitness' and 'conviction' (Fogerty 1929: 190) the *inherent* value in the dramatist's voice.

In more general terms, however, Guido and Fogerty speak to a shared cultural interest – that of the enhancement and development of the relationship between the voice of the actor and the authorial voice in the art of textual interpretation. Where, historically, theatre has long instructed in its voice manuals on the development of a spoken aesthetic for verse speaking, it is interesting to note that Guido draws attention to the newness of this for contemporary interpreters in linguistic disciplines who are more familiar with the adoption of a critical and analytical position that is both 'passive and silent' (Guido 2013: 13).

SHAKESPEARE AND THE VOICE

It is important, though, to return to Fogerty's book *The Speaking of English Verse*, in order to further examine the value she places on the function of poetry in the spoken arts in the twentieth century and, in particular, the position afforded Shakespeare. Fogerty regards Shakespeare as a 'primary' poet, the one she charges with the capacity to generate an elevated and profound cultural understanding in both speaker and listener. The term 'elevated' is a contested one but, for now, it allows the thought that Fogerty was one of countless members of her class for whom Shakespeare was *the* exemplary verse dramatist. The reasons for this are complex and will not be explored at length here, but I can, in part, suggest that this regard for the elevation of Shakespeare is a way of equating the arts with notions of the sublime, even the divine:

> The arts of song and of speech owe less homage than any arts to the need for material wealth, they touch the most human, and therefore the most divine, of our capabilities.
>
> (Fogerty 1929: 241)

Fogerty holds with the belief that an encounter with Shakespeare's work, particularly his verse, will effect something transformational for both speaker and audience. The greater part of one of her chapters in *The Speaking of English Verse* is spent on extolling the range and depth of his writing, in particular his capacity to expertly evoke the machinations of character. This she adopts wholesale from the work of William Poel:

> Mr William Poel, whose intimate study of the whole question of Shakespearean performance, auditive as well as visual, makes him in this as in all such questions the one supreme authority.
>
> (Fogerty 1929: 194)

She draws on Poel's view about the importance of giving voice to Shakespeare's lines in order that the actor receive all necessary expressive information. This suggests an adherence to the order, rhythm and content of thought in the verse, as it not only evokes the character, but, as for many commentators, actually *is* the character:

> It is plain that the function of verse as Shakespeare uses it can only be maintained if the true rhythmic significance be audible throughout. To reduce it to the level of prose, as the actor so often does, is to sacrifice the essentially ideal effect intended by the poet, and so to diminish the extraordinary sense of transcendent significance which attaches to his characterisation. To deliver the verse as if it were lyric, with no sense that behind its cadences lies the music of actual speech, is to confirm a public delusion that plays in verse must be dull and unnatural.
>
> (Fogerty 1929: 194)

The attention paid to the characteristics of verse over prose also alerts the actor to a set of expectations in relation to the delivery of vocalized sound in Shakespeare. Although Fogerty sets verse apart from everyday conversational exchange, she also advocates that the actor upholds 'the music of actual speech'. In this way she positions the art of voice in theatre on a spectrum that answers to both conversational spoken norms and culturally determined vocal aesthetics of theatre. This says a lot, too, about Fogerty's expectations for everyday speech and the ways in which she holds out ambitions for the enhancement of its 'musical' properties.

SCIENCE AND INSTRUCTION

Chapter ten of Fogerty's *The Speaking of English Verse*, for example, builds on the technical instruction set out in her previous chapters and goes to some length to reposition spoken English as a musical language against a backdrop of its regard as an 'unmusical, inharmonious' sound (Fogerty 1929: 227). Fogerty rebuts the dominance of European musical interpretation over her favoured idea of a 'pure melodic tone' (Fogerty 1929: 228), and locates the influence of Gilbert and Sullivan in changing perceptions of English tonality, particularly at the level of the vowels:

> The great school of oratorio and festival singers at the end of the last century stood out as magnificent examples of rather formal diction, but it is, I believe, to the Gilbert and Sullivan operas, with their matchless blending of music and speech, that we owe the first perception that a singer could be audible and rapid, delicately accurate and simply expressive, in singing English, without sacrificing conviction or character, and without departing from the true phonetic values of his [sic] native tongue.
>
> (Fogerty 1929: 229)

Fogerty's contribution to spoken voice development is here further demonstrated in the link she makes with Gilbert and Sullivan's singing aesthetic and the opportunity it provides to redress some of the negatively held ideas about the English vowels. Her recognition of vowel function as it forms a 'succession of musical resonances for the voice' (Fogerty 1929: 231) captures an idea drawn from the resonator scale work of the early twentieth-century phonologist, Dr W.A. Aiken. His work, underpinned by the 'science of vocal sound' (Aiken 1951: 1), enshrines a controversy that persists into the twenty-first century about the necessity for an adherence to a set of basic rules about sound that are closer to singing principles than the actual practice of everyday speech.

Phonology, as it observes the action of the speech organs that make sound and ensures that 'the principles of sound, and the natural behaviour of the organs, are properly applied to it' (Aiken 1951: 3), renders vowels in spoken English as clear as those in sung English under the strict management of the 'respiratory forces' (Fogerty 1929: 108). The role of the phonologist as 'referee' in the aesthetic outcome of the voice based on phonological laws, however, sets up the sometime tyranny of enforceable standards. The observations, based on Aiken's cultural assumptions and observations about the sound of the voice in 'most people' (Aiken 1951: 52), generate conclusions about the most effective shape of the resonators from a starting point with 'the vowel-sound *ah*' – the shape of the neck, the space in the throat, the shape of the mouth cavity, that 'all tend to divide the resonant vibrations into two' (Aiken 1951: 49). As such they are valuable objective reference points. However, they also form a prescriptive basis for sound production that has overshadowed the subjective sensory experience of the voice. Discussion about the merits of both continue to feature in the ongoing debate about voice, accent and the virtues or not of standardization and their association with the aesthetics of sound values.

It is important to note that Fogerty was not alone in her embrace of phonological principles in the underscoring of a commitment to the 'beauty of vocal tone' (Fogerty 1937: 108). Nor was she the first to give primacy to the influence of poetic form in shaping the voice. The debt she owes to her contemporaries, the writer and dramatist Harley Granville Barker (1877–1946) and William Poel, as already stated, is significant in this regard and is examined in Chapter 3. But it is her discursive and pedagogical legacy in drawing upon synthesized evidences from both the sciences and the humanities that stands alone. Her articulation of both a philosophical and a practical rationale provided key validation for the development of training strategies in voice for UK theatre voice work in the twentieth century. Her two major publications were seminal with regard to their discursive effect but left unresolved questions concerning effective student usage of the books for future generations of authors.

GWYNNETH THURBURN (1899–1993)

In both the teachings of Gwynneth Thurburn and her book, *Voice and Speech* (1939), published in London a few years before she became principal of the Central School of Speech Training and Dramatic Art in 1942, we see a consolidation of Fogerty's legacy, although still no definitive answer to questions about the effective use of the voice manual. Dedicated to her predecessor at Central, Thurburn, like Fogerty, similarly gives thanks, in her foreword, to Dr W.A. Aiken 'whose scientific approach to the study of the voice forms the basis of Speech Training, and to whom all who care for the human voice as an instrument of sound must ever be grateful' (Thurburn 1939: vi). We see in this book, as referenced earlier, evidence of the ways in which, on the one hand, medical science knowledge about breath and the function of the larynx, as well as speech science knowledge about the acoustics of speech, continues to provide the 'glue' for the speech and voice rationale in the training of the actor in the UK; and on the other, continues to be outshone by far less scientific, but none the less significant, information relating to the actor's physical inhabitation of the voice.

It is important to consider, though, that as voice practice develops, the voice manuals that account for it continue to remain problematic. Not only are they hard to follow as actual instruction, but also they are less than transparent as repositories of meaning. Outstanding questions remain, for example, about the criteria used to measure the outcomes of the voice in theatre. It is not clear if these are set by the manual writer, the theatre audience, the trainer, the producer, the speech scientist and so on. In total, this was a troublesome legacy for the development of the theatre voice manual. And in its wake, it was often the personality of the practitioner that exerted the stronger influence over the less codified but no less important ways of framing and valuing an actor's expertise in voice that was to become a signature of voice practice later in the century and beyond.

Thurburn aimed her book at teachers and trainers of speech and voice, and it is possible to see glimpses of the criteria set for vocal outcomes in the mutable boundaries identified between theatre and science. She partially solves the question by making no specific mention of the ways in which speech for theatre performance might differ from other kinds of social speech. In so doing, she implies approval for a standardization of outcomes that are bolstered by the rules of science, over those that are emergent from individual experiential immersion more favoured in psychophysical approaches to acting. She is clear, however, about her articulation of an enlightened pedagogical frame. Her philosophy of teacher–student engagement would not be out of place in many late twentieth- and early twenty-first-century theatre studios, in which a positive, student-centred approach is implemented to foster development:

It is important in teaching people of all ages that they should be encouraged to think, not of the mistakes they are making, but of building up a new set of habits.

It is of the greatest psychological importance that all training in speech should take a positive and not a negative form.

(Thurburn 1939: 14)

She is at great pains to demonstrate, however, how this underscores the primary characteristic of her pedagogical approach, already noted above, with its reliance upon agreed scientific and anatomical vocal principles (or 'laws' as she calls them) over individual preference:

[I]t must be borne in mind that without a foundation upon physiological and physical laws the sounds made are apt to be governed either by habit or individual preference.

(Thurburn 1939: 22)

This shows the ways in which a reliance upon 'physical laws' gives rise to a vocal aesthetic that steers the individual away from their own vocal propensity in order to be 'free from all conscious effort … to give full powers of expression and interpretation' (Thurburn 1939: 26). It is an aesthetic that purports not to be one and enshrines, instead, a paradox. It asks that an individual erase all distinctive signs of their class, region and background as well as their personal vocal habit in order to better free themselves in the realization of the authorial voice. Speaker self-effacement thus becomes the template for vocal 'truth', and its resultant 'neutrality' the means by which the voice conceals the origins of a perceptual hierarchy.

THE LONDON THEATRE STUDIO

Fogerty, in the introduction to the fourth edition of *The Speaking of English Verse*, argues, like Thurburn, against 'artificial recitation' and 'conscious effort':

Above all, we must throw away the horrible false tradition of 'recitation', which stood self-condemned in that it never succeeded in interpreting anything but the worst, the most vulgar and meaningless of verse, because in that it could find room for the personal self-assertion which destroyed all true faculty of poetic interpretation.

(Fogerty 1937: xii)

It is a view that remains at the heart of the voice practitioner script throughout the twentieth century and is closely aligned to contemporaneous actor-training methodologies and performance values in which the aesthetics of tension-free sound – and tension-free acting – are highly valued. The example for actor training set by the London Theatre Studio, founded by Michel Saint-Denis in 1938, provides at least as significant an influence for

Thurburn's views as that provided by Fogerty. Thurburn is reputed to have said that 'Central is the product of a shotgun marriage between Elsie Fogerty and Michel Saint-Denis' (Susi 2006: 145) and Saint-Denis's advocacy for the separation between voice and speech was one mirrored in the approach taken at Central:

> Vocal study, consisting of voice production, diction, and speech became as important as movement. The three disciplines (voice, speech, movement) taught by different instructors, while overlapping with each other, were kept distinct, in line with the Saint-Denis philosophy.
>
> (Baldwin 2010: 88)

The distinction of Thurburn's approach, as opposed to that taken by Saint-Denis, was in her advocacy for a remedial speech role. This she developed to international acclaim:

> By 1942, Central was recognized as a leading institution for actor training, and the respect earned by Thurburn in the fields of speech therapy, speech and voice training for teachers helped maintain a high profile for the School.
>
> (Susi 2006: 86)

The main influence of the London Theatre Studio was in its provision of a training context in which an 'organic and integrated approach to acting' aimed to free actors from the 'frivolous fare performed in an outmoded style' that prevailed on the London West End stage (Baldwin 2010: 87). The use and practice of voice, as underpinned by 'physiological and physical laws', was well suited to their training mission. Practice that involved the neutral mask found its equivalency in practice based on a stripped-down 'natural' voice and both were utilized to confront and eradicate 'cliché mannerisms' in the actor (Baldwin 2010: 91).

CLIFFORD TURNER

Turner was one of the UK's foremost voice teachers in the middle of the twentieth century, and his seminal voice book, *Voice and Speech in the Theatre*, first published in 1950, links theatre, voice and physiology in a way that is closely reminiscent of the Thurburn and Fogerty approach, principal amongst which is the reliance on rib-reserve breath work. Whilst this is now largely regarded as outmoded in contemporary voice practice, it was a key feature of many early twentieth-century practitioners. As a student of Fogerty's, Turner's belief in the usefulness of rib-reserve (in which the ribs are held in suspension and kept separate from abdominal and diaphragmatic processes) is hardly surprising. Like his predecessors, he, too, positions voice at the epicentre of the actor's craft and focuses upon the enablement of a durable vocal technique. Whilst the notion of 'technique' is often challenged for its apparent masking of 'truthful' acting, in which 'a naturalistic emphasis on simulating the surface aspects of daily social existence often obscured a more profound level of Truth [*sic*]' (Wolford 2010: 200), this was not Turner's view. He firmly believed in the practical importance of technique as a means to provide the actor with the primary tools to gain and sustain employment.

Theatre director Terry Hands notes Turner's pragmatic approach in the following account:

> His job, as he saw it, was to provide the actor with a means of communication that would support whatever challenges he or she might face in their subsequent careers. Those challenges might come from the avant-garde, the classical or the new – in 2000 seaters, studios, films or television – in dialect or RP. 'You must intend to be heard' he'd say. 'The intention is paramount but don't neglect the equipment'. He was formal, kindly and above all practical.
>
> (Hands 2007: v)

Turner echoes this view in his own words:

> When the technical equipment of the actor is considered, voice and speech are of paramount importance. The actor's art, it is true, consists of much more than the delivery of the lines, but take away the element of voice and very little is left. Even if the actor were to forget the aesthetic implications of his or her craft, mere economics compel perfection and care of the voice, and the acquisition of control over speech ... The very highest manifestations of any art are always characterized by a technique so flawless that it is unnoticeable and become one with the art itself.
>
> (Turner 2007: 1)

What is of particular interest here is Turner's paradoxical aim in the application of vocal technique to conceal the effort of the art. What after all is technique but effort? This, however, is illustrative of a much wider tension that runs throughout twentieth-century theatre training in which debates about the truth *in* art and the art of *being* truthful relate to points of view in which existential questions are raised that lie beyond questions of craft and call upon wider philosophical, political and educational belief systems. This is echoed, too, in the now familiar binary represented by the 'natural' voice and a voice under the influence of 'technique' that has, consequently, persisted as a touchstone for debate amongst voice trainers on both sides of the Atlantic right into the twenty-first century.

A matter, however, about which many diverse practitioners agree is that of the importance of an individual's disciplined attendance to the process of repetitive and developmental exercises, regardless of whether they support concepts of existential 'truths' or other more artful truths. The actor at the centre of Turner's approach is expected to dedicate themselves in a focused and consistent way to the development of their voice as instrument.

This inevitably resulted in a range of outcomes for the individual for whom, of course, success or failure was subject to a number of variables that included self-perception, regional influence, class privilege, gender, ethnicity and so on. The excerpt from Turner below shows just how problematic he knew the process to be:

> Voice and speech for the majority are haphazard affairs, but what passes in everyday life will not stand the test of performance in the theatre, and the qualities that are essential for the actor cannot be acquired overnight, let alone during the process of rehearsal. The voice and speech of the embryo actor, then, are already determined before acting begins. Unfortunately, difficulties often arise when bad habits have to be discarded and prejudices overcome before the new habits can be substituted. In many ways it would be simpler for all concerned were he or she in a position to start from scratch.
>
> (Turner 2007: 2)

Turner, then, whilst acknowledging the challenges, provides a clear endorsement for the inestimable values of both psychosocial and vocal change. In his view, the acquisition of vocal technique offers the additional promise of personal transformation and even the disguise of class origins. Those students for whom it was effective felt that the technique offered both inspiration and industry staying power:

> There was no 'voice beautiful' nor psycho-babble – just simple clarity. He was the best of the best – the Godfather of the voice.
>
> (Hands 2007: vi)

Turner's book is brilliant, according to Malcolm Morrison, the editor of his third edition: 'It is a unique volume by a teacher of rare skill, whose influence on the work of many actors is incalculable' (Morrison in Turner 1981: v). It is certainly one of the most enduring representatives of the how-to voice genre examined thus far, and has been usefully enhanced by Morrison's inclusion of suggested 'Daily Routines, following Mr Turner's principles' (Morrison in Turner 2000: note to the Fifth Edition). Turner's aim, from the title through to the contents, was to establish a concise foundational voice training system:

> which will put at the actor's command a technique of voice and speech; a technique which will embody the essentials of the art, but which cannot in the nature of things be in any way final or conclusive. A technique matures only with the development and maturing of the imagination by which it is controlled and whose servant it is.
>
> (Turner 2007: 3)

It is of note that it is only in subsequent editions of the book that self-help aspects of the work are addressed. Early editions offer objective instruction, illustration, exercise reference and dramatic text extracts but no explicit concession to teacher–student engagement. Direct instruction to the reader about the content and sequencing of the work was left to the editor, Morrison, in later editions, particularly the fifth one.

In its various incarnations it has not been out of print since its first publication in 1950 and I suggest that the impact of Turner's presence in the studio has contributed to the longevity of this work. Morrison echoes this view when he writes about the importance of 'enhancing and sustaining the reputation' of its author (Morrison in Turner 1981). It is a belief he shares with many of Turner's contemporaries:

> Former students of Turner bear witness to the profound influence he had upon their careers. Some of them regard his teachings as among the most significant in their actor training …
>
> Many also speak fervently of the impact of Turner himself. His physical presence was striking, at well over six-foot-four with … 'a wonderfully resonant deep voice which we all tended to imitate'; professional verse reader and founder of Speak-a-Poem Betty Mulcahy, similarly remembers, '[He] had a magnificent voice, and was always aware of the sound,' whilst actor James Dodding goes so far as to refer to his 'God-like influence'. Of his voice, again, Pensotti memorably adds:
>
> > … it was magical. There's no other word for it. His own voice was so unforced, having a musical quality that I can still recall so clearly. Certainly it was one of the most distinctive voices I've ever heard.
> >
> > (Boston 2007: vii–viii)

Thus, Turner, at the middle of the twentieth century, is representative of a number of his contemporary practitioners in that he stresses both the importance of vocal technique and the means to disguise it. This results in work that has the appearance of being effortlessly born. On one hand, he insists that improvements to the voice for theatre require the discipline of training not normally available in civic life; and on the other, he leaves open the possibility that the mind in response to the imagination will have the greater influence over the voice. His suggestion that instrumental vocal changes can be exceeded by the mind fails to address that this option is, surely, available to everyone. He had it both ways and he wasn't sufficiently interested in addressing these contradictions.

Like other voice practitioners of his generation, Turner seems content with the example set by his own voice, teaching structures and book as the means to provide the most effectual vocal instruction. Individual differences, embodied perceptions and canonical investigations in voice practice stand at a far remove from this view and do not become relevant for several decades to come. Notwithstanding these shortcomings, in mid-twentieth-century voice in UK theatre, Turner stands out as one of its key practitioners and authorial models. His work at RADA and Central, amongst other London drama training schools, positions him as 'one of Britain's foremost voice experts' (Susi 2006: 51). His own voice was synonymous with his pedagogy and this suited a theatre ethos interested in the celebration of the persona in the voice. After all, he and his voice provided the constituent ingredients of a kind of equivalent vocal 'stardom' that was commensurate with many wider mainstream theatre values.

CICELY BERRY

A somewhat less demonstrative, but no less significant, vocal and pedagogical example is supplied by Cicely Berry, one of the leading voice practitioners of the mid to late twentieth century. She also possesses a vocal instrument of note, shaped by years of diligence to the art of reading poetry aloud, although it is less frequently referred to as such. There are few written accounts of the impact of her voice, except in this author's testimony to its flexible musical range and warmth of tone, but in the main, it is the accounts she provides in her published texts, along with the impact of her voice directorship at the Royal Shakespeare Company, that are most influential to UK theatre voice and beyond.

It is in the texts and the teaching presence that we learn most about the principles Cicely Berry brings to bear on mid to late twentieth-century 'classical' acting. Her national and international work on voice is underpinned by a democratic belief in opening access to the Shakespearean canon. Jacqueline Martin, in her book *Voice in Modern Theatre*, sees this as part of a shift in theatre voice training in the post-war period of 1945 onwards, often identified with the opening of Osborne's seminal play *Look Back in Anger* in the West End in 1956. Whilst the symbolism represented by the date must be regarded as something of a cliché, it is interesting to note just how many social commentators continue to use this as shorthand for a perceived change in theatre and social values in the UK. It is possible that this reflects a wish for a greater social shift in emphasis than actually occurred. Whilst this ushered in a wider appeal for a range of social sounds on the stage, the necessity for the acquisition of vocal technique with its indelible class associations was never far away:

> Voice and speech training underwent enormous changes in the fifties, when the theatre changed so radically in Britain with John Osborne's *Look Back in Anger* (1956). Suddenly and quite fundamentally, the whole question of accents and social classes disappeared and with it the need for an upper-class 'beautiful' voice, according to Cicely Berry, who admitted to deliberately changing her approach to the demands which the new theatre made, where the emphasis was placed on 'what' was said rather than on 'how' it was said.
>
> (Martin 1991: 171)

Martin sums up the importance of Cicely Berry's role as voice director from the 1970s at the Royal Shakespeare Company. In broad terms, this post meant she was able to contribute to a shift of emphasis with regard to Shakespearean performance voice, referred to earlier, and was able to reflect a wider range of class and social backgrounds. Her work was no less technical than that of Turner, but in a 'new' way, it emphasized the importance of embracing a wider spectrum of vocal styles outside the metropolitan upper- and middle-class contexts. Her actual pedagogy, though, influenced by a deep interest in poetry, rendered her interest in formalizing the work on voice in ways that remained very reminiscent of previous traditions:

[I]t is her untiring dedication to finding ways of making people listen again to the music of language and to its poetry, and not only to grasp its literal meaning, that is so unique about Cicely Berry's contribution to vocal delivery in the modern theatre.
(Martin 1991: 175)

Whilst it is also true the 'what' of theatre's message had become of more interest to Berry post-Osborne, as opposed to the stylistic 'how', she continued to engage with the music-like sound of Shakespeare's language. The idea that access to certain kinds of texts could impact on the mind and expand the imagination of an actor still predominated, albeit represented through a democratic prism, and this placed Berry in direct line with her predecessors, Fogerty, Thurburn and Turner. Theatre voice, marked by sweeping movements of pitch, tonal range and rhythmic emphasis as inflected with the iambic pentameter, was clearly not yet ready for a final divorce from the musicality of its sound. What differed in the postmodern era, however, was an increase in the range available for the expressive voice from the 'heightened' to the 'natural'. Indeed, Berry makes much of an insistence that both music and individual vocal verisimilitude are important in contemporary performance, particularly in Shakespeare.

In her influential work *Text in Action*, aimed in particular at a readership of actors and theatre directors, Berry outlines a philosophy of voice and text work. I operate under the assumption that this is because she felt that theatre directors needed to know more about the relationship between the voice and the actor than was already customary. In this sense, we can regard Berry as a champion of the role of the voice teacher within the professional theatre-making process. In the following extract she discusses an idea about the actor's function as one of custodianship for specific values in language, both within the cultures of theatre and within society more widely. For Berry, the actor becomes a motor for the enhancement of public communication:

The role of the actor today is more important than ever: the more techno-speak takes over, the more we will disable our belief in language. Words have the power to disturb, surprise, delight and provoke, and they are happening in the moment – and between people. We must never forget this.
(Berry 2001: 5)

In the following quote, she identifies the stylistic influence of public-speaking on theatre voice. She draws attention to problems faced by both actors and trainers when older traditions of voice practice carry over into different cultural epochs and conflict with social norms. She talks, specifically, about managing a change in vocal tastes that relate to the attitudes and values about tonal qualities that were carried over from the instruction on the singing voice in a previous era:

> In the last century and in the beginning of this, voice work for actors was closely aligned to that of the singer – and indeed was usually undertaken by singing teachers. I believe the actor then saw his/her work in a much more public way: I do not think it was regarded as being declamatory, but it had a much more public air to it, and the music within the language was integral to the actor's speaking – that is what the audience came to hear. And I think they would have felt cheated if that quality had been missing.
>
> (Berry 2001: 29)

Berry's identification of a dominant musical aesthetic, as it carries over into the spoken voice and becomes attached to a social elite, provided further insight for her 'new' multifaceted method for the spoken voice. It meant that she gave a little more prominence to individual vocal variety:

> And so the speaking slowly began to change as more attention was paid to the nuances of meaning and literary allusions: it was becoming more finely drawn and perhaps more personalized – i.e. actors were starting to speak rather than declaim – but the music and shaping of the rhetoric was still central to the speaking.
>
> (Berry 2001: 31)

Text in Action is a clear departure from the ambitions of Turner's descriptive voice manual and is closer in style to that of Fogerty and Thurburn. In it, Berry sets out not only a sequence of vocal exercises but also a history and a philosophy of voice, spanning personal story and social observation from within theatre practice. She notes that the practical exercises for working on text in rehearsal are 'the reason for the book' (Berry 2001: 67), but, significantly, gives over the first third of the book to her ethos and philosophical reasoning. Notable, too, is the attention she gives to the social context of voice work in a range of international environments, in particular that of Brazil and her work with Augusto Boal on his Forum Theatre processes (Berry 2001: 55) and with the group 'Nos de Morro' in Vidigal outside Rio (Berry 2001: 56). This demonstrates not only her strong interest in the application of voice to contexts outside those of the commercial theatre but also her recognition of it as a socially transformative tool.

In this text, too, there is a shift of position about the voice teacher's role within society and theatre. It no longer suggests that a voice is trained to reinforce the values of theatre's status quo. Instead, she regards voice as part of a wider social activity designed to align invigorated artistic values with the interests of disenfranchised groups. Here the 'high' and 'low' culture divisions are dissolved in favour of a 'new' interest in the capacity of voice and language to enable wider social mobility. Not only is society within Berry's sights but so, too, is the organization of the theatre industry in which, as seen earlier, she is keen to give the voice practitioner a more prominent profile.

ANGLO-AMERICAN VOICE MANUALS

Berry's textual style and content anticipate those of a number of Anglo-American voice manuals in the last third of the twentieth century. In these, there is a similar twinning of social critique and vocal instruction along with a foregrounding of theatre processes, in which the voice practitioner is designated an invigorated collaborative position. Nan Withers-Wilson, for example, a vocal director in US theatre from the 1990s onwards, offers a hybrid account of voice in theatre, not dissimilar to that of Cicely Berry, with its combination of ethos, historical overview and models of voice approaches. In this, she identifies a need for vocal standards bespoke to the American cultural setting and an explanation about 'how the theatre voice specialist functions as a collaborative artist within the production process' (Withers-Wilson 1993: xi). Her desire is to define the voice practitioner's function against a historically fraught backdrop associated with professional role demarcation in the theatre-making process. As such, it echoes many of Berry's concerns about the status of the voice practitioner, particularly in relation to that of the theatre director:

> In this text the title 'vocal director' is utilized rather than the more frequently employed designation 'vocal coach.' The title 'vocal coach' is a limited one, for the word 'coach' meaning to 'instruct or train,' infers that the theatre voice specialist works solely with the actors during the rehearsal period. This inference has been a source of much confusion to stage directors and has had a negative impact upon the effective use of vocal directors within the production process.
>
> (Wilson 1993: xii)

Linda Gates' *Voice for Performance: Training the Actor's Voice* (2000) similarly acknowledges the potential for voice work to be misunderstood within actor training, echoing the concerns of Withers-Wilson and Berry. Gates, though, attributes the misunderstanding in part to Anglo-American relations and not to the theatre profession alone, and raises issues about nationality and 'authenticity' when it comes to speech in theatre training on both sides of the Atlantic, the institutional aspects of which are taken up in Chapters 1 and 5:

> Today, even as many American actors are criticized for failing to measure up to the vocal skills of their British counterparts, voice and speech classes often do not receive a sufficiently prominent place in the curriculum of many American theatre training programs.
>
> (Gates 2000: 1)

The stated purpose of Gates is to 'cut through some of the mystery and confusion surrounding voice and speech training for actors' (Gates 2000: 1). It is possible that this 'mystery' is a representative term for many of the issues already touched upon pertaining to the anxieties about the status and function of the voice practitioner in theatre practice. It is interesting that Gates sees it as her job to clarify the aims of the voice trainer. By so doing, she returns us to the issue of voice as an instrument of the individual who, she believes, needs to be separated from their personal thoughts and vocal habits in order to best express the primary meanings of the writer. The work on voice, then, is about the instrument in service of the author:

> Its aim is to develop a flexible vocal instrument that can convey the ideas, thoughts and feelings of the playwright in such a way that they can be easily heard and understood by an audience in the theatre.
>
> (Gates 2000: 1)

This book, with its clarifications and codification of a range of voice exercises, sits fair and square in the how-to genre of the voice-training manual. Its aim is to support a training ethos that exists outside the manual and is assumed to run alongside it, in the belief that the reader will readily understand and appreciate the function of the exercises. Although it falls short of an examination of the underpinning principles upon which these sequences are based, it offers clear credentials about a transatlantic theatre voice tradition in its recognition of both Edith Skinner, mentioned earlier in the book, and Cicely Berry.

In Chapter 1, the actor's voice is defined in relation to a musical aesthetic for the actor's voice that, as I have shown on numerous occasions, is a common feature of the twentieth-century voice manual:

> The actor's voice is developed in much the same way that one learns to play a musical instrument … the human voice is, in fact, the most sublime musical instrument of them all.
>
> (Gates 2000: 3)

The largest portion of the book gives a precise account of each of the standard American speech sounds. Whilst Gates acknowledges the controversies about the teaching of Standard English at the Central School (Gates 2000: 176) and elsewhere, her support for teaching standard sounds resounds, particularly in relation to the experiences gained as a student under Edith Skinner, who encouraged her to lose her regionalism. The 'Southernisms' in her own sound were ironed out under Skinner but, without offering a critique of the reasons for the necessity of one regional sound's domination over another, as part of a wider story that also includes class and race, she avoids her own complex experience. She chooses, instead, to concentrate on factors important to the market-led context of the actor and concedes, thereby, the pragmatics of the profession:

> It comes down to employability. The more skills you have: good voice and speech, ability to handle a variety of textual material, dialects, and trained singing voice – all increase your chances in a very overcrowded and highly competitive profession.
>
> (Gates 2000: 180)

THE ACTOR'S STUDIO

It comes as no surprise, then, that within actor training there are counter-reactions to the interventionist standards set by Skinner and others. The strongest of these alternative views sets out to elevate or promote rather than iron out the demotic voice. In the USA, broadly speaking, these views get tied up with the aims and ambitions of exponents of the Method. The Method in the USA, built in part on the legacy of Stanislavski's Moscow Arts Theatre teachings, as they were interpreted in New York from the early 1920s onwards, was an area of theatre practice that directly eschewed the prescriptions of standardization in speech. Lee Strasberg's later iteration of The Method, seen in the version he devised in New York in 1951 at the Actor's Studio, took this further. He based his work upon a range of psychological and inward-looking processes, many of which concurred with a preference for the 'natural' demotic vocal aesthetic that became associated with theatre authenticity or 'truth'. This, of course, raised problems for the actor who had questions about squaring up to a vocal technique that was anti-technique and yet was the representative sign of a culturally attractive acting ethos:

> Many American actors who studied the Method struggled to find a way to sustain the 'truth of the moment' while simultaneously honouring vocal technique. For a while many Method actors discarded their vocal training altogether, believing it to be detrimental to their acting process. How could they focus on forming perfectly shaped vowels while connecting with an emotionally charged memory and its ensuing expression? How could they adopt Good American Speech, which was not their native pronunciation, and still maintain a sense of truth?
>
> (Saklad 2011: 8)

Chuck Jones, a voice trainer at the Actor's Studio in the USA, provides no direct answer to the question about the paradox of voice techniques that are anti-technique. He gets close, however, in his discussion about whether the voice is best regarded as an instrument to be perfected or rather as a 'natural' sounding expression of the individual persona. In the preface to his how-to book, *Make Your Voice Heard: An Actor's Guide to Increased Dramatic Range through Vocal Training*, Jones states that his approach is one that both allows individuals to develop their own 'truthful' voice, as against one that is illustrative of any particular stylistic, and is capable of coping with the wide-ranging demands of theatre. It is notable that he lays his credentials on the table with clear market-led efficiency and leaves the reader in no uncertain terms as to the authority of his vision, the viability of his exercises for the jobbing actor and its status as a 'breakthrough' approach. This latterly shores up the book on the market as a standout how-to text with sufficient credentials to make a difference to the individual who buys it:

> Actors who follow my advice have often told me that:
>
> - Their voices improve in power and range.
> - They have more vocal stamina.
> - They are more focused in their acting …
> - Their auditions have gotten better results and are more satisfying.
>
> (Jones 1996: 11–12)

Jones, unlike many of his earlier UK twentieth-century counterparts, writes vividly about his belief in the effectiveness of the work and lays out his reasons for a selection of exercises in relation to their viability in a fast-moving marketplace: 'my goal as a teacher has been to develop time-efficient exercises – effective and fast-working' (Jones 1996: 14). The economic interests involved in 'selling' a voice method are distinctly more evident in Jones and Gates than in the earlier works by Fogerty, Thurburn and, later, in Berry. I assume that in an earlier historical period, the philosophical and scientific credentials provided a more than adequate sales rationale. Fogerty, for example, in her text *Rhythm* (1937), prefers to align her work grandiosely with 'Natural Law' (Fogerty 1937: 23), similarly echoed in Thurburn, rather than with commercial success. Berry, in a different but related vein, expresses an antipathy towards advanced capitalist venture throughout her oeuvre.

Jones speaks to a feature of the voice manual that is shared jointly on both sides of the Atlantic, and that is its direct relationship to the marketplace. I suggest that the commercial and often polemical characteristic of the contemporary voice manual, in particular, as it must sell its uniqueness to the marketplace, keeps it at somewhat of a remove from the debate and discussion afforded other kinds of writing in the academy. This factor also draws attention to a wider problem in which the eclecticism of voice manuals, as they make passing reference to linguistics, aesthetics, literature and philosophy, for example, shores up a persistent cultural binary in which practical instruction is regarded as inferior or less significant than discourse that is of a theoretical nature.

KRISTIN LINKLATER

This brings me, finally, to the work of Kristin Linklater in the last third of the twentieth century and into the twenty-first, in which she addresses and resolves many of the persistent binaries discussed concerning theory versus practice, the voice as instrument or as individual, technique versus the 'natural' and so on. Of a similar generation to Berry, but primarily operating in the USA, Jacqueline Martin credits Kristin Linklater's work with bringing theatre voice into a new phase by building upon the seminal work of psychophysical voice practitioner Iris Warren. According to Martin, she added 'psychological principles to the physiological principles which Elsie Fogerty had established in the first twenty-five years of this century, when she systematized a method of speech training based on accurate physical mechanics of voice' (Martin 1991: 175).

Key to the success of Linklater's work is her integration of the psychological principles she had witnessed under her tutelage with Iris Warren at the London Academy of Music and Dramatic Art:

> In moving from 'external' controls to internal psychological ones, Iris Warren was able to help British actors avoid straining their voices when expressing strong emotions – by helping them 'unblock'. All this pioneering work ran counter to the 'voice beautiful' ideals of the day, but was supported by Michel Saint-Denis and movement teacher Litz Pisk, at the Old Vic Theatre School after the Second World War, when the main teaching direction was towards organic training.
>
> (Martin 1991: 175)

Linklater frames a synthesis of Fogerty's principles and Warren's psychological awareness and develops them during her fifty years of practice in the USA. Theatre practitioners embraced her approach at a time of cultural shift in the 1960s where the beautiful or 'trained' voice was, in some quarters, valued less than that of the individual's raw vocal expression. (Her interview in Chapter 5 of this book testifies further about the unique historical circumstances she found in the USA in the early 1960s):

> Her approach to voice training is based on psychotherapeutic principles, emphasizing that in order to unlock the mind, one must unlock the body. Building on the premise that the 'inner muscles of the body must be free to receive the sensitive impulses from the brain that create speech', she has evolved a system of vocal training, psycho-physical in nature, where the emphasis is placed on the relationship between mind and body.
>
> (Martin 1991: 176)

Freeing the Natural Voice is Linklater's key text and was an international bestseller when it was first published in 1976. It is the most recent edition of 2006, however, that I examine here, as it provides an example of a voice text/manual that has evolved to satisfy both the *how to* and the *why*. This sets it apart from the majority of its predecessors and speaks to a reader who has the capacity for both thought and practical action. By so doing, it extends the ambitions of the voice text beyond the usual binary reinforcement and opens up the possibilities for 'newer', more fluid, embodied encounters with it.

Linklater draws direct attention in her preface to the difficulties presented in other voice publications, and raises questions about the relationship between practice and authorship rarely cited by other writers:

> In the following chapters I have tried to capture the work that Iris Warren said should never be written down and that I use daily in the classroom. It is intended, by its nature, to be conveyed orally, and it is dangerous to confine and define it in printed words. I resisted writing the original edition of this book for years, but its value has been proven over the past thirty years and the risk of its being misunderstood outweighed by the many experiences of understanding. The additional material must now stand the test of publication.
>
> (Linklater 2006: 10)

Her work, spanning over fifty years from 1963 to the current day, is a vivid example of the ways in which traditions from both the USA and the UK have successfully intertwined to move voice training in the West towards psychophysical synthesis and application:

> The language I inherited from Iris Warren was easily translated into the emotional and psychological terminology of, for instance, the Method and other acting methodologies that had branched off from those of the Group Theatre.
>
> (Linklater 2006: 2)

Linklater's work, overall, deserves the attention of the academy and the voice practitioner communities on both sides of the Atlantic in higher education and the theatre profession, precisely because its weave of commentary, ethos, philosophy, illustration and exercise progression renders it discursively transparent and deeply accountable to the practice it describes at one and the same time. In drawing attention to a multiplicity of sensation and awareness in the enactment of any given vocal event, her instruction provides a key step forward in the task of defining the relationship between the knowledge contained in the publications on voice and their intended effects in embodied practice. The book marks a significant step forward in challenging the hierarchies of knowledge in education, in particular, and suggests that theatre practices contain their own knowledge that it is important to recognize and discuss outside the frame of their inception in the studio. As a text it moves beyond the generalized hybridity of previous examples and establishes a new phenomenon – the voice text that is more widely discursive and one capable of holding its own under both academic and professional theatre scrutiny.

Linklater's work returns me to the themes of the chapter that start, with theatre's open arms to science in the guise of Fogerty and ends with Linklater's hybrid arts–science-philosophical synthesis. Fogerty's work clearly establishes credibility for the craft of spoken voice, but it also marks the beginning of a more complex discussion about the object, that is, the vocal instrument, and the subject manifested *in* vocal expression. The relationship between the more abstract principles of sound making and the specifics of their individual embodiment, under the influence of theatre, society and family, now becomes the 'new' story of voice in theatre.

In the voice manual, some of the anxieties about the responsibility for safeguarding the function of voice within theatre production are made evident. This 'exposure' sits at the heart of a wider discussion about the organizing principles under which theatres operate. In the overlap between the roles of director and voice practitioner, competition is revealed about control over the production values and its outcomes to which the voice is susceptible.

I suggest that the location of theatre voice on a spectrum that involves both the givens provided by conversational vocal values at one end, and ones that are highly trained and specialized at the other, offers the possibility for better understanding voice in the pluralistic demands of context. This works alongside the other model established for reading the voice manuals themselves in which the descriptive vocal manual sits at one end of a spectrum and the socially triangulated embodied experience of voice, manual and teacher sits at the other. Taken together, these models help to provide better understanding about the signs of vocal meaning utilized in any given vocal manual, training studio or theatre production and the hierarchies of interest to which they all three pertain.

AN INTERVIEW WITH CLAUDETTE WILLIAMS, 4 JULY 2017

CW – Claudette Williams

JB – Jane Boston

JB: So, Claude, this is an interview in relation to a voice reader that I'm writing. As you've played a key role as a voice practitioner in actor training in the UK for many, many years, it is important that you are here to speak to me today. Firstly, I want to ask, what is important about voice and why does voice remain important to you in a theatre and theatre training context?

CW: I think theatre has always been for me about the spoken word and the spoken word as far as story and orality is concerned and that for me is the beginning of all theatre; theatre is not, for me, about a building but a gathering of people exchanging stories. And theatre, for me, began really, you know, in my mother's kitchen in which groups of women would get together and tell stories. It is about the voice and what the voice does to listener transformation. I grew up to hushed tones of thoughts which were dangerous for a young listener to hear – thoughts and words you had to grow into hearing/using. Dangerous thought/words that, when said, unmasked various realities. The said, unsaid, gestured and the silence all played their part in an aural delight. Stories so intoxicating that it awakened myriad sensual and emotional responses that still live with me today. So, theatre becomes this magical place of potency as far as words are concerned and the many multifaceted levels of meaning.

JB: I think that's absolutely brilliant and I just wonder if you feel that you came to theatre first or second? I mean I think you've indicated here that it was at your mother's table in a way and through your mother's ear, and so does that history predate your connection with modern theatre, is that really what you're saying?

CW: Yes! I'm saying that all theatre begins with the voicing of a story. And that is how voice operates within traditional storytelling as a tool of invocation. It was believed that whatever is spoken manifests itself into sight. This invoking of the voice shaped each scene, each turn of phrase, so that the word gets empowered with the notion of shapes, texture, space as well as meaning. The voice of the storyteller constantly shifts from the first person to the voices of characters; as the story journeys to the listener, it renders the hearer better able to perceive that they alone are the object of attention, with its ability to shape worlds.

JB: It is not incidental that Kristin Linklater says something similar in her interview in this book in which she says that to have a voice in theatre is partly about, if not all about, the ability to tell the story in theatre as with people in ancient times; if you like, it was the people that emerged out of the storytelling group that developed the special communication skills we know as acting.

CW: I spoke to an African storyteller about his craft and he said the most important performative skill needed was the ability to entice the ear of the listener. So it's that ability to engage an audience in 'Communal listening'; to provide intimacy and connectedness.

JB: How do you develop this? Is the ability to spatially get that listener engaged something individuals have very early on – is it something that is trainable, for example?

CW: I remember my daughter, she was two and she took delight in sound making. One day we were on the bus and she said quite loudly, 'I just love to talk'; the whole bus just fell about laughing which did not deter her.

What she loved was the physical engagement of communication. A communication that was inclusive, it included her and the listener or all the listeners. To her it was an act of being – an act of power. So I think sometimes it's deeply innate within you. My daughter felt the power the act of speech gave her. With young actors the task is to release them to the possibilities of their voice. There are those first moments in Year One of training, when the actor experiences to its fullest the power of the intentional breath, connectivity and word shape within the situation of need. It is in those moments of shifting energies that the voice of the speaker and the hearer engage in conversation. There is a oneness of breath exchange between all who are present and meaning is not only heard but felt.

JB: Would you say the child, then, say at the point of your daughter's development – if the child at that point had not really got any feedback or received any attention – might that have given her a very different sense of direction about herself would you say? Did she get a lot of recognition?

CW: Yes, she did.

JB: She did, the people on the bus. Marvellous. So, there is an emergent sense of the child who is capable of taking a delight in moving the voice and feeling it. Obviously, though, there are going to be students with different relationships to such formative experiences in voice training groups. I would like to know where you started to find that delight for yourself or interest in catching the ear of the listener?

CW: It started as a child with me also. I grew up in the Caribbean and on Sunday evenings we would have concerts, performances in church of poetry, proverbs, riddles, songs, dramatic text and stories. I recognized very early on that the power of words gave you social and communal power.

JB: Now, you mention the proverbs and the riddles in your Caribbean upbringing. Can you talk a bit more about the ways these words were constructed?

CW: Their construction is part of an education for the community. The linguistic forms, as I remember, were really formulaic. What I do is to transfer this awareness of form in order to help my students recognize form of all kinds and how to interpret it. What's fantastic about understanding form is that it's not static, it does not belong to any era, it's about what is given.

JB: The understanding of the 'riddle' within your community gives you an advantage in terms of interpreting the words that are exchanged in all kinds of public domains. I'm wondering how you identified with that sense of being different – of being able to decipher what was going on?

CW: It was exhilarating.

JB: That's so interesting. So, in a sense, you were more fully educated to hear the form than perhaps a young white English person who, it was assumed, should 'know' but who did not? You possibly had form embedded within you in spades – perhaps more than many white English people. I can only speak for myself – educated in, about a similar time, a little bit earlier – when I experienced a sense of let's ignore form because it has oppressive connotations and let's look for other freedoms here. So, in a sense, a lot was thrown out by certain white educators in order to free the child, to free the spirit to find something 'other'; thrown out by one part of the culture whilst it was still held up on the other with the assumption that 'everyone' would understand the biblical reference and the Shakespearean references. Perhaps the education you had at home and in the Caribbean actually gave you a unique ability to hear and to translate? I don't know, I'm just thinking about that – it's very interesting and I wonder how you put it all together? Are you saying that, in theatre, your voice found its way; that in discovering the voice you found your way to the theatre – but it wasn't the theatre that gave you the voice? If I'm understanding you, you felt equipped in many ways with the internal capacity and the need and you wanted to tell the story.

CW: Yep and that need led me to drama school.

JB: Where did you go?

CW: I went to Guildhall [London]. The training was exhilarating emotionally and physically and demanded the ability to work from different perspectives and to make connections by defining a practical methodology that worked for you in all the classes given. I was actively engaged in determining the artist I wanted to be. And the actor I wanted to be held a specific worldview. I had no expectation of diversity within the training. I knew why I sought to train and whilst studying I began my own cultural education, reading the plays of prominent American writers, working on accents and going to the theatre to see emerging British Black theatre.

JB: It's interesting, isn't it, that as a black woman in the UK you found a place and a voice through the Afro-American voice? I can identify with that in a way that has similarities and differences: the Afro-American writers spoke to me as a white woman growing up in the Midwest where I was looking for those writers who could put something different on their tongue if you like, put something different on the page. Were there things that came to you because you had an education in any case and then you found those writers; did it come out of Guildhall – did they point you to these writers?

CW: No.

JB: So you got your training in theatre, but it wasn't the theatre that gave you the voice?

CW: No. Not at all. I don't think anybody comes to the theatre to find a voice in that sort of way; I think you have to have a voice to come to the theatre.

JB: [Laughing]

CW: You have to have that embedded – that embodied understanding. There are things we can train but we can't train *that*. We can release the right to speak but the rest is up to the student's ownership of *self*.

JB: Okay, thanks – so on to the next question about how do you describe a voice that works in theatre? You know, what is it that makes the voice work in theatre?

CW: When the voice is heard as an opening of the intellect and emotion and it enlivens the imagination of all. When the voice unmasks the defences of the listeners and demands to be heard. It is the ability to recognize that language has to be heard – a heard voice is articulate, free and intentioned – it's the ability to hear with your own being in order to speak.

JB: So has that, in your view, changed? Is that something that you feel has shifted in contemporary culture: the capacity of the young actor to know what listening is?

CW: I think so because it's such a huge act of humanity, it's an act of just being present within a moment and I think with all that's going on for our students at times, they are not able to be present to themselves. Our education system does not allow failure – so in the act of *doing* students are preoccupied with getting it right but not with the experience of the *doing*.

JB: And where do you think they have to go, or do go? What preoccupies them away from the *being* and *doing*?

CW: The education system and self-belief. Students feel they cannot change the 'industry' and they are frustrated by the lack of performative opportunities that allow them to develop their artistry. Many are frustrated by older actors and their perception of voice within the training – those older actors are the product of the rep system that allowed them to hone their craft. Where do they go to do that? Employability is difficult unless you have a profile.

JB: Yes. So, I'm hearing you say that the wider framework for theatre relates to a star culture on one side and a particular kind of spectator on the other. So, bearing that in mind, as you are a trainer of voice for theatre, can you give us an indication of how you have to shift your voice training to meet the modern actor, the modern young student?

CW: The ability to communicate now is so different. As trainers we're looking at young actors who do not read, and who lack any understanding of how language works, and whose understanding of the performative voice is televisual.

JB: Can I ask you – just as an aside – how would you define the televisual voice?

CW: I think it's the voice of, well, it's a conversational tone of TV and film, in which you can get a close-up on the internal thoughts. In theatre there's no close-up – you have to be present – and so it's about how do you teach a voice that has to do that, that has to be projected, and also has to be heard.

JB: The ordinary conversational voice, or the everyday voice, is perhaps not what it seems to the young actor – is there more to it in your view? Would you say that theatre voice is not just a snapshot of being ordinary? Does something *else* happen to the voice in theatre?

CW: Well, I think there has to be embodiment; it has to be slightly heightened by thought-energy, then intentional need and sub-textual resonance within a thought. It's about voice that understands the dynamics of space without amplification.

JB: Can I ask you, then, what do you feel that your training at Guildhall gave you – what was the key training point? Was your background and/or drama school the more important influence?

CW: I think it was both. Students enter training today from an intellectualized and technological learning environment that has led to a lack of physical embodiment. Their imagination is one of concrete imagery and it is not sensory. The engagement of reading books has lessened so the felt/words/imagination triggers are not there. Speech training is now paramount within training to enliven the student's imagination with regard to what words do.

JB: And it feels as if you had a predisposition to negotiate form because of what you had heard and what you had experienced, am I right?

CW: Yes, yes, so in that sort of way it was about how language was spoken in a different time period and frame. And when you talk about 'freedom', it is, you know, also about the *freedom* that is to be found within the text of Rattigan and many others.

JB: Yes, that is a wonderful point and speaks to a big, big existential position that I feel you point to and that is about a paradox; such that the constraints of form are there to guide you to find an extraordinary expanse – is this correct?

CW: Yes, yes.

JB: Now that is a complex ask for the young person.

CW: It is, it is – but the change occurs with the embodying of the thought ... Yesterday I worked with a young man who was reading a Ginsberg poem and when it hit his breath there was a moment of transformation when the poem became this wild horse that was taking him to places.

JB: Was it Ginsberg's *Kaddish*?

CW: Yes, it was *Kaddish* – and it took him to places that, when he finished, gave him the sensation of transformation.

JB: That is so exciting, I feel the goosebumps …

CW: And it's that – the language is able to transform through the breathing of it. He allowed the breath to get engaged and he went on a journey like it was an exorcism charged with spontaneous thought – moving from one topic to the next, to the next, to the next and it, yeah, it was intoxicating, he was alive, his breath became essential to him. I think we all watched him engaged in a, I don't know, a level of spiritual connection that was beyond him and so the residue that was left for him was that his breath had extended his life in a huge way.

JB: Wonderful, wonderful.

CW: And so that's what language gives you …

JB: As you're speaking I'm just going, yes, yes, yes – I understand what you're saying about the relevance of versed text in the actor training experience – where at first it may seem wholly outside the purpose of theatre, but it seems to me that the way you're talking about verse places it right at the core of something that facilitates change; it can speak to us and then do something to us, yeah?

CW: Yeah, so it's really about taking young actors to that level of the spoken word and how it transforms them internally in order to make choices about how they go on then to use what they have experienced.

JB: So that brings me to a complex question – do you feel that voice is becoming sidelined as a part of theatre today?

CW: The Internet has changed humankind in many ways, but most importantly in its communicative behaviours. The continuous inducement of digital technology has possibly fashioned a generation that requires continuous visual stimulation. We don't live in an aural culture anymore when you went to the theatre to experience and participate in a relationship with the audience. We are at a crossroad with regards to professional vocal usage by trainee actors. Judi Dench has been very outspoken about the actor's voice: If you're not going to be heard, then stay at home and do it in your living room. It doesn't require shouting; it requires learning about it and learning where your voice comes from, where your diaphragm is and how to use it.

The BBC drama *Happy Valley* angered audiences because of the 'mumbling' and actress Siân Phillips feels that the only thing that hasn't improved with time is the audibility of the voice, which is a great problem for younger actors. Young actors seem to think it is more natural to talk quietly, more realistic, but in the theatre the trick is to be natural enough to be heard. You must be heard.

These comments need addressing. Why is this happening and what can we do?

There is ever more demand for training the contemporary performative voice in theatre, film and television. Students leave drama school with the knowledge about how the voice works – articulation, placement, support/ use of words, sentence structures, thoughts, intention, dialogue, need, the imaginative and poetic nuances of thought/character/intent and the physical/verbal demands of voicing various performative modes. But, professionally, students struggle! Why? Do we need to do more extensive microphone technique classes run by voice teachers? Surely we do so with the Carleton Hobbs [BBC radio] competition? Do we now need more vocal coaching or vocal directors working on theatrical productions or TV and film productions? Where is the discrepancy? Is there a tension between acting training and voice training; if so, where and how can we resolve this? Are we in crisis regarding theatre and theatre voice – in fact voice within all the creative mediums?

JB: These are big and important issues that you so rightly bring to the surface and it is important that all involved in performance training give deeper consideration to them for the future.

CW: Yes.

JB: I'm not going to let you stop just on that. I want to say: what is the legacy you feel you give to theatre today, in voice, theatre voice today?

CW: I don't know really, I mean, I hope to give students ownership and the ability to reveal the emotional nuances of a word, a thought, and a speech in ways that will affect the psyche of the listener:

'Praise of the Word'
The word is total:
it cuts, excoriates
forms, modulates
perturbs, maddens
cures or directly kills
amplifies or reduces
According to intention
It excites or calms souls.

(Praise song of a bard of the Bambara Komo society, quoted in Louis-Vincent Thomas and Rene Luneau, *Les religions d'Afrique noire, textes et traditions sacres*; as cited in Gleason xxxvii)

JB: Marvellous. I think that is a modest claim, Claude, a modest claim! I was going to comment, for what it is worth, that I see you as brilliant in the way you negotiate and facilitate the actor's voice. It is one of things that I see you do so beautifully.

CW: I don't know – you try.

JB: You do, you do, I mean that's what you embody. Thank you, Claude, thank you so much.

CW: My pleasure.

JB: Thank you, I appreciate that so much.

Extremities: Experiments in Theatre Voice

VOICE: A RADICAL SIGN

Voice is key to a number of twentieth-century theatre practices in which literary theatre, authorial privilege and commercialism are challenged. Although new forms of speech practices arise in late twentieth-century theatre practice for many of the same reasons, it is the potentiality of voice as a radical sign that I examine here. Voice in radical theatre practice is animated by many of the key social and cultural theories across the century that champion process over product and devised work over work on extant text. It provides an important counterbalance to the account given more widely in the book about voice in interpretive theatre practice.

But, first, a word in brief about Verbatim theatre projects. A number of late twentieth-century practices favour theatre content and expression that is activated by demotic speech, principally the Verbatim theatre projects of the past quarter century. Whilst it is not my intention to examine them in any further detail, partly because they relate, in the main, to theatre making that uses documentary speech content in order to engage in social and political comment, and not voice per se, I want to register the importance of the ways in which they pose a direct challenge not only to the canon, but also to notions of the 'trained' voice.

There is a paradox in the fact that Verbatim theatre is itself a technique based on the speech forms of the everyday. The use of the inflections of 'real' people who are steeped in pre-existing regional speech forms is its trademark aesthetic. I consider that the values of spoken 'ordinariness' in Verbatim stand in marked contrast to the self-conscious sound values of the trained theatre voice and this raises several questions about the merits of the trained voice over the non-trained voice. The 'real' speech trend in contemporary theatre, film and television realism contains traces of Diderot's familiar eighteenth-century theory about the paradox of acting in which the 'real' voice and the trained voice compete as to which holds the greater veracity. It is a discussion that shows little sign of diminishing.

The voice as a radical theatre sign, however, is the primary focus of this chapter and I want to examine a few of the ways in which it enters into the fields of theatre meaning independent of its 'reasoned' association with speech. As part of a number of radical theatre interventions 'tracked back to the emergence of a Modernist avant-garde at the beginning of the twentieth century, with Alfred Jarry and, especially Antonin Artaud as founding fathers' (Shepherd 2012: 171), voice offers a key signature. An account of Jarry's play *Ubu Roi* in 1896, for example, describes vocal extremities of volume, duration and word distortion not unfamiliar to radical art and theatre laboratory practices in the middle of the twentieth-first century:

> Ubu was uncompromising. Indeed, with its opening neologism spouted by the vulgar, obscene grotesque Père Ubu – '*Merdre!!!!*' – it immediately announced its intentions. 'It was,' says Brotchie, 'as though a modernist play from the middle of the next century had been dropped on the stage without all the intervening theatrical developments that might have acclimatized the audience to its conventions.'
>
> (Moorcock 2012)

THE DISMANTLEMENT OF LOGOS

Voice and the dismantlement of logos are also prominent features of the twentieth-century hybrid art practices of Dadaism. Making its first appearance in early twentieth-century Zurich in 1916, Dadaism later spread across Europe and beyond. It relied heavily on voice as a means of evoking potent disruption within a range of mixed media outputs. The key features of postmodern twentieth-century work, 'the deconstruction, anti-textuality, hybridization and heterogeneity' (Sidiropoulou 2011 cited in Shepherd 2012: 171) ensured that the voice (and speech) was deliberately estranged from the conventions of 'ordinary' communication. The ways in which voice effects disorientation in the audience and becomes a tool for the expression of powerful anti-bourgeois feelings lead to further consideration about how and why voice has the capacity to evoke and enact social rupture.

In order to examine such issues, I start with an identification of three of the key political and philosophical events and principles that intersect with theatre and helped to shape many of the rationales for radical or 'extreme' voice. The first is *psychoanalytic* theory, the second is the *avant-garde* of the early twentieth century and the third is the *countercultural* activism of the 1960s. I examine here, in brief, some of the ways in which voice, under the influence of these events and principles, is a key element in non-mainstream theatre practice and consider why, for many, it is the principle experimental sign. I consider, too, why voice holds the promise of the radical and the new as it connects with the 'belief that words possess intrinsic physical strength,' in which 'incantation could therefore be a powerful weapon' (Hayman 1977: 134). A common feature of radical theatre practice is the way that voice acts as both a signal and a transmitter to effect the estrangement of spoken norms. This capacity is underpinned and informed by a number of notable performance laboratory experiments in Europe during the mid-twentieth century, many of whose practices subsequently cross over into the mainstream theatre.

THE THEATRE LABORATORY

The theatre laboratory context acts as a crucible in which several behavioural theories and political 'countercultural' ideas converge. Supported by communal values, devised and lived outside the mainstream, the labs take the form of a series of lifestyle experiments out of which a number of distinctive embodied voice practices emerge. The experimental theatre lab, as I have shown, is not new to the twentieth century but, as theatre historian James Roose-Evans argues, this fact is not to diminish the importance of the need for it to be remade for each generation. He suggests that Artaud's same act of rebellion against mainstream fashions in art is reproduced to great effect in many subsequent theatre iterations across the twentieth century:

> It is important to remember that Artaud … was rebelling (like Copeau) against a particular kind of rhetorical acting then fashionable at the Comédie Française. He was attacking a French theatre particularly dominated by words and by reverence for the author. In place of the poetry of language he proposed a poetry of space, employing such means as music, dance, painting, kinetic art, mime, pantomime, gesture, chanting, incantations, architectural shapes, lighting.
> (Roose-Evans 2001: 76)

One of the consequences of the spotlight placed on individual experience in this new 'poetry of space' noted by Roose-Evans is the fact that the voice emerges as an important agent in the expression of self-discovery. Central to this are the sensations of the 'lived' self that are highlighted in phenomenological approaches. Actors use these to construct their own testimony, drawing 'on the deepest and most secret experiences of their own lives, articulated in such a way that this act of revelation' … can 'serve as a provocation for the spectator' (Wolford 2010: 204). This is a far cry from the theatre practice that focuses on the interpretation and reproduction of the authorial voice. It is primarily in laboratory-style work, such as Grotowski's, for example, that an actor's engagement with the embodied voice serves as the means by which the audience is invited to 'measure him/herself against the truth revealed in the performance' (Wolford 2010: 204).

The provocations and interventions made by Artaud and his contemporaries aim to highlight values that celebrate the liveness and aliveness of the actor in the moment of performance:

> Artaud was attacking the kind of minority culture that depends on the printed word and has lost contact with the primitive sources of inspiration. He saw that the dualistic rift between mind and body, intellect and feeling, must be healed.
> (Roose-Evans 2001: 77)

Although a generalization, there is enough in this description that resonates specifically with the now familiar themes in voice practice wherever challenges are made to the mind–body binary. And in many ways, Artaud's work exemplifies all attempts made to resolve this binary in theatre. Towards the end of his life, for example, his work gets as much infused with his psychological state as with his unique physical capacities. In fact, the two are hard to separate. An account of his appearance at the Theatre of the Vieux–Colombier, on 13 January 1947, vividly recreates the charged atmosphere of a poetic vocal performance that takes place in the company of many leading writers, poets and philosophers of the French avant-garde. As an act of mesmeric transgression it is compelling and, at the same time, hard to comprehend, partly because there is little in the public domain against which to appraise it:

> According to an article by Maurice Saillet in *Combat,* there were about 700 people in the theatre, a hundred of them standing in the back. The majority were young, but the audience included Gide, Barrault, Breton, Paulhan, Adamov, Camus, and Roger Blin. 'Artaud made his entrance, with this emaciated, ravaged face resembling both Edgar Allan Poe's and Baudelaire's … his impassioned hands flew like two birds round his face, groping at it tirelessly … he began to declaim his beautiful, scarcely audible poems with his hoarse voice broken by sobs and tragic stammers'.
>
> (Hayman 1977: 134–135)

VOICE AS RUPTURE

In this account, the eruptive and disruptive voice of Artaud's performance is given prominence. Its 'sobs' and 'stammers' provide examples of a voice 'freed' from the obligations and conventions of interpretation. His use of paralinguistic vocal features, as they fall outside the traditions of theatre voice aesthetics, serves, in many ways, as a direct challenge to the canonical grip of the theatre elite. His voice, generated with rupture at its heart, in turn effects disruption for the audience, parallel evidence of which lies in Zygmunt Molik's aims for voice work with Grotowski later in the century. In this work:

> there is a deep connection between the physical shaking, the physical shocks and the voice, that stressing the body physically opens the channels to liberating the voice.
>
> (Campo 2010: 3)

In the adoption of some of Artaud's paralinguistic vocal features, many of the twentieth-century laboratory theatre practices introduced a 'new' primal element that in and of itself registered a challenge to bourgeois theatre values. The constrictions, the static and the turbulence generated by such sounds ran counter to the mellifluous vibratory tones of the 'trained' vocal instrument that most audiences had grown accustomed to.

As with the sob and the stammer, additions of the cry, the laugh, the shaken sound and the sigh of relief also constitute regular features of paralinguistic voice work. Even in the more formalized contexts of frameworks established by practitioners such as Kristin Linklater, these features often play a key formational role in the enablement of an individual's discovery of hitherto unknown facets of their voice, here evidenced in the laboratory work of Zygmunt Molik:

> I just said to him: 'Cry out now!' And he did, and then later, once opened, it was easy. Once I had opened the voice … he could keep this voice. I repeated it and told him: 'Cry out, take a breath and cry out, keep on shouting'. And he did it, and then I just regulated it, I put it into a normal channel and he started signing with his full voice.
>
> (Molik in Campo 2010: 2)

I suggest that, in all these instances, voice is instrumental in bringing specific kinds of energy or life 'force' into the theatre. Molik names this simply as the capacity to find life in the voice:

> [F]or the first few days the point is just to work on the breath … Afterwards they can go more into the unknown, when the Life has been found. Everybody finds the Life in the self. The Life is something connected with everyone's life, his memories, or even his dreams. This is what I call 'the Life'. It's difficult to explain. The Life, when it's found, has its physical and vocal shape.
>
> (Molik cited in Campo 2010: 5)

VOICE AND THE MIND: WOLFSOHN

Voice, in its potent and 'irrational' way, therefore, is central to a number of theatre rationales set in place to replace old beliefs. They are informed, as I suggested earlier, to no small degree by theories in the field of psychoanalytic thought, principally the archetypal work of the Swiss psychotherapist Carl Jung (1875–1961). One of the key examples of the ways in which Jungian-based psychoanalytic theory is incorporated into 'radical' performance practices is evident in the work of German psychoanalyst and singing teacher Alfred Wolfsohn (1896–1962), earlier in the twentieth century. Wolfsohn suffered auditory hallucinations after bearing witness to the suffering of the wounded in the trenches of World War I, and later devised a way to overcome his trauma. Upon his discharge from hospital in 1919, he devised a set of vocal processes for the restoration of the voice based upon his psychological and singing expertise:

> [I]n the ten years following his release from the hospital, one of the first means that he pursued to restore his health was to try and re-find his lost voice. He went to a number of highly reputed singing teachers but none of them were able to help him.
>
> By 1930, he was sufficiently himself again to be able to continue his pre-war work as a singing coach for professional classical singers. They came to him to

redress their vocal problems. In working with them, he began to realise that their vocal problems, like his own, were based not on their physical condition but on their psyche. At this time psychology was in its infancy, so those interested in the subject, like Alfred himself, were all searching. He soon began to get some very encouraging results; and many of his pupils showed sustained improvements in their singing capacities, as well as in their psychological condition.

(Centre Artistique International Roy Hart website 2016)

Wolfsohn's psychological insight supports the subsequent work of the Roy Hart Theatre Company, founded in the mid-1970s and 'renowned for going beyond the vocal limits of what is considered acceptable sound' (Kalo, Whiteside and Midderigh 1997: 185). Regarding themselves as practitioners of life, as much as theatre, voice as a form of therapeutic release provides a paradigm for the company's entire oeuvre (Kalo, Whiteside and Midderigh 1997: 189).

It is important to be reminded that although extremities of pitch, dynamics of volume and other paralinguistic features have radical potential, they are not, of themselves, radical. Extreme pitch range on its own terms, for example, sets up listener disturbance and is effective as a means of drawing attention to other levels of existential significance in any given performance, but does not communicate literal meaning on its own. Dependent on the ways in which it is deployed, it is able to effect responses that fall outside linguistic sense structures. Yet only where it is instrumental to the exploration and expression of individual meaning does it have the potential for radical intervention. Pitch disconnected from intention has an effect, but it carries fullest meaning when it is connected to the individual actor in an expressive context. In the following extract about Wolfsohn's beliefs, it is clear that he regarded the voice as crucial to the well-being of not just the body but also the psyche:

Believing that the voice is the audible expression of a man's inner being, he [Wolfsohn] devoted his life to trying to discover why, in most people, the voice is shackled, monotonous, cramped. Through his research he learned that the voice is not the function solely of any anatomical structure, but the expression of the whole personality. Working with a great variety of people he proved that the human voice is restricted only by the psychological problems of the individual and that, conversely, the voice is a way through which all aspects of an individual can be developed. His work with singers and actors and ordinary people led to an increase in the vocal range, irrespective of sex, from two to eight octaves, and even nine … It was this link between the voice and the psychological growth of the individual that perhaps marked Wolfsohn's most important discovery.

(Kalo, Whiteside and Midderigh 1997: 181–182)

HART, GEORGE AND STEEN

Under the influence of Wolfsohn, Roy Hart's work raised new questions about the relationship between the practice of extended pitch work and the ways in which it contributes to a development of the 'whole' person. Whilst the voice is experienced by many as an indelible part of self, for others plural notions of selfhood also pertain. I suggest, then, that it is more useful to reflect on voice as it comprises multiple interactive events, rather than just a singular one. The work on extended pitch is one such example. It gives rise to a range of feelings and sensations associated with third-party exhortations, self-beliefs and opinions, only parts of which are linked to a unified sense of self.

Whilst it was Wolfsohn's specific research into the extreme sounds of the voice in the World War I trenches that informed Hart's own vocal discoveries, it was Hart himself who took the work right to the core of theatre and made invitations for participatory 'release' in the audience. With parallels in shamanic practices across cultures, he took a lead role in the orchestration of both individual and audience transformations. This has links to other related theatre laboratory processes, as the interview with Grotowski's voice specialist, Zygmunt Molik, upholds. He describes his voice role as requiring the insight of the 'shaman, trying to make the impossible possible' in his work with an actor who showed strong resistance to change (Campo 2010: 2).

Roy Hart company actor Hywel Jones, in his utterance of one word, *Light*, during a seminal contemporary performance, provides vivid evidence of a moment of vocal change as it is an act of catharsis. It is exemplary of many such desired effects in this type of work:

> [T]he actor's sense of release from the claustrophobia of death (interior death and physical death), the awareness of space and freedom and illumination, finally culminated in a sound that became the word 'Light!' With the final articulation of the word-sound-image, the actor turned to the other coffins and, throwing off their lids, cried out the word repeatedly, like a trumpet summoning the dead to the day of resurrection ...
>
> Into that one sound the actor poured all the intensity of his own life experience. The image was personal to him, and yet re-explored at each performance. The vibrations of that one sound, charged with the actor's own research and life experience, conveyed to the spectator who had ears to hear something of the essential darkness of death, and of the awe and wonder of being delivered up from this experience into that of a rebirth.
>
> (Roose-Evans 2001: 179–180)

Hart's work also drew, in part, on Jungian archetypes, with their offer of a 'bridge between the conscious and the unconscious, the male and the female, the feeling and the intellect, the dark and the light, within every human being' (Kalo, Whiteside and Midderigh 1997: 183). Hart, like Artaud, was not as interested in the interpretation of existing modalities as he was in stretching existing forms beyond the borders of the 'known' within the boundaries of an experience:

As the actor stripped away his lies and evasions, his defences, word by word, movement by movement, gesture by gesture, the audience had to be led through the experience with him.

(Benedetti 2007: 226)

A signature of the work is a high degree of self-examination. It relies on the removal of an actor's conventional mask to reveal inner states that, as such, have the capacity to make links to similar expressive states in a number of other world theatre cultures. Interpretive theatre, in which the authorial voice retains the dominant position, is largely eschewed in this work. In its place, the voice as symptom of the mind, and, once explored, as an instrument of individual and communal repair, is uppermost.

What does the voice sound like when worked extensively under similar holistic values, but applied to work with the dramatic text? The following extract about Ros Steen's voice work – under the influence of Nadine George (who was herself a founder of the Roy Hart training school) – for a play by Linda McLean gives an indication of some of the specific kinds of vocal texture or *character* that result when embodied vocal intentions are invoked and prioritized:

The empowered ensemble demonstrated how a performance training where the voice work is embodied and holistic can seep into the fabric of the production to produce a living organism, a breathing whole:

Imagine a string quartet, but with actors instead of musicians. In place of a score, a set of overlapping monologues. As they riff on similar themes, they could be from a family of musical instruments, each with her own timbre and pitch, but each part of the ensemble. Phrases echo like a melody from one performer to another, sometimes dissonant, sometimes in harmony, taking on different meanings according to their setting.

(Birch 2013: 15; the quoted extract in Birch [2013] is from a review by Mark Fisher for the *Guardian*, 16 October 2012)

Nadine George's own system, again with its echoes of Jung, consists of a series of core exercises that concentrate on four qualities of pitch that cover the spectrum of the male and the female voice. The female voice starts at middle C and the male voice starts on the C below middle C. Her warm-up moves through language taken from Shakespeare in such a way that both men and women are invited to experience a full range of vocal pitches that cross conventional gender divides. Individual awareness and development are activated by intense experiences of pitch duration drawn from a wide spectrum of sound.

Common to the work of all the laboratory-based voice practitioners I have cited are the ways in which the extremities of voice are utilized as the basis for not just technique, but individual self-determination. In some circumstances, under often extreme laboratory conditions, the voice is placed under pressure that is at a remove from the conventions of ordinary conversational exchange. In this work, the individual's life experience often replaces the conventional author, and a highly developed expressive range of vocal exercises replaces conventional speech exercises. Audience reception, in turn, is encouraged to accept vocal exhortations that fall outside those of rational conscious interpretation.

At times, the contemporary lineage from Hart, traced through George to Steen, moves effectively into mainstream theatre production and the publicly funded conservatoire environment. It is remarkable that many of the precisely wrought laboratory voice principles endure. These include a premium placed on embodied, organic voice under the influence of strong democratic and utopian values. Taken together, they support the development of the 'richness and variety to be found in each voice' where 'all voices hold the potential to become a celebrated force for good' (Birch 2013: 14).

As I have shown, one of the other trademark features of the work is pitch. Ordinary communication requires audibility and conventional pitch use such that:

> [The] fundamental frequency of vocal fold vibration is one of the most important aspects of larynx activity as far as speech and language are concerned. It varies continuously during speech and consequently the pitch of the voice never remains the same for any appreciable time. This is the essential difference between singing and speaking, for in singing the pitch of the voice is held steady for the length of one note, whether long or short and changes of pitch are made between notes.
>
> (Fry 1979: 68–69)

With the basic principles of ordinary pitch movement in mind, I argue that it is the manipulation of these principles under extensive laboratory experimentation, using the lived experience of its participants, that renders the output of experimental theatre expression radically different to the realistic forms that aim to replicate the conventions of communication. The performer who transgresses the spoken pitch norms outlined above for whatever reason is readily detected and the effects of disturbance, disruption or transformation are ones that are intended to dominate over and above those of speech-modulated interpretive performance practices.

BROOK AND A NEW THEATRE LANGUAGE

The transgressive nature of the work means that it is not always well received and commercial theatre has remained, on the whole, sceptical. Of Hart it is said that '[t]here were those who could not accept his pioneering break from classical Western music; they were not able to "hear" him' (Kalo, Whiteside and Midderigh 1997: 192). Many audience members, however, took inspiration from its characteristic urgency and intensity. The theatre of difference and disruption, too, caught the attention of the young Peter Brook in the early 1960s when he 'first visited the Roy Hart Studio in London and was much impressed and excited by what he found' (Kalo, Whiteside and Midderigh 1997: 180–181). In Brook's case, he professed he was attracted by the opportunity to make theatre essential to everyday life, 'as necessary as eating and sex' (Roose-Evans 2001: 174), and this led him to develop work based upon research into a new theatre language. For reasons that have resonance with the work of Artaud and Hart, Brook's interest was not just in the disruption of norms, but in the formation of something new: a new set of processes that, in themselves, might lead to a new international theatre language:

> a work of theatre that will make total sense, regardless of language, wherever in the world it is played. Month after month, at this centre in Paris, he found that the most powerful expression in sound and movement always came through shedding more and more outward forms – or masks. His is an attempt to make the greatest impact using minimal means. Brook's training methods are like those of a Zen master rather than a conventional theatre director. This is why he insisted, during the long journey through Africa, that the camp would be seen by the actors as an extension of their work. In their lives as well as in their acting the actors had to strive for the kind of spontaneity which can come only from an arduous and sometimes agonizing process of self-exploration.
>
> (Roose-Evans 2001: 183–184)

There are two things of note here that connect Brook to the longitudinal intensive laboratory processes of his predecessors. First, is his desire to create something new out of expressive means that are based on a fresh perception of the conventions of communication. Second, is the social and political context within which his early work is created, that is not dissimilar to the radical context of Europe in the early twentieth century. In the countercultural environs of anti-Vietnam war and anti-establishment feeling in the mid to late 1960s, rather than attack the status quo, however, Brook set out an agenda to provoke audiences out of their habitual responses in order to be enlivened by the in-the-moment actions of the actors. His work posed a twin challenge. First, to the audiences, and second, to a number of mechanistic and outworn working theatre processes. In time, his work became attractive to mainstream theatre managements who sought to revitalize their stock, transform their relationship with audiences and also enhance box-office takings.

Again, there is a distinctive vocal stylistic in the work that includes an experimentation with spoken norms and theatre language in its entirety. More than many other British directors in the mid-twentieth century, Brook's work is marked by a fusion of voice, breath function, emotion and the spoken word. His view of the actor as a 'medium for words' marks a departure from speech-based theatre as it shifts attention to the body of the actor away from an exclusive focus on the author, thereby injecting theatre with a new embodied sensibility that recharges an approach to words. One instance of the work in action is provided by the international theatre experiment he orchestrated in the early 1970s:

> This openness to words was to be a vital principal of the very creation of the play that was performed ... in Persia. In the programme for Persepolis, Brook inserted a quotation from *The Empty Space*: 'A word does not start as a word – it is an end product which begins as an impulse, stimulated by attitude and behaviour which dictate the need for expression. This process occurs inside the dramatist; it is repeated inside the actor. Both may only be conscious of the words, but both for the author and then for the actor, the word is a small visible portion of a gigantic unseen formation ... the only way to find the true path to the speaking of a word is through a process that parallels the original creative one.'
>
> (Smith 1972: 27)

Brook collaborated at Persepolis with the English poet Ted Hughes, and together they created a new language, Orghast, and a play of the same name, which was performed at the 1971 Shiraz Festival: 'This production, *Orghast*, is a big leap forward for the theatre, from representational to abstract, abandoning the meaning of words for their sound' (A. Smith 1972: 120).

Their project marks a turn away from the voice in extremis towards work that sought meaning in a fusion of voice, speech and language forms out of which a new textual language emerges. Not satisfied with the existing acting stylistics, Brook aimed to bring the best of theatre experiment and improvization to the work. In many ways this seemed to suggest an anti-acting stance. His desire to close the gap between the word and reality prompted a challenge to the conventions of acting that only seemed to make it wider.

In Brook, however, a bridge is made between the old and the new – between the extant authorial dramatic text and the new charged embodied processes of the acting laboratories. Most of all, his position at the heart of the British artistic establishment offered invigorated solutions for the theatre as well as reconciliation between those who believed the acting and voice stylistic in an experimental capacity had moved too far beyond readily available comprehension. His work returns the voice to the word, albeit a reconsidered word, that, when investigated, represents an outpost of the feeling, emotion, practice, exercise, discipline, history and thought that lies underneath. No postmodernist then, Brook believes in the effects of the word and to this end he returns to the position of the early modern period in which the actor who held to the purpose of the word also held the power in both its sacred and its secular context. In harnessing the work of Ted Hughes, he also brings me back to the discussion about the material of textual voice practice that forms the basis of much of the training in voice in the UK's conservatoire where voice and speech are reconciled together. In Brook, the laboratory comes full circle in bringing voice and speech into a closer working partnership of meaning.

CATHERINE FITZMAURICE

The countercultural experimentation period of the late 1950s and 1960s that informed Brook's experiments also informed those of Catherine Fitzmaurice in the development of her experimental voice work known as Destructuring/ Restructuring. It is a strand of voice training developed out of the rules and conventions of UK voice work and the countercultural climate of the 1960s in the USA, with its attendant challenge to conformity at all levels of society. Fitzmaurice's work, in particular, equates with the experimental voice work of Artaud and Hart, more than with the work of Brook, and takes its strongest cues from the psychoanalytic work of Sigmund Freud, Wilhelm Reich (1897–1957) and the mind–body work of Reich's student Alexander Lowen (1910–2008) who developed bioenergetics analysis, a form of mind–body psychotherapy, with his then colleague John Pierrakos (1921–2001). It draws upon early twentieth-century voice training at the Central School of Speech and Drama in London and elsewhere, but is ultimately less focused on the literary or dramatic textual traditions of interpretive acting, and more on the psychophysical processes that place the body under specific forms of duress in order to *release* more possibilities for individual vocal expression than are customarily afforded. The voice in this context is regarded as an integral part of a sophisticated psychophysical sensory process and, as a key signature of the work, provides the means for a distinctive expressive outcome based upon specific individual perceptions about their state of being. Again, the voice is more than an instrument for the fulfilment of theatre purposes; it is, instead, an intimate litmus paper for the state of mind and body of the individual, whatever the role they choose to perform in theatre or elsewhere.

Fitzmaurice encountered the work of Wilhelm Reich early in her career through a group David Kozubei founded in London in 1965. During that period, she was also a teacher at the Central School of Speech and Drama:

> I returned there to teach before coming to the United States in 1968. It was the lack of ability in most of my students in both countries to isolate, without undue tension, the breathing actions of the vocally efficient rib swing and abdominal support that caused me, not to give up the idea of technique as others have done in response to the perceived difficulty, but to look for methods of reducing body tension in faster and more radical ways than the voice work or the Alexander Technique which I had experienced at the Central School, so that the breathing isolations could become effortless and therefore economical, limber, and effective. The rib swing and abdominal support actions are, in fact, what an uninhibited body does during speaking.
>
> (Fitzmaurice 1997: 249–250)

In Fitzmaurice voice work there is a coalescence of many traditions born out of British conservatoire voice practices, along with the radical rupture of convention and authority that is represented by many of the expressive practices discussed earlier. In her work, the voice links to similar principles held by Artaud, in which an actor's emotions get located in specific areas of the body and are associated with the psychophysical systems of breath. The actor under these conditions requires a kind of 'emotional athleticism that correspond[s] to the art of the wrestler' (Benedetti 2005: 226):

> Artaud is restating the age-old notion of the relationship of mind and body and their interaction. Just as inner feelings produce actions so actions produce inner states. The actor can work either way.
>
> (Benedetti 2005: 227)

The body *as* voice gets its clearest iteration in Fitzmaurice Voicework™. In its systematic focus on the body it has the aim of getting close to the desired 'liberated' state common to many radical movements of 1968, where the voice of the disenfranchised individual receives and is able to respond to the invitation to be 'free'. It is a body of work that inflects both towards and away from theatre practice. As such, it is emblematic of multiple strands of voice work that speak to the holistic and the transformational possibilities of individual expression that fall both *within* but also *outside* mainstream theatre practice. In its concentration on physical processes it is not too far-fetched to connect Fitzmaurice voice work to notions of dramatic authorship elsewhere. In her case, the body stands in as author for a text that, in turn, gives licence for the individual to account for and sign up to their own capacity for artistic expression. With its specific body work cues, it invites an individual to know themselves, both as a functioning psychophysical instrument and as an idealist, who can puncture given sensibilities. Whilst it is sometimes at odds with the status quo, its ways of prompting vocal expression are linked to ideas of truth seeking and the visionary. With an inheritance drawn from a mix of secular, sacred, radical and conventional voice work, it places supreme value on the utterance of voice in ways that ensure it is 'written' on and from the body's own script:

> My own adaptation for voice work of bioenergetics tremors and Yoga stretches exists in their combinations and in a focus on a fully relaxed torso to allow maximum spontaneous breathing movement, and, more specifically, in the use of sound on every out breath, no matter how the body is breathing, without changing the placement or rhythm of that breathing … Then, after carefully integrating the unconscious (autonomic nervous system) patterns with the conscious (central nervous system) pattern of rib swing/abdominal support, speech sounds and then speech are introduced as an extension and application of the primary breathing function of oxygenation.
>
> (Fitzmaurice 1997: 250)

Fitzmaurice voice work completes the circle for this discussion about theatre voice with its now familiar acknowledgement of the interiority of voice, in the psycho acoustic home of the body, and the external voice, shaped and positioned by multiple social and cultural systems of knowledge and practice, some of which are regarded as repressive. These have been common themes throughout. The desire for vocal expression in a body re-habituated to instinct, impulse and freedom is one shared with many radical theatre and social movements. In its reliance on body memory to engender an active relationship between voice, speech, breath and impulse, it serves as a key aesthetic for those interested in the potentialities of a challenge to the limitations not just of theatre protocols, but of society's regulatory power mechanisms. The cycle of connectedness that links Fitzmaurice's work to many of the vocal styles I have examined also echoes Artaud's original, poetic belief that breath as part of impulse can influence the soul: 'if the knowledge of breath illumines the colour of the soul, it can even more rouse the soul and allow it to blossom' (Benedetti 2005: 227). The last word, therefore, lies with vocal practice (even as the concept fails to recreate the conditions it seeks to describe). It is provided in Fitzmaurice's account of the process of Restructuring that follows on from the work on spontaneous breathing described earlier. In this process, the ideal is for an actor to be in full receipt of the capacity to enact supported, unforced, proactive vocal expressivity *as if* in complete ownership of their own psychophysical script. It evokes an actor with a licence to both perform as themselves and as a conduit for the authored canon. As such, the work is radical, almost heretical, and, strangely, traditional, at one and the same time, with its paradoxical (and familiar) invitation for the free expression of voice within the known and structured container of the body:

Restructuring gives the actor control over the timing and the variety of delivery choices of pitch, rate, volume, and tone, and allows approximate repeatability without loss of either spontaneity or connection to impulse.

(Fitzmaurice 1997: 250)

AN INTERVIEW WITH PATSY RODENBURG, 1 DECEMBER 2015

PR – Patsy Rodenburg

JB – Jane Boston

Professor and Head of Department: Patsy Rodenburg at Guildhall School of Speech and Drama

JB: A few questions for you about voice in theatre: why is voice important within theatre both today and yesterday?

PR: Well, I think it matters that we hear every word – it is an essential part of good storytelling. You have to hear every word – especially when text is very structured and it is not casual – and particularly in the contemporary climate. I think actors will always train – audiences now are very polite, but in my memory audience members would shout out if they couldn't hear.

JB: In a professional, mainstream West End context?

PR: Yes, yes – 'I can't hear you!' [A heightened form of received pronunciation (RP) imitated by Patsy.]

And of course you go to *hear* in the theatre – the audience are the listeners. In a contemporary context, although you might go more for the spectacle, the voice is still required to operate at an enormously athletic level. So, even if you have a good voice, it is not necessarily going to reach 800 people and you need to have athleticism; you need to have a connection to your body and a connection to a free and open placed voice which is not necessarily used in everyday circumstances.

So clarity is critical and I suppose the other level is – and I am sure Shakespeare's actors knew that in doing a show every day it was putting the voice under pressure – you have to be vocally fit. You have to have range and the physical manifestation of passion is range – either intellectual or physical. So we need a voice that can do it all to the point where we don't worry about the voice or we feel that the voice is abrasive or too loud.

JB: I'd like to go back to your historical memory about theatre – to ask where you locate your traditions of theatre voice?

PR: James Shapiro in his book *1599: A Year in the Life of Shakespeare* [Shapiro 2005] tells about the moment when Shakespeare got rid of his great box-office draw Will Kempe because he wouldn't stick with the text and then, if you look at Hamlet and his advice to the actors, it is all about the voice. And so we know that it mattered to Shakespeare and maybe that is as far back as I can go, although some years ago I was working with the National Theatre of Greece and they said that Sophocles had a weak voice and had to give up acting. The consciousness was there that if you spoke important plays to an audience you needed to work on your instrument.

My journey started, in part, due to the trouble I found with speaking as a child, so it has always intrigued me – and in time I went to the Central School, to learn how to teach. Audrey Laski [Director of the Teacher Department at Central in 1972] and Helen Wynter [Teacher Department staff member] – both great teachers – were there, and Cicely Berry would also come in. I later developed a close personal relationship with the principal Gwynneth Thurburn ['the second longest-serving Principal after Fogerty' (Susi 2006: 45)]. She talked to me – apparently she didn't talk to many people at that time, but she chose to talk to me. When I got to Central they were, quite rightly, getting rid of *overblown* delivery – the rather pompous 'I don't know what I'm saying or why I'm saying it voice, but I'll pretend I do' – you know these big voices …

JB: Like a big sob.

PR: The big sob, and what I call 'the woofers' that Cicely Berry brilliantly understood you had to change; not only because there was a new theatre coming in but because there were also actors coming from working-class backgrounds – not just the privileged sectors – so a huge adjustment was underway.

JB: Just to put in a historical marker, this was Central in the 1970s?

PR: Early '70s.

JB: Early '70s, so we could say that – in a way – voice work has only relatively recently transformed?

PR: Yes – though the origins precede this time and go back to the 1960s when, quite rightly, Central abandoned a lot of the old traditional exercises, which included rib reserve. They also abandoned a lot of craft repetition; I had a fantastic training there but I had also been taught elocution as a child.

JB: Just as an aside, I was surprised and shocked to hear from a student in the United States that she was being taught by a teacher of thirty-five years standing who is still insisting on the most archaic form of Edith Skinner – you know elocution – and I was kind of fascinated and appalled to hear that that repetition laboratory level of restriction was being taught still – so pockets of this type of teaching still exist?

PR: Yes – and I do think that if you repeat, it has to be organic. I mean, you don't learn a craft without some repetition and that's as simple as it gets. With reference to this, I had a lot of old-fashioned teachers before I got to Central. When I eventually got there, I found there was also a lot of very free and fantastic work going on, including a lot of work on poetry with Pauline Meddings and Gerard Benson [Teacher Department staff member], to name a few of the teachers. When I finished at Central, I was asked to go back to teach at Central and I thought, well, no, no, no, I must move away. I deliberately sought out an older, very traditional voice teacher, Sheila Moriarty [Member of the Association of English Singers and Speakers 1980] because I wanted to find out what had been dismissed and she was, in a way, one of those grand divas. I tell my teachers this story and I thank her every day for this, although it was very unpleasant going through it. I taught for her in various places, including the Royal Opera House, Webber Douglas Academy of Dramatic Art, to a certain extent Arts Educational – various places – and she got me into teaching at Lucie Clayton College [A 'Finishing' School founded in 1928, now known as Quest Professional].

JB: She kept an eye on you throughout, did she?

PR: Well, yes – if I remember correctly, I had seven groups for her at one time. I think there were even more at some points, but I remember noting that I had seven groups, each for an hour and a half a week, which amounted to more than ten hours of teaching per week under her. I was teaching in other places, but under her, she insisted that I do the exact set of exercises every class, and that if you came in at ten minutes past the hour you could guarantee that I would be on a specific exercise every time. I did that for five and a half years and I have to say, I learnt a huge amount. I hated it but then I went through a sort of wall when I thought, actually this has given me such an incredible grounding in basics. I don't do many of those exercises any more, although they taught me something that I took on, and I have tried to wed the two worlds together ever since. I have to say that a year ago in the subway in New York a man came up to me and he said, 'Are you Patsy Rodenburg?', and I said, 'Yes', and he said, 'Oh, I loved your classes; you were at Webber Douglas', and he was the first batch I'd ever taught and I think that was 1976, and I said, 'Was it so boring?' and he said, 'I never noticed'. So, I did somehow make it my own.

JB: I'd like to know what Sheila Moriarty's lineage is – what was her pedagogical background?

PR: Well, I think she was a singer, an opera singer, and she had a lot to do with poetry, and knew T.S. Eliot. In fact, she said, and I can't verify this, that he used to get her voice to try things out.

JB: On his dramatic verse?

PR: Yes.

JB: That's interesting, isn't it? And her work obviously provided you with a valuable contrast to the other voice teachers who were positioned under the influence of the 'rebellious' '60s where many of the more 'formal' structures of voice teaching were thrown out.

PR: And I deliberately went to find it, you know, and I thought, I can't just go back to Central; and through my friend John Roberts I met all sorts of amazing actors and by talking to them – a lot of them became mentors of mine – it became a very rich period of my life. They would talk about their voice work and they would talk about what they did and Glen Byam Shaw once told me that at the Old Vic Theatre in London somebody couldn't hear him and he heard a man very clearly cry out from the gods – I think he was playing Macduff – 'Macduff, I can't hear you. If I can't hear you show me your prick', and he said that this was the moment when he started to take voice work seriously …

JB: Marvellous.

PR: I have to say something else.

JB: Oh do, do.

PR: When I was at Central, I don't know how I managed it, I had a friend who was teaching in HM Prison Pentonville and he was an absolute loser because he kept on not turning up for work so he had this brilliant idea that I would deputize for him and I did. I don't remember going through any security checks, but I had the most amazing epiphany about teaching and how important voice was because the epiphany was that actually the inmates had *lost* their voices. And I realized then that voice work was incredibly important – and I've always done voice for non-actors as well so that the two feed each other. In fact, it occurred to me a while ago, that in the theatre we listen to the actor but there are a lot of people that I deal with to whom nobody listens at all – so in fact for them voice work is even harder.

JB: You speak to a strong and significant strain of teaching at Central, in Gwynneth Thurburn, Cicely Berry and others and through to your work, and I wonder, is this work unique to the UK where the particular circumstances of class and inequality have led to the necessity to claim the right to speak in both a metaphorical and actual sense?

PR: Because we have a very fluent middle class who have always wanted to speak better, speaking and being able to converse has always been part of the British way. I think, though, that it also has got a lot to do with the freedom that we've had with the English language; the English language has not been constrained by an academy like the French, Spanish or the Portuguese classical languages, so Shakespeare could, you know, mix sound and sense; fun and wit have always been very important and none of these things can work unless you speak!

JB: Of course. So leading on from that, you've got to be able to speak; you've got to have something to say and I suppose you've got to have been listened to at some point, so, in all that, what are the terms by which you'd describe a voice that can succeed in theatre today?

PR: As I say, the voice has to have strength and athleticism and you have to know the work so well you forget it, which is why we do repetition; you mustn't be standing on your stage worrying about your voice and that takes time, that takes about a year of training. It has to be able to respond to language and connect to language; it has to be fully present and it has to be authentic.

JB: Do you feel that there are any contemporary factors, in terms of the digital environment, where perhaps the full spectrum of sound is less important? Or, is there anything you can point to that might be involved in changing expectations about the perception of the voice?

PR: Oh yes, I mean bodies are changing – the breath too – I think part of it is to do with the pressures of urban living where we're being shoved so much together that we don't have space to take breath. I think, too, that pounding pavements is distorting the body – I'm also very excited, you know this about me, about the science coming through …

JB: The neuroscience, yes.

PR: And without any doubt, as you speak and engage with poetic language, the right side of the brain engages; perception of metaphor is part of our humanity. I did a session with Ian McGilchrist [Psychiatrist Iain McGilchrist, author of *The Master and His Emissary: The Divided Brain and the Making of the Western World* (2009)] and without any doubt, we can now prove this.

JB: I'm sorry I wasn't there, I heard about it – my students came.

PR: Oh, did they?

JB: Yes.

PR: Did they find it interesting?

JB: Yes, oh yes, very much so.

PR: You see, we don't even need to dispute it. I'm also working with a man, Gordon Guigan, based in Australia and he found that people who speak remember the knowledge longer. Now we know all this so I am an optimist in the sense that I think we need to speak, and, although we might feel disconnected from speech because of text messages and emails, there is a shift in the higher levels of the corporate world where they realize that you don't get anything done with an email. You have to have a dialogue and actually it's going to come full circle. We need our voice, it connects us to ourselves and the world. It connects us to sound and language – it is part of our humanity and so we have to fight this and so my experience with young people is that they all yearn to speak, and they all want to be heard. It's not something that's going to go away, it's so deep in our DNA. Anthropologists tell us that using our voice and singing was what kept a community together

JB: You'll be interested to know, I interviewed Claudette Williams for this book (Senior Voice Lecturer at the Royal Central School of Speech and Drama) and she spoke about a moment when her young daughter celebrated 'being a person'. It was a notable point when she physically exercised the act of talking in her public surroundings and evidenced sheer pleasure in doing so.

PR: Sheer joy! That's why audiences went to Shakespeare. They wanted to hear and experience joy and be shocked by language, so it's critical. When I've worked in prisons, for example at Broadmoor Hospital with Murray Cox [Psychotherapist (1931–1997)], people said the most extraordinary things like, 'Oh, I could speak about it rather than do it'. It is a release. In the beginning was the word.

JB: So you're not pessimistic and that's grand and I feel that most people I speak to are optimistic. But there's often an abiding sense that something has been lost in relation to voice practices of the past.

PR: I don't think they've been lost, I mean fashions come and go. You can go all over the world as a teacher and people are speaking and telling stories although it is, I mean, it's politically dangerous to speak of course, and we're facing that now. We need to find our voices again because we need to speak things that have to be spoken.

JB: They're difficult.

PR: They're difficult.

JB: It's all we have really, until you start sending in the bombs. But I'm interested, politics aside, in the fact that there … we are perhaps more led by a visual culture – a strong, dominant, physical, visual culture; and you know I've been in higher education for a while and on certain days it almost feels as if the voice teacher is at the bottom of the theatrical pile; the scenographer, the director, the writer, the lights, the sound – a lot of other elements in theatre seem to come to the fore, and the voice, it's a bit like: oh, maybe we need someone to come and do a little bit of 'fixing' something, you know – I just wondered what you thought about that?

PR: Well, yes. I mean, I remember the first time at the National when I was there – the depression was when the set got the loudest applause and I thought, uh oh. But, interestingly enough, the speaking of poetry is getting more audiences. I think we'll go back to our natural place – I think we will. I mean in the corporate world, I've done it in certain companies, you know, the *bloody* PowerPoint presentation; I said: 'You don't want a PowerPoint, you'll just put them to sleep; you have to come out and speak from yourself' – and there are whole companies that are doing it because it works better.

JB: Well, I must say you are really brilliant at that, you really are; you come out and it seems as if you extemporize without any notes. Do you memorize?

PR: No.

JB: How do you organize the flow of your talks?

PR: I prepare structurally. But I do it a lot, it's again about practice … I care; all you have to do is care. I think the work we're doing is incredibly important and you're right, it's under threat, it's being eroded; but all I can say is you can go into the most cynical group of Wall Street bankers and suddenly you get them speaking and something breaks open, you see their humanity.

JB: I absolutely concur with that. My partner also works in training where, in one sense, we have come full circle and business leaders and civil servants are taking up the same disciplines as theatre/ drama schools did a while ago. In the meantime, drama schools are now paying more attention perhaps to the more scenographic factors.

PR: Well, we also have to be honest and say that the training we do, because it is about, to a certain extent, repetition, is expensive. I think it boils down to that, to a certain extent.

JB: In a brutal sense.

PR: In a brutal sense, such that it seems that to teach a group of designers is easier in a way, whereas the one-to-one, the group sessions that are needed in voice, are not and the joke is, voice is under threat and so we need more voice work, but we get it cut back, so we have to go on that political journey.

JB: I mean there are very few professional theatres with resident heads of voice.

PR: Yes, I was the first one at the National.

JB: When were you appointed there?

PR: 1990. I stayed for seventeen years. And then there is Stratford, Ontario. They always had voice people and that's because, I think, the actors that went over in the '50s to set up that company had been trained by Gwynneth, and the older actors in that company all came to the voice warm-ups. The other very controversial thing – and I have to say it – but I think you know it, is that the only trouble I've ever had with an actor not doing voice work is that they've had somebody who's been cruel to them in the voice world. There's still a lot of cruelty in the voice world I think.

JB: I wonder why specifically – do you have a view on that?

PR: Well, I think it's easy to be. I mean, what did somebody tell me the other day? I was stopped at a party in New York in October by a woman who was very angry that her daughter was at a leading drama school and she said a voice teacher had been so hurtful about her voice – so it's still there.

JB: I abhor that to the very core of my being.

PR: If they come into my workshops in New York, and they talk about why they're there, a huge reason is that they've worked up the courage to come to a voice person because they've been so negated – their voice, and their accent, has been accused of being 'squeaky', or 'strident' – and this is before they have done any work on their instrument. It's outrageous … now don't get me on it – I get so angry. But I had it, it was at Central when I was there.

JB: I've experienced that in my career and I decided I would do everything in my power…

PR: Not to teach like that … But I sometimes think that I explain too much, um, and then you have to say, now you do a bit of work.

JB: It's a balance, isn't it?

PR: Yes, everything's a balance.

JB: Scaffolding is the great key – if you can give enough scaffold so that they can climb.

PR: And then, a key – you know, one key. As soon as you give somebody one key and they can open a door, then they're off.

JB: But you're never sure, that's the great wonder of teaching – you're never sure which key will open which door.

I am aware we're getting close to the end of the interview and I wanted to ask if you had any key predictions about the future of voice. I think I have a sense about what you might say, but I'd love to hear you say it. Where are we going?

PR: Where are we going? Hmm, I think there is a big battle ahead. I am optimistic, which is why I'm wedding myself a lot to Ian McGilchrist's work. We have a scientist there saying that the only way to keep the brain healthy is if we embody, breathe and speak in relationship with each other. So, I'm going to spend the rest of my life dedicating myself to saying this. And I have no fear in saying this. You can't fully educate people without doing this work. You can't understand a great text without speaking it fully – not whispering it or muttering it but *out loud*. The evidence suggests that, actually, the artists are right …

JB: That's magnificent really, isn't it?

PR: So, we have this amazing tool in neuroscience that's landed over the last fifteen years or so and, with the evidence getting stronger and stronger, we have to just take the fight to the people who don't want to hear this.

JB: Voice has dropped out of teacher training almost completely now, hasn't it?

PR: Yes. And we now know that there's something called 'Friday afternoon voice' when teachers lose their voices, so it is a battle with lines drawn. I think there is a need for clear language. I do a lot of work, and I'm sure your partner does, about humanizing language in the workplace. The corporate world doesn't have *human* language as such – it has a language that I'm trying to get them to humanize.

JB: Wonderful … My last question: what do you feel is your particular legacy for the field of voice in theatre?

PR: I don't know really, I don't. I mean I hope it's to do with being decent to students; I hope it's to do with that. I hope it's to do with inspiring them to do incredibly, sometimes, boring exercises that young people do not want to do. Maybe teaching a work ethic. I always find myself saying you've got to do the work – you've got to do the work. I suppose the only other thing I'll say is, I think if you went into my brain you'd find it quite a boring place in the sense that all I think about is education. I think about it, even though I've been teaching the same classes for thirty-five years. I don't ever go into that classroom without trying to work it, find the better way of teaching it, doing it better. I'm continually obsessed with how to get something better. I change my exercises; I need time before I teach every day just to think – yes, I'll do that ... well, maybe I'll actually do that – so I have a continual dialogue about voice.

JB: The reflective practitioner incarnate.

PR: Well, I'm working on that. I suppose it links back to what I said about not having so much fear of saying certain things because I've thought about it all a tremendous amount.

JB: You have consistently maintained – at the highest level – your passion and your connection to the subject.

PR: Yes, and I don't mind doing the boring bits. I have tremendous trouble finding teachers who want to do the true, hard, what I call 'plough the field' work. You've got to plough the field in there and some teachers just want to do the interesting bits, the text, which is great. I love doing that, but the fundamental thing is that we have to get them fully engaged, present and in their bodies, on their breath and that takes time.

JB: You're absolutely right about time and it takes energy and it takes a particular key for each student. I was just thinking about a student I had yesterday who seems to be so disassociated from knowing what her physical sensations are; I don't think she knows if she's up or down, so there's a physical orientation that has to be had.

PR: Yes.

JB: And continually, continually worked at.

PR: And you have to start at the same place every day and you can't be frightened of that. I've thought a great deal about it and I've done it – I've done a lot of work on it.

JB: Well, congratulations – I feel that. I have a huge respect for where you've got us to. One last thing, which one of your publications stands out?

PR: Well, I've done a new edition of *The Right to Speak*. I think *Presence* is a very powerful book all over the planet. It's been translated into huge numbers of languages; it does speak to people and I think I managed to codify something that, again, I've been working on for over thirty-three years. I'm slow of study in the sense that I chip away at something.

JB: Well, marvellous – I appreciate that. Thank you, too, for letting me interview you.

PR: My pleasure, my pleasure.

References

Aiken, W. (1951). *The Voice: An Introduction to Practical Phonology*. 2nd edn. London: Longmans, Green and Co.

Baldwin, J. (2010). Michel Saint-Denis: training the complete actor. In: A. Hodge, ed., *Actor Training*. 2nd edn. London: Routledge, pp. 81–98.

Ball, P. (2010). *The Music Instinct*. 1st edn. London: The Bodley Head.

Bambach, A. (2017). Anatomy in the Renaissance. In: *Heilbrunn Timeline of Art History*. New York: The Metropolitan Museum of Art, 2000. [Online]. Available at: http://www.metmuseum.org/toah/hd/anat/hd_anat.htm [Accessed 17 August 2017].

Barton, R. and dal Vera, R. (2011). *Voice: Onstage and Off*. 2nd edn. London: Taylor & Francis.

Benedetti, J. (2007). *The Art of the Actor*. Abingdon: Routledge.

Berry, C. (2001). *Text in Action*. London: Virgin.

Birch, A. (2013). Reflections on the Centre for Voice in Performance. In: R. Steen, eds., *Growing Voices: Nadine George Technique: The Evolution of Its Influence in Training and Performance*. Glasgow: Royal Conservatoire of Scotland.

Blair, R. (2008). *The Actor, Image, and Action: Acting and Cognitive Neuroscience*. London: Taylor & Francis.

Bloom, H. (2005). *Harold Bloom's Literary Criticism Twentieth Century Anniversary Collection*. Philadelphia: Chelsea House Publishers.

Boston, J. (1997). Voice: The practitioners, their practices, and their critics. *New Theatre Quarterly*, 13(51), pp. 248–254.

Boston, J. (2007). Introduction. In: C. Turner, ed., *Voice and Speech in the Theatre*, 6th edn. London: Methuen, pp. vii–xv.

Boston, J. (2009). Breathing the verse: An examination of breath in contemporary actor training. In J. Boston and R. Cook, eds., *Breath in Action: The Art of Breath in Vocal and Holistic Practice*. 1st edn. London: Jessica Kingsley Publishers, pp. 199–214.

Brooks, H. (2015). *Actresses, Gender, and the Eighteenth-Century Stage Playing Women*. 1st edn. London: Palgrave Macmillan.

Brown, J. (2002). *Shakespeare and the Theatrical Event*. 1st edn. Houndmills: Palgrave Macmillan.

Bush-Bailey, G. (2009). *Treading the Bawds*. 1st edn. Manchester: Manchester University Press.

Butler, J. (1999). *Gender Trouble Feminism and the Subversion of Identity*. 10th edn. New York: Routledge.

Campo, G. and Molik, Z. (2010). *Zygmunt Molik's Voice and Bodywork*. 1st edn. London: Routledge.

Carey, D. and Carey, R. (2008). *Vocal Arts Workbook and DVD*. 1st edn. London: Methuen Drama.

Cavarero, A. (2005). *For More than One Voice*. 1st edn. Stanford: Stanford University Press.

Centlivre, S. (2017). *Full Text of 'A Bold Stroke for a Wife: A Comedy'*. [Online] Archive.org. Available at: https://archive.org/stream/aboldstrokefora00centgoog/aboldstrokefora00centgoog_djvu.txt [Accessed 24 August 2017].

Cibber, C. (2017). *Full Text of 'An Apology for the Life of Mr. Colley Cibber'*. [online] Archive.org. Available at: http://www.archive.org/stream/apologyforlifeof01cibb/apologyforlifeof01cibb_djvu.txt [Accessed 24 August 2017].

Connor, S. (2000). Dumbstruck: A Cultural History of Ventriloquism. Oxford: Oxford University Press.

Coveney, M. (2015). *Maggie Smith*. London: Weidenfeld & Nicolson.

Craigie, D. (1838). *Elements of Anatomy, General, Special and Comparative from Encyclopaedia Britannica Seventh Edition*. Edinburgh: A&C Black.

Dayme, M. (1993). *Dynamics of the Singing Voice*. 2nd edn. New York: Springer-Verlag.

Dayme, M. (2009). *Dynamics of the Singing Voice*. 5th edn. New York: Springer-Verlag.

Declercq, N. and Dekeyser, C. (2007). Acoustic diffraction effects at the Hellenistic amphitheater of Epidaurus: Seat rows responsible for the marvelous acoustics. *The Journal of the Acoustical Society of America*, 121(4), pp. 2011–2022.

Derrida, J. (2010). *Writing and Difference*. London and New York: Routledge.

Dillon, J. (1998). *Language and Stage in Medieval and Renaissance England*. Cambridge: Cambridge University Press.

Dillon, J. (2006). *The Cambridge Introduction to Early English Theatre*. Cambridge: Cambridge University Press.

Fisher, J. and Kayes, G. (2016). *This Is a Voice*. 1st edn. London: Wellcome Collection.

Fitzmaurice, C. (1997). Breathing is meaning. In: B. Acker and M. Hampton, eds, *The Vocal Vision*. 1st ed. New York and London: Applause.

Fogerty, E. (1929). *The Speaking of English Verse*. 2nd edn. London and Toronto: J.M. Dent and Sons.

Fogerty, E. (1937). *The Speaking of English Verse*. 4th edn. London: Allen & Unwin.

Foucault, M. (1977). *Discipline and Punish: The Birth of the Prison*. London: Allen Lane.

Foucault, M. and Rabinow, P. (1984). *The Foucault Reader*. London: Penguin Books.

Fry, D. (1979). *The Physics of Speech*. Cambridge: Cambridge University Press.

Gates, L. (2000). *Voice for Performance*. New York: Applause.

George, N. (n.d.). *My Life with the Voice*. [Online] Available at: http://www.voicestudiointernational.com/files/3212/.../My_Life_with_the_Voice_article.pdf [Accessed 23 June 2017].

Goldhill, S. (1986). *Reading Greek Tragedy*. Cambridge: Cambridge University Press.

Greenblatt, S. (2004). *Will in the World: How Shakespeare Became Shakespeare*. New York: Norton, W. W. & Company.

Gross, J. (1994). *Shylock*. 1st edn. London: Vintage.

Guido, M. (2013). *The Acting Interpreter: Embodied Stylistics in an Experiential Perspective*. 1st edn. New York, Ottawa and Toronto: Legas Publishing.

Hampton, M. and Acker, B. (1997). *The Vocal Vision*. New York: Applause.

Hands, T. (2007). Foreword. In: J. Turner and J. Boston, ed., *Voice and Speech in the Theatre*. 6th edn. London: Methuen, pp. v–vi.

Harris, R. (1986). *The Origin of Writing*. London: Duckworth.

Hayman, R. (1977). *Artaud and After*. Oxford: Oxford University Press.

Hodgdon, B. (2007). Shakespearean stars: stagings of desire. In: R. Shaughnessy, ed., *The Cambridge Companion to Shakespeare and Popular Culture*. Cambridge: Cambridge University Press, pp. 46–66.

Hulbert, H. (1912). *Voice Training in Speech and Song*. London: London University Tutorial Press.

Ihde, D. (2007). *Listening and Voice: Phenomenologies of Sound*. 2nd edn. Albany: State University of New York Press.

Jackson, R. (1994). *Victorian Theatre*. 1st edn. Franklin, NY: New Amsterdam.

Jones, C. (1996). *Make Your Voice Heard: An Actor's Guide to Increased Dramatic Range through Vocal Training*. New York: Back Stage Books.

Kalo, L., Whiteside, G. and Midderigh, I. (1997). The Roy Hart Theatre: Teaching the totality of self. In: B. Acker and M. Hampton, eds, *The Vocal Vision: Views on Voice*, 1st edn. New York and London: Applause.

Karpf, A. (2007). *The Human Voice: The Story of a Remarkable Talent*. London: Bloomsbury Publishing.

Kayes, G. (2000). *Singing and the Actor*. 1st edn. London: A&C Black.

Kelleher, J. (2006). Human stuff: presence, proximity and pretence. In: J. Kelleher and N. Ridout, eds., *Contemporary Theatres in Europe*. 1st edn. London: Routledge. pp. 21–33.

Kennedy, D. (1985). *Granville Barker and the Dream of Theatre*. 1st edn. Cambridge: Cambridge University Press.

Kennedy, F. (2009). The challenge of theorizing the voice in performance. *Modern Drama*, 52(4), pp. 405–425.

Kitto, H. (1986). *Greek Tragedy, etc. (Second Edition.)*. 1st edn. Methuen & Co.: London.

Lawrence, B. (2016). Billie Piper will make you numb with pity in Yerma – review. *The Independent*, 5 August.

Linklater, K. (2006). *Freeing the Natural Voice*. London: N. Hern Books.

Lord, A. (2000). *Albert B. Lord The Singer of Tales*, ed. by Mitchell, S. and Nagy, G. Cambridge, MA and London: Harvard University Press.

McAllister-Viel, T. (2009). Voicing culture: Training Korean actors' voices through the Namdaemun Market projects. *Modern Drama*, 52(4), pp. 426–448.

McCollum, J. (1961). *The Restoration Stage*. 1st edn. Boston: Houghton Mifflin.

McIntyre, I. (2001). *Garrick*. 1st edn. London: Allen Lane/Penguin Press.

McKibbin, R. (1998). *Classes and Cultures*. 1st edn. Oxford: Oxford University Press.

Manvell, R. (1970). *Sarah Siddons*. 1st edn. London: William Heinemann.

Martin, J. (1991). *The Voice of Modern Theatre*. London: Routledge.

Moorcock, M. (2012). A review of Alfred Jarry: *A Pataphysical Life* by Alastair Brotchie. *The Guardian*, 4 January.

Morgan, F. (1981). *The Female Wits*. 1st edn. London: Virago Press.

Nicoll, A. (1949). *World Drama from Aeschylus to Anouilh*. London: Harrap.

Nelson, J. (2015). The Voice Exercise Book. London: National Theatre.

Ong, W. (1982). *Orality and Literacy*. London and New York: Routledge.

Onions, C., Coulson, J., Fowler, H. and Little, W. (1965). *The Shorter Oxford English Dictionary on Historical Principles/Prepared by William Little, H. W. Fowler,*

J. Coulson. Revised and Edited by C. T. Onions. 3rd edn. Oxford: Oxford University Press.

Pascoe, J. (2013). *The Sarah Siddons Audio Files*. 1st edn. Ann Arbor: University of Michigan Press.

Pavlovskis, Z. (1977). The voice of the actor in Greek tragedy. *The Classical World*, 71(2), p. 113.

Powers, M. (2014). *Athenian Tragedy in Performance: A guide to Contemporary Studies and Historical Debates*. New York: University of Iowa Press.

Praise song of a bard of the Bambara Komo society, (qtd. In Louise-Vincent Thomas and Rene Luneau, Les Religions d'Afrique noire, textes et traditions sacres; & cited in Judith Gleason, ed. Leaf and Bone: African Praise-Poems, (New York: Penguin, 1994), xxxvii.

Rodenburg, P. (1992). *The Right to Speak: Working with the Voice*. London: Methuen Drama.

Rodenburg, P. (1993). *Need for Words*. 1st edn. [S.l.]: London: Methuen Drama.

Roose-Evans, J. (2001). *Experimental Theatre from Stanislavski to Peter Brook*. London: Routledge.

Roy-hart-theatre.com. (2017). *Centre Artistique International Roy Hart*. [online] Available at: http://roy-hart-theatre.com/ [Accessed 26 August 2017].

Rufford, J. (2015). *Theatre and Architecture*. 1st edn. Basingstoke: Palgrave Macmillan.

S, C. (2017). *Bold Stroke for a Wife*. Google.

Saklad, N. (2011). *Voice and Speech Training in the New Millennium: Conversations with Master Teachers*. 1st edn. Milwaukee: Applause Theater and Cinema Books.

Sanderson, M. (1984). *From Irving to Olivier A Social History of the acting profession 1880–1983* 1st edn. London: The Athlone Press.

Shapiro, J. (2005). *1599: A Year in the Life of William Shakespeare*. London: Faber and Faber.

Shaughnessy, R. (2007). *The Cambridge Companion to Shakespeare and Popular Culture*. Cambridge: Cambridge University Press.

Shepherd, S. (2012). *Direction: Readings in Theatre Practice*. New York: Palgrave Macmillan.

Sidney, P. and Bellings, R. (1724). *The Works of the Honourable Sr. Phillip Sidney, kt., in Prose and Verse*. London: Printed for E. Taylor, A. Bettesworth, E. Curll, W. Mears, and R. Gosling.

Sleigh, S. (2016). Theatre review of *No Man's Land*. *Evening Standard*, 21 September.

Smith, A. (1972). *'Orghast' at Persepolis*. London: Eyre Methuen.

Smith, B. (1999). *The Acoustic world of Early Modern England*. 1st edn. Chicago: University of Chicago Press.

Strauch, T. and Stengel, I. (2000). *Voice and Self*. London: Free Association Books.

Susi, L. (2006). *The Central Book*. 1st edn. London: Oberon.

Taplin, O. (1978). *Greek Tragedy in Action*. London: Methuen.

Taylor, P. (2016). Theatre review: Yerma, Young Vic, London – 'Billie Piper gives a performance of devastating emotional force'. *The Independent*, 8 August.

Thurburn, G. (1939). *Voice and Speech*. 1st edn. London: Nisbet & Co.

Trott, L. (2012). Elizabeth Pursey obituary. *The Guardian*, 20 February.

Turner, J. and Morrison, M.(ed.) 1981. Voice and Speech in the Theatre. London: A&C Black Ltd.

Turner, J. and Morrison, M. (ed). 2000. Voice and Speech in the Theatre. London: A&C Black Ltd.

Wallis, M. and Shepherd, S. (2004). *Drama, Theatre, Performance*. New York: Taylor & Francis.

Webb, B. (1979). *Poetry on the Stage William Poel, Producer of Verse Drama by Bernice Larson Webb*. 1st edn. Salzburg: Institut fur Anglistik und Amerikanistik Universitat.

Wiles, D. (2003). *A Short History of Western Performance Space*. Cambridge: Cambridge University Press.

Williams, R. (1976). *Keywords: A Vocabulary of Culture and Society*. London: Fontana Press.

Withers-Wilson, N. (1993). *Vocal Direction for the Theatre*. New York: Drama Book Publishers.

Wolford, L. (2010). Grotowski's vision of the actor: The search for contact. In: A. Hodge, ed., *Actor Training*. 2nd edn. London: Routledge, pp. 199–214.

Zarrilli, P. (2009). *Psychophysical Acting: An Intercultural Approach After Stanislavsky*. 1st edn. London: Routledge.

Index

in nineteenth-century theatre, 55, 78–79
social influences, 13, 34, 35
sociocultural need for, 36
vs. voice as instrument, 24–25, 141
vs. voice stylistics, 119
interiority, 11, 165
interlocutor. *See* audience; listener
International Phonetic alphabet (IPA), 100
internet, 149
Irving, Henry, 54, 57, 58–59
Isabella, or the Fatal Marriage, 52

J
Jarry, Alfred, 152–153
Jones, Chuck, 24, 139–140
Jones, Daniel, 120
Jones, Hywel, 158
Jordan, Dora/Dorothy, 47
Jouvet, Louis, 116
Jung, Carl, 156, 158, 159

K
Kaddish, 149
Karpf, Anne, 27
Kayes, Gillyanne, 113
Kean, Edmund, 38
Kelleher, Joe, 71
Kempe, Will, 35, 75, 166
Kennedy, Dennis, 59, 78
Keywords: A Vocabulary of Culture and Society, 6
King's Men, 34, 75
Kozubei, David, 163

L
Laban, 105
Lambert, Catherine, 99–100
language, 95, 170. *See also* logos; speech; texts
for describing voice, 46
in dramatic structure, 34, 87, 88
norms of, 55
producing meaning, 29, 84, 89, 93
in radical practice, 162
in workplaces, 172–173
Laski, Audrey, 166
Lefebvre, Henri, 70
Leigh, Mike, 52

Les religions d'Afrique noire, textes et traditions sacres, 150
Linklater, Kristin, 100–109, 141–143, 144, 156
Freeing the Natural Voice, 10, 11, 118
and neuroscience, 12
psychological awareness, 11
resolving binaries, 8, 141
listening, 13–14, 166, 169. *See also* audiences; theatre spaces
communal, 144
vs. looking, 65
norms of, 64
and reception of voice, 74
in theatre spaces, 64–65
Little Theatre movement, 57–59
logos, 83–100. *See also* language; silence; texts; voice
in ancient Greek theatre, 29
dismantlement of, 153
duplicity of, 30
in print-oral binary, 86–88
radical approach to, 162
significance and context, 89
as stylistic element, 84
in theatre spaces, 69
London Academy of Music and Dramatic Art (LAMDA), 123, 141
London Theatre Studio, 129–130
Look Back in Anger, 104, 134
Lorca, Federico García, 47
Lord Admiral's Men, 33
Lord, Albert B., 90, 91
Lowen, Alexander, 163
Lucie Clayton College, 167
Luneau, Rene, 150

M
Make Your Voice Heard: An Actor's Guide to Increased Dramatic Range through Vocal Training, 140
Manvell, Roger, 52–53, 54
market influence, on voice training, 4, 140, 172
Martin, Jacqueline, 26–27, 134–135
materiality of voice, 9, 13
at Epidaurus, 69
gender shaping, 55
obfuscated by power constructions, 88